The Church Lads' Brigade in the Great War

The Church Lads' Brigade in the Great War

The 16th (Service) Battalion, The King's Royal Rifle Corps

Jean Morris

Pen & Sword
MILITARY

First published in Great Britain in 2015 by
PEN & SWORD MILITARY
An imprint of
Pen & Sword Books Ltd
47 Church Street
Barnsley
South Yorkshire
S70 2AS

Copyright © Jean Morris, 2015

ISBN 978-1-78346-358-9

Typeset by Concept, Huddersfield, West Yorkshire, HD4 5JL.
Printed and bound in England by CPI Group (UK) Ltd, Croydon CR0 4YY.

Pen & Sword Books Ltd incorporates the imprints of Pen & Sword Archaeology, Atlas, Aviation, Battleground, Discovery, Family History, History, Maritime, Military, Naval, Politics, Railways, Select, Social History, Transport, True Crime, and Claymore Press, Frontline Books, Leo Cooper, Praetorian Press, Remember When, Seaforth Publishing and Wharncliffe.

For a complete list of Pen & Sword titles please contact
PEN & SWORD BOOKS LIMITED
47 Church Street, Barnsley, South Yorkshire, S70 2AS, England
E-mail: enquiries@pen-and-sword.co.uk
Website: www.pen-and-sword.co.uk

Contents

Acknowledgements vi

Foreword viii

Introduction x

1. The Raising of the Regiment 1

2. The Brigade in Times of War 27

3. Eight Good Men and True 44

4. Becoming one of the King's Men 62

5. 1915: The 33rd Division 95

6. 1916: The Battle of the Somme 112

7. 1917: The Battles at Arras 162

8. The Race to the Sea 196

9. 1918: The Battle of the Lys 204

10. Armistice 223

11. Those Who Came Home 230

Appendices

1: Line of Descent 244

2: Order of Battle of the 33rd Division 245

3: The King's Royal Rifle Corps: Great War Battle Honours 1914–18 . 248

4: Comparison of Casualties from major Western Front Battles 250

Bibliography 251

Index 252

Acknowledgements

Firstly, I must thank Pen & Sword Books for commissioning this book about the Church Lads' Brigade, and in particular Roni Wilkinson who guided me through my many initial questions about submitting the manuscript; his advice and understanding were invaluable.

Without a positive idea of how I would tackle the story of the Church Lads' Brigade in the Great War I realized that, for my own satisfaction, I needed to know how and when the King's Royal Rifle Corps was raised and how and when the Church Lads' Brigade was founded. My research led me through an incredible history of personal courage, suffering and endurance over almost two centuries of warfare.

My very special thanks go to Zoe King who regularly tours the war graves throughout Europe, and to Jeremy Banning who agreed to make a detour during his visit to the graves of the Arras Offensive so that Zoe could take a picture of the grave of Rifleman Lomas. Additional thanks to Zoe for writing the Foreword to this book.

I am profoundly grateful to the families and various local historical societies and publications that helped in my search for the backgrounds of my 'eight good men'.

Pete Hawking, editor of the Tideswell and District *Village Voice* newsletter, posted my request on their website and the response was overwhelming. Special thanks are due to Corrine Hoban for allowing me to use pictures and a letter from her grandfather, Rifleman Harry Barber; also to Julie Mills and Malcolm Burton, the granddaughter and nephew of Rifleman Sydney Goodwin; to Denise Hadjipetrou for information about her grandfather, Captain Jesse Brightmore; and to Alan Beresford for the photos of the Tideswell CLB and the ex-servicemen's club. My thanks to the Reverend Bill Rigby of St George's Church, Mickley, who passed my request on to Jim Standish who supplied information about Matthew Ferguson from a 1916 copy of the Mickley Parish Magazine. Also to Ken Pearce, Chairman of Uxbridge Local History Society, for sending me information about Denham Camp from a 1919 edition of the *Middlesex Advertiser and Gazette* (Uxbridge edition) and the 2005 article by Terry Hissey in the *Uxbridge Record* about Walter Mallock Gee. My thanks to John Sullivan for his story about Willie Chappell.

Unfortunately I was unable to find further information about Rifleman Gwinnell and Lance Corporal Norman other than that published on the usual family history sites, the 1911 census and births, deaths and marriage records.

Another special thank you goes to Rob Bolton, Chairman of the CLB Historical Group. Rob showed me around the CLB National Memorial Garden at Alrewas and gave his permission for me to include the pictures of the dedication. Thanks also for details from the 'Looking Back' pages of the story of the CLCGB.

For details of the 16th (Service) Battalion The King's Royal Rifle Corps and its journey through the four-plus years of the Great War, the Rayleigh Library in Essex referred me to Mike Davies of the Rayleigh Historical Society, who gave me an insight into how the battalion fared during its stay in Rayleigh.

Thank you to the King's Royal Rifle Corps Association, the Western Front Association, the Royal Green Jackets Museum, The National Archives at Kew, the Commonwealth War Graves Commission and to Forces War Records (www.forces-war-records.co.uk).

My most sincere apologies to anyone I might not have mentioned, and any mistakes are, of course, down to me. I must include extra special thanks to my daughter, Lorraine Ward, who spent so many hours researching the lives of so many lads included in this book, and to my whole family, who must have tired of listening to me talking about the Church Lads' Brigade.

Foreword

There is something remarkably humbling about standing before the pristine grave of a 26-year-old who has given his life for his country. This particular 26-year-old was Reginald Lomas, a member of the 16th (Service) Battalion, The King's Royal Rifle Corps. When Jean Morris heard that I was planning a return trip to the Somme in October 2013 to learn more about those who fought and died in the First World War, she revealed that we shared a passion and asked if I could possibly visit and take a photograph of Reginald's grave.

Jean rightly asks the question: what made these young men sign up for duty to a country that did not even grant them a vote? Even the most superficial examination of the Great War throws up endless questions. Why, for instance, did those who advocated the formation of Pals Battalions not consider the possible consequences? Of course young men would be more likely to join up if they were told they could serve alongside their friends and neighbours, but what about the downside? When such battalions were involved in enemy action, it was friends and neighbours who would be killed or injured. Thus English villages and towns would be likely to lose a disproportionate number of their young men at a stroke. As the war continued, many Pals Battalions were decimated following heavy losses and their members conscripted into other units. The truth inevitably emerged, and with the introduction of conscription in 1916, the idea of Pals Battalions had lost favour.

Reginald Lomas joined the army in 1914 aged 22, and died of his wounds just a month or so before the Armistice. He is buried at Awoingt British Cemetery in France and lies next to Lieutenant Colonel the Honourable Harold Ritchie of the 11th Battalion Scottish Rifles (Cameroons), who died two days after him and was presumably at the same dressing station with him. This fact gives lie to the usual assumption that officers and men would always be buried separately. What gave me further pause for thought at Awoingt was the fact that against the left-hand boundary wall was a row of twenty-two graves of German officers and men. It was very noticeable, however, that these graves were relatively untended whereas the British graves were almost manicured, most being planted with species with strong British identities such as roses and Michaelmas daisies. Anyone visiting graves in France or Belgium is likely to see teams of gardeners tending the graves, but these men always disappear into the shadows if visitors appear.

Looking at other First World War cemeteries in the area, one cannot help but be struck by the number of shared graves and the number of gravestones bearing the legend 'Known unto God'. These are perhaps the most poignant of all. All Stones of Remembrance feature the words 'Their Name Liveth For Evermore', which strikes a particular paradox for me. I also never fail to be moved by the tablets on boundary walls bearing the words 'Known to be buried here', or 'Believed to be buried here', the former indicating that perhaps a dog tag or some other means of identification has been found alongside otherwise unidentifiable remains.

No visit to the First World War battlefields area is complete without a trip to the Thiepval Memorial to the Missing on the Somme. This for me is the most moving memorial. The sixty-four stone panels of this massive structure bear the names of over 72,000 officers and men from United Kingdom and South African forces, most of whom died in the 1916 Battles of the Somme between July and November and have no known graves. Designed by Sir Edwin Lutyens, the scale of the structure truly brings home the scale of the war and its casualties. Scouring the columns of names, every now and again one comes across spaces in the listings where names have been erased. These spaces indicate that the remains of the person previously listed have been found and identified. Even today, some 100 years after the events, remains regularly turn up as farmers plough their fields. Thanks to the dedication of the Commonwealth War Graves Commission, they are treated with the kind of dignity and respect befitting those who sacrificed their lives in the service of their country.

Zoe King
Chair of the Society of Women
Writers & Journalists, 2011–14

Introduction

In the early part of the twentieth century Britain's youth were acutely aware of their heritage of being born within a sovereign state. To honour one's king and country was instilled into every boy's learning, as was the meaning of 'The British Empire' and what it stood for. Schools, church groups and other recreational societies usually included Britain's heritage in lessons, sermons and topical discussions.

On Sundays families attended church services to hear messages of hope rooted in the Bible, God and Jesus, but influential Christians became worried about the poor spiritual and physical development of Great Britain's young people.

Every year, hundreds of juvenile novels were published and filled with stories that romanticized and glorified the exploits and adventures of Empire-builders. Dozens of illustrated periodicals provided readers of every social class with imperialistic articles and cartoons. In 1878 *The Boy's Own Paper* was raised by the Religious Tract Society, both as a means to encourage younger children to read and also to instil Christian morals during their formative years. The first issue went on sale on 19 January 1879 and within the space of four years had achieved circulation figures of about 250,000.

By 1914 Great Britain had a basic educational system, though for most school-children it did not take them beyond the elementary age limit of 12. However, thousands of youngsters belonged to various associations through their partnerships with local churches. The Brigade movements were popular as they prevented the great loss of young Sunday school members who would otherwise be leaving day school and going into paid employment. In 1891, the Church Lads' Brigade was formed as the movement most associated with the Anglican Church. Its intention was to give young men an interesting, recreational and purposeful social life.

It was while I was sorting through family photographs and papers after my mother died in 1991 that I came across a very tattered page from an August 1917 copy of the brigade magazine. The heading on that page said 'SOME OF OUR WOUNDED MEN' and showed eight photographs of lads of the Church Lads' Brigade who, as soldiers in the King's Royal Rifle Corps, were fighting in the Great War. One of those lads was my mother's brother Joe, the eldest and much-loved child of my grandparents, Mary and Joseph Boller. My mother was aged 10 when Joe went to war and had often told me about a brother who appeared to be worshipped by his five sisters. Her stories told me a little about him, but I wanted to know more. Why was this mainly gentle, pacifistic lad ready to fight for his

SOME OF OUR WOUNDED MEN.

RIFLEMAN M. FERGUSSON,
C. 1647,
C. L. B. BATT., K.R.R.
(Late St. George's, Middl'x.)

RIFLEMAN T. H. GWIN-
NELL, C. 1316,
C. L. B. BATT., K.R.R.C.

RIFLEMAN J. BOLLEN,
C. 720,
C. L. B. BATT., K.R.R.C
(Late Bishop Ryders Com-
pany.)

RIFLEMAN R. LOMAS,
C. 423,
C. L. B. BATT., K.R.R.C.
(Late Tideswell Company.)

SERGEANT J. BRIGHT-
MORE, C. 436,
C. L. B. BATT., K.R.R.C.
(Late Tideswell Company.)

RIFLEMAN R. BARBEE,
C. 428,
C. L. B. BATT., K.R.R.C.
(Late Tideswell Company.)

LANCE-CORPORAL J. H.
NORMAN, C. 657,
C. L. B. BATT., K.R.R.C.
(Late Tideswell Company.)

RIFLEMAN S. GOODWIN,
C. 432,
C. L. B. BATT., K.R.R.C.
(Late Tideswell Company.)

Page from *The Brigade* magazine, August 1917.

country, and what about those other seven lads? Who were they and where did they come from?

So it was, with this meagre snippet of information that my mother had kept and treasured for over seventy years, that I started to write about Rifleman Joseph Isaac Boller, a soldier in the 16th (Service) Battalion The King's Royal Rifle Corps and his comrades, in the 'War to end all wars', namely the Great War.

Jean Morris
2014

Chapter One

The Raising of the Regiment

When I first started my research, I was truly amazed at how far back in time I had to go to get to the origin of the formation of a British army regiment that would eventually become the King's Royal Rifle Corps.

Seven years in British history is of England's war with the French and Native Americans in North America. Great Britain had 'Thirteen Colonies' plus Nova Scotia, while France ruled a vast area known as 'New France'. Both frontiers were fighting ferociously against each other.

There had been several wars between the two empires in the years preceding the so-called French-Indian war. King William's War of 1689–97, Queen Anne's War of 1702–13 and King George's War of 1744–48 were all parts of the War of the Austrian Succession. Great Britain and the Dutch Republic, who, at that time, were the traditional enemies of France, supported Austria.

By 1754, Britain controlled 1.5 million colonists in North America with France having only around 75,000. Expansion of the area was pushing the two boundaries closer together. Arguments behind the war were about which nation would eventually dominate those areas. A British infantry regiment was originally raised in North America called the 'Royal Americans' and recruits were engaged from the colonists living within North America. Its purpose was to defend the colonies against attack by the French and their Native American allies. The history of this regiment is so colourful and exciting that its many battles have been written as scripts for epic technicolour movies from Hollywood and played on the 'silver screen'. In 1826, James Fenimore Cooper wrote the book *The Last of the Mohicans: A Narrative of 1757*. This novel was one of the most popular of its time. Written in English, it remains widely-read on American literature courses and has been adapted numerous times for films, television and cartoons.

Edward Braddock (*c.*1695–1755) was a major general in the British army. He was dispatched to America in 1754 to restore and strengthen British positions in the Ohio Valley and the Great Lakes region. Braddock was born in Perthshire, Scotland and was the son of Major General Edward Braddock of the Coldstream Guards. His military career started at the age of 16 when Queen Anne commissioned him as an ensign in his father's regiment. He was acting brigadier of the Guards Brigade under the Duke of Cumberland during the 1745 Jacobite rebellion when Bonnie Prince Charlie tried to recover the British throne for the House of Stuart.

In 1746/47, Edward Braddock became a lieutenant colonel and commanded the Coldstream battalions in the abortive expedition against the French during the War of the Austrian Succession. In 1753, he resigned his Coldstream

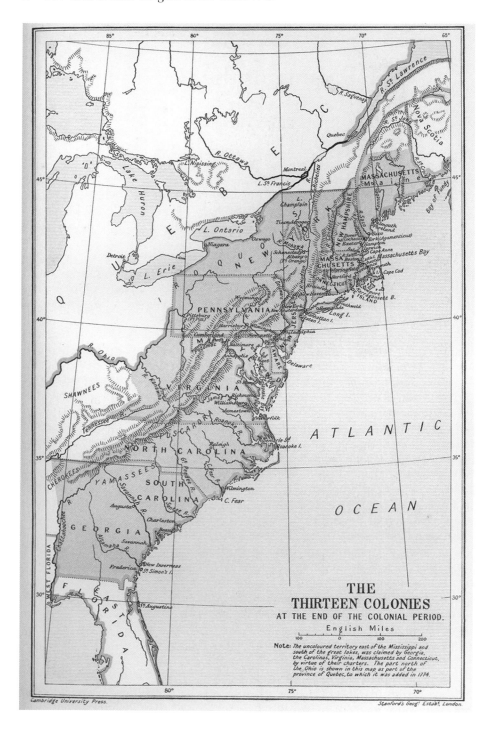

THE
THIRTEEN COLONIES
AT THE END OF THE COLONIAL PERIOD.

English Miles

Note: *The uncoloured territory east of the Mississippi and south of the great lakes, was claimed by Georgia, the Carolinas, Virginia, Massachusetts and Connecticut, by virtue of their charters. The part north of the Ohio is shown in this map as part of the province of Quebec, to which it was added in 1774.*

Major General Edward Braddock.

commission to become colonel of the 14th Regiment, which was stationed in Gibraltar, where it seems he served briefly as commandant and acting governor. On the Duke of Cumberland's recommendation, he was recalled to London and in 1754 was promoted to major general to become commander-in-chief for North America at the start of the French and Indian War (the Seven Years War).

Braddock landed in Virginia on 19 February 1755 with two regiments of British regulars. He met with several of the colonial governors, but neither he nor the British War Office had any idea about North American recruitment, communication or supply problems. The north-eastern part of North America was like a giant chessboard with French and British forts making up the many pieces.

Native Americans, who were allies of the French, were quite at home in their temporary skin and bark tepees that were pitched around the French forts. Fires smoked, dogs barked, children laughed or cried and the women worked at chewing and sewing animal skins or stirring pots of simmering food. The men sat in silence, smoking their white clay pipes and listening to others telling stories of the bravery of one or another that had gone to fight in the war.

On 14 April 1755, Braddock was persuaded to undertake intense action against the French and four separate initiatives were planned.

The four-part plan and Braddock's defeat
William Shirley (*c.*1694–1771) was a British colonial administrator and also the longest-serving governor of the province of Massachusetts Bay (1741–49 and

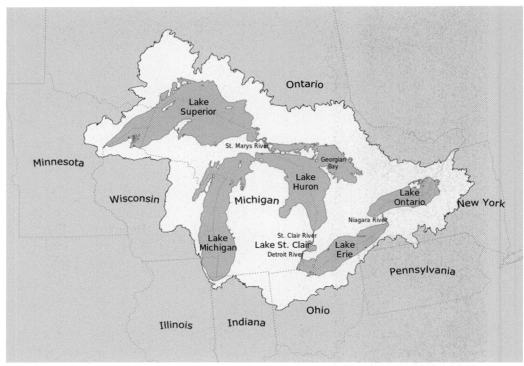

The Great Lakes.

1753–56). Now honoured with the commission of a general from the king, it was intended he should take action for the reduction of the French fort of Niagara with a force composed of American regulars and friendly natives. Fort Niagara stood at the mouth of the Niagara River and was vital, as it controlled access to the Great Lakes and the westward route to the heartland of the North American continent.

Shirley led the unsuccessful attack on the French position in what today is upstate New York. In 1756 he was relieved of duty and returned to England to answer charges of treason and incompetence. Shirley made a successful self-defence and in 1758 was named governor of the Bahamas. He enjoyed this posting for a decade before surrendering it to his son. He returned to Massachusetts to live in Shirley Place in Roxbury, where he died at the age of 77. He was buried at King's Chapel in Boston.

General Sir William Johnson 1st Baronet (*c.*1715–74) was an Anglo-Irish official of the British Empire. Johnson was appointed as the British agent to the Iroquois. He had lived for many years alongside the Mohawk nations and had learned their language and knew their customs. He was in command of the Iroquois and the colonial militia forces that were to attack at Crown Point (so called by the French). This was part of a chain of British and French forts along

William Shirley.

the important inland waterway and occupied a key forward location on the frontier.

In the summer of 1755, under Johnson's command, 3,500 New England provincials marched to the frontier outpost of Fort Edward, close to the headwaters flowing from the source of the Hudson River. The campaign was meant to expel the French from Lake Champlain. Johnson put his men to work opening up a road that ran 15 miles north, through the wilderness, to the lake known as Lac Saint-Sacrement. Johnson renamed this Lake George in honour of King George II.

From the head of Lake George, it was thought that Johnson's army would be able to travel almost entirely by water to the strategic fort held by the French at Crown Point. The provincials and their Mohawk allies had been at Lake George for only a few days, when they learned that a force of French and hostile Native

Americans was nearby. Some 200 Mohawk warriors arrived to join the campaign against the French. The Battle of Lake George on 8 September 1755 was one of the bloodiest encounters along that great warpath during the French and Indian War.

Johnson's Mohawk ally, Hendrick Theyanoguin, was killed in the battle and, Baron Dieskau, the French commander, was captured. Johnson prevented the Mohawks from killing the wounded Dieskau and the compassionate rescue became famous in a painting of the event. The painting is by Benjamin West and is now housed in the Derby Museum & Art Gallery in England.

This battle brought an end to the expedition against Crown Point. Although it was counted as a victory for the British, the momentum of the campaign against Crown Point was broken. During that battle, Johnson was wounded by a bullet that was to remain in his hip for the rest of his life.

Johnson's army built a fort at the head of Lake George to strengthen British defences. It was named Fort William Henry in honour of both Prince William, Duke of Cumberland (younger son of King George II), and Prince William Henry, Duke of Gloucester (grandson of George II). In December of that year (1755), tired of army life, Johnson resigned his commission as major general.

Robert Monckton (*c.*1726–82) was an officer of the British army and a colonial administrator in British North America. He was second-in-command to General Wolfe at the Battle of Quebec and had a distinguished military and political career. He was later named governor of the province of New York.

General Sir William Johnson.

Robert Monckton.

The British conquest of all of France's North American territories began on 4 June 1755 when a force of British regulars and New England Militia from Fort Lawrence attacked Fort Beauséjour. Located off the northern coast of Maine, Fort Beauséjour is on the Bay of Fundy. Although Monckton was to have some regular soldiers with him, the force was principally made up of 2,000 colonial 'provincials'. They were eventually mustered at Boston and were formed up into two battalions. One battalion was under John Winslow and the other under George Scott. These New Englanders were to be transported to the coast in 'sloops' and 'schooners'. However, there was some delay as they were obliged to wait for a shipment of muskets arriving from England.

The richness of the area was only one factor accounting for the determination of the British attempt to capture the district and of the French to retain it. The Isthmus was a long-used route of travel from the Gulf of St Lawrence to the Bay of Fundy, familiar to both the Native Americans and the French. Furthermore, the area had a strategic value as offering the shortest possible front line for the opposing forces.

There would not have been much time to shore up defences at Fort Beauséjour before the English armada made its appearance in the Fundy basin. The descent of such a force could mean only one thing and the fears of the French were considerably heightened. A call went out to all able-bodied Acadian men in the district to come into the fort for its defence. Approximately 300 men responded. At the time the British commenced their attack, Fort Beauséjour had twenty-one cannon and a mortar and was manned by 165 officers and soldiers of the French regular army. A French officer, who was behind the walls of Beauséjour at the time, wrote:

It was known, however, that their coast-guards had captured and taken to Chebucto a French ship, which had been loaded with munitions and food-supplies at Louisbourg for the King's post on the St. John river. We also learned about this time, that great preparations for war were being made throughout New England, and that all merchant ships had been held in their respective ports; even those which habitually brought provisions to their fort in this neighborhood, early in April, were being detained until June 1st. The confidence that peace would continue was so deeply impressed on the minds of those who lived in the district, that none of these reasons sufficed to awaken the slightest alarm, and we continued to enjoy a sense of security as perfect as though we were residing in the centre of Paris.

On June 2nd we realized our mistake. At 5 o'clock in the morning a settler who lived at Cape Maringouin, in the Bay of Fundy, about 2 leagues from Point Beauséjour, came to warn M. de Vergor du Chambon, Commandant of the Fort, that an English fleet of about forty vessels, laden with men, had sailed into the cove on the inner side of the Cape, and was there awaiting the turn of the tide to enter Beaubassin. The commandant, who could no longer doubt the intentions of the English, dispatched couriers to Quebec, the St. John River, Louisbourg and the Island of St. John to solicit aid. The

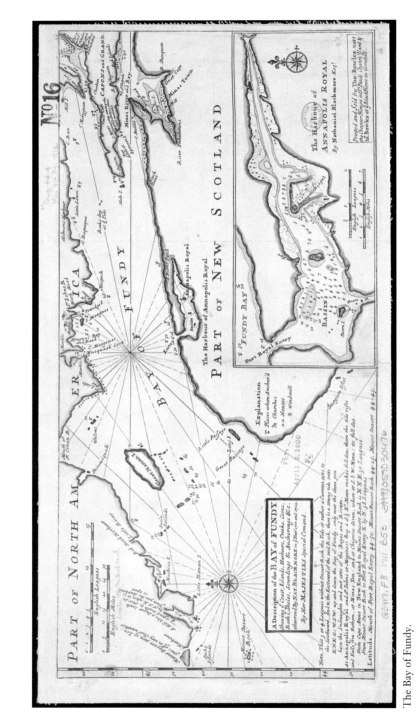

The Bay of Fundy.

inhabitants from rivers dependent on this post and, from the surrounding country, were summoned to the Fort, raising to about six hundred the number of men under orders to take up arms and fire on the English whenever they should attempt to set foot in the King's domain, or to make an attack on our fort.

At 5:30 in the afternoon, the enemy's fleet composed of 37 sail made its appearance; three frigates, a snow, and two other vessels, equipped for fighting, which served as an escort, anchored at the entrance to Beaubassin; the transports were run aground close to Fort Lawrence, the English post, 1,450 fathoms from our own. The troops landed at about 6:30 in the evening and the great majority of them passed the night under arms.

The British seized the high ground to the north of Fort Beauséjour. Among their preparations was the opening-up of the siege trenches to within 700 feet of the walls of the French fort.

The men crept closer and closer within the protection of their trenches that sappers had dug under the cover of night. Their fellow infantrymen lay on their bellies ahead of them, ready to return fire. The trenches were started on 12 June 1755 and, once advanced, a '13 inch mortar' was moved along under cover.

It is likely the British thought they had weeks, maybe months, of work ahead, when out of the gates came a group of French officers under a flag of truce. The British were surprised to learn that the French wished to surrender. What they did not know at the time was that the French defenders were a very disheartened group. The British-led force took control of Fort Beauséjour by 16 June 1755, after which they changed its name to Fort Cumberland.

Terms of an agreement were worked out with the usual to-ing and fro-ing of arguments. The French were allowed to march out with their bags and guns, their flags flying and their drums beating. They retired with honour and were allowed to go to Louisbourg with transport being laid on by the British. Another condition was that there should be no retribution against the Acadians found behind the walls of the fort.

General Braddock was to lead an expedition against Fort Duquesne at the forks of the Ohio River. The name 'Ohio' comes from the Iroquois Indian word meaning 'good river' or 'large river'. The Ohio River is a principal tributary of the grand Mississippi River and was of great importance to both the Native Americans and the settlers, as they expanded westward.

After some months of preparation, in which he was hampered by administrative confusion and lack of resources, Braddock took the field with a hand-picked column. Future American president George Washington, then just 23 years of age, knew the territory and served as a volunteer aide-de-camp. As commander-in-chief of the British army in America, General Braddock led the main thrust with a column some 2,100 strong. His command consisted of two regular line regiments, the 44th and 48th, with about 1,350 men that included 500 regular soldiers and militiamen from several of the British-American colonies. There were also other support troops and artillery.

Fort Duquesne US commemorative
postage stamps, 1958.

With these men, Braddock thought it would be easy to seize Fort Duquesne and then push on to capture a series of other French forts. Benjamin Franklin, who at that time was deputy postmaster general of North America, helped procure horses, wagons and supplies for the expedition. Among the wagon-drivers was Daniel Boone, later to become a legend in American history.

The column crossed the Monongahela River on 9 July 1755 and, with only a few miles left to reach its target, was ambushed by the French and their Native American allies. Braddock was completely surprised and constantly tried to re-route and rally his men. Finally, after four horses had been shot from under him, he fell and was mortally wounded. Braddock was carried off the field and died on 13 July 1755. He was buried at Great Meadows, where the survivors of the column had halted on its retreat in order to reorganize.

Incompetent subalterns blamed Braddock for the disaster, but George Washington said his character was treated much too harshly. The Braddock expedition, more commonly known as 'Braddock's Defeat', was just one of a line of massive British offensives against the French in North America that summer. It was a failed British military expedition during its attempt to capture the French Fort Duquesne. The defeat was a major setback for the British in the early stages of the war with France and has been described as 'one of the most disastrous defeats for the British in the 18th century'. Only one of the four planned take-overs was a success.

During the week of 10 August 1756, a force of regulars and Canadian militia serving under General Montcalm, commander of the French forces in North America, captured and occupied the British fortifications at Fort Oswego. In spite of its military vulnerability, it was one of a series of French victories. The 50th (Shirley's) and 51st (Pepperrell's) foot regiments were removed from the British Army Roll after their surrender at the Battle of Fort Oswego.

Back to the drawing board
After Braddock's defeat in 1755, royal approval for a new regiment was granted by Parliament just before Christmas 1755; hence the regiment's traditional birthday of Christmas Day. It is reported that Parliament voted that the sum of

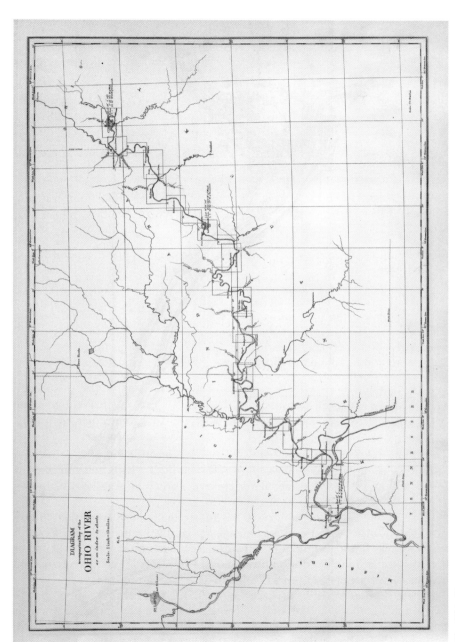

The Ohio River.

£81,000 would be provided for the purpose of raising a new regiment and approved an act:

> To enable His Majesty George II to grant commissions to a certain number of foreign Protestants, who have served abroad as officers or engineers, to act and rank as officers or engineers in America only, under certain restrictions and regulations.

Major General John Campbell, 4th Earl of Loudoun (*c.*1705–82), became the newly-appointed commander-in-chief of the forces in North America and was appointed colonel-in-chief of the new regiment.

Certain parliamentary delays meant that it was 4 March 1756 before a special Act of Parliament created four battalions of 1,000 men each (to include foreigners) for service in the Americas. The idea for creating this unique force was proposed by a friend of Prince William, Duke of Cumberland. William was the king's third son and was commander-in-chief of the allied forces. Jacques Prevost, a Swiss soldier and adventurer, recognized the need for soldiers who understood forest warfare, unlike the regulars who went to America in 1755 with General Braddock. The regiment was intended to combine the characteristics of a colonial corps with those of a foreign legion. Swiss and German forest fighting experts, American colonists and British volunteers from other British regiments were recruited. These men were Protestants, an important consideration for fighting against the predominantly Catholic French. The officers were not recruited from the American colonies but consisted of English, Scots, Irish, Dutch, Swiss and Germans recruited in Europe. It was the first time foreign officers were commissioned as British army officers. About fifty officers' commissions were given to German and Swiss volunteers, but none were allowed to rise above the rank of lieutenant colonel.

Among those given commissions was Henri Bouquet, born in Rolle, Vaud, Switzerland (*c.*1719–65). He entered the British army in 1756 as a lieutenant colonel. He was a prominent British army officer whose ideas on tactics, training and man-management included the unofficial introduction of the 'rifle' and 'battle-dress'. Bouquet was commanding officer of the 1st Battalion and, with his fellow battalion commanders, set about creating units that were better suited to warfare in the forests and lakes of north-east America.

In February 1757 the regiment was renumbered the 60th Regiment of Foot (Royal American Regiment) and was made up largely of members of Pennsylvania's German immigrant community. The regiment consisted of 101 officers, 240 non-commissioned officers and 4,160 enlisted men. The battalions were raised on Governors Island, New York.

The new regiment fought at Louisbourg in 1758. On the Atlantic coast of Cape Breton Island was the bastion guarding the entrance to the Saint Lawrence River and access to French Canada. Before the British could conquer the French colony, Louisburg had to be captured.

In 1758, after leading the Royal Americans to Charleston, South Carolina to bolster that city's defences, the regiment was recalled to Philadelphia to take part

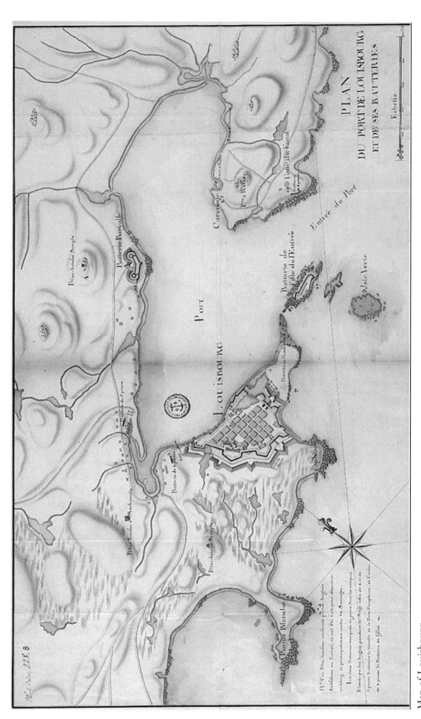

Map of Louisbourg.

Major General John Campbell.   Henri Bouquet.

in General John Forbes' expedition against Fort Duquesne. As they travelled from Fort Bedford, French and Native Americans attacked Bouquet's troops at Loyalhanna, Pennsylvania. However, the attack was repulsed and they continued on to Fort Duquesne, only to find it razed to the ground by the fleeing French.

In 1759, conventional battles were fought on the European model. The Quebec campaign finally forced Canada from France. By 1760 France was defeated and the British had seized all of its colonies. In September, Governor Vaudreuil negotiated a surrender with General Amherst.

Vaudreuil requested that French residents, who chose to remain in the colony, be given freedom to continue worshipping in their Roman Catholic tradition and, with continued ownership of their property, would remain undisturbed in their homes.

The British provided medical treatment for the sick and wounded French soldiers. French regular troops were returned to France aboard British ships with an agreement that they were not to serve again in the present war. Bouquet ordered the construction of a new British garrison on the site. He is given credit for naming the new garrison Fort Pitt and the village that quickly grew up around it as Pittsburgh. The Seven Years War finally ended in 1763. Great Britain was left with an insurmountable mountain of debt, but its army was still kept there.

The Native American uprising
The fighting during Pontiac's Rebellion in 1763 was of a very different nature from anything that had ever been known before.

The new frontier war threatened the British control of North America. At first the new 60th (Royal American) Regiment lost several outlying garrisons, but finally proved its mastery of forest warfare under Bouquet's leadership at the victory of Bushy Run. The 60th were uniformed and equipped in a similar manner to other British regiments with red coats and cocked hats or grenadier caps, but on campaigns, swords were replaced with hatchets and coats were cut down in length to make movement in the woods less of a problem.

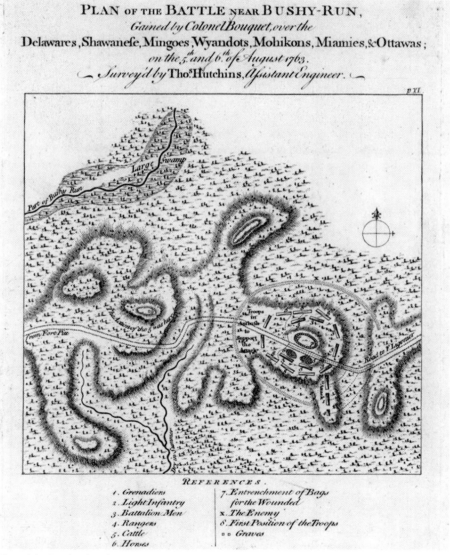

Plan of the Battle of Bushy Run.

'Pontiac's Conspiracy' or 'Pontiac's Rebellion' was named after the leader of the Ottawa tribe. He was the most prominent of many native leaders and declared war on the British in May 1763. After the British victory in the French and Indian War, Native Americans, primarily from the Great Lakes region, Illinois Country and Ohio Country, were dissatisfied with British post-war policies. Warriors from numerous tribes joined the uprising in an effort to drive British soldiers and settlers out of the region. A number of British forts and settlements were attacked, with eight forts being destroyed, hundreds of colonists killed or captured and many more fleeing the region.

Pontiac urged the defeated Indian tribes that had been allied to the French to unite and continue the fight against the British. He initiated attacks on frontier forts and settlements, believing the defeated French would rally and come to his aid.

The conflict began with the siege of Fort Detroit on 10 May 1763. The Native Americans quickly overran Fort Sandusky, Fort Michilimackinac, Fort Presque Isle and numerous other frontier outposts. Several frontier forts in the Ohio Country had fallen to the Native American tribes and Fort Pitt, Fort Ligonier and Fort Bedford were besieged or threatened.

Henri Bouquet, who was in Philadelphia, threw together a hastily-organized force of 500 men, mostly Scottish Highlanders, to relieve the forts. On 5 August 1763, near a small outpost called Bushy Run, warriors from the Delaware, Mingo, Shawnee and Wyandot tribes attacked the relief column. In a two-day battle, Bouquet defeated the tribes and Fort Pitt was relieved. That battle marked a turning-point in the war. It was during Pontiac's Rebellion that Bouquet gained a certain infamy and is best known for his victory over Native Americans at the Battle of Bushy Run.

Over the next two years, warfare on the North American frontier was brutal with the killing of prisoners, the targeting of civilians and other widespread atrocities. In what is now perhaps the best-known incident of the war, British officers at Fort Pitt attempted to infect the besieging Native Americans with smallpox by using blankets that had been exposed to the virus. The ruthlessness and treachery of the conflict was a reflection of a growing divide between the separate populations of the British colonists and Native Americans.

By the autumn of 1764, Bouquet had become the commander of Fort Pitt. To subdue the ongoing Native American uprising, he led a force of nearly 1,500 militiamen and regular British soldiers from the fort into the Ohio countryside. On 13 October 1764, Bouquet's army reached the Tuscarawas River. Chiefs from the Shawnee, Seneca and Delaware tribes came to Bouquet to petition for peace.

As part of the treaty, Bouquet demanded the return of all white captives in exchange for his promise not to destroy the Indian villages or seize any of their land. The return of the captives caused a lot of bitterness among the tribes because many of them had been forcibly adopted into Indian families as small children and living among the Native Americans had been the only life they remembered. Bouquet was responsible for the return of more than 200 white captives to the settlements back in the east.

Native Americans were unable to drive away the British, but the uprising prompted the British government to modify the policies that had caused such a conflict. This series of attacks on frontier forts and settlements required the continued deployment of British troops. Hostilities came to an end after British army expeditions in 1764 led to peace negotiations.

Contrary to popular belief, the British government did not issue the Royal Proclamation of 1763 in reaction to Pontiac's Rebellion. The proclamation was issued on 7 October 1763 by King George III following Great Britain's acquisition of French territory in North America. It forbade early colonists from settling past a line drawn along the Appalachian Mountains. The purpose of the proclamation was to organize Great Britain's new North American empire and to stabilize relations with Native North Americans through regulation of trade, settlement and land purchases on the western frontier. This proved unpopular with British colonists and may have been one of the early contributing factors to the American Revolution.

The Royal Proclamation continues to be of legal importance to the First Nations in Canada and is significant for the variation of indigenous status in the United States. There are currently over 630 recognized First Nations governments or bands spread across Canada, roughly half of which are in the provinces of Ontario and British Columbia. It eventually ensured that British culture and laws were applied in Upper Canada after 1791, which was done to attract British settlers to the province.

In 1765 Bouquet was promoted to brigadier general and placed in command of all British forces in the southern colonies. He died in Pensacola, West Florida, on 2 September 1765 from what was thought to be yellow fever.

The Seven Years War nearly doubled Britain's national debt. The Crown looked for sources of revenue to pay off the debt by attempting to impose new taxes on its colonies. These attempts were met with increasingly stiff resistance until troops were called in so that representatives of the Crown could safely perform their duties. These acts ultimately led to the start of the American Revolutionary War.

The Napoleonic Wars
During the Napoleonic Wars the regiment saw action in the Peninsular War. The first four battalions had been raised as regular line battalions, but in 1797 a 5th Battalion was raised and later equipped entirely with the Baker rifle.

Officially known as the 'Infantry Rifle', the Baker rifle was a flintlock type used by the rifle regiments of the British army during the Napoleonic Wars. It was the first British-made standard-issue rifle accepted by the British armed forces. Ezekiel Baker, a master gunsmith from Whitechapel in London, first produced it in 1800. The rifle was used by what were considered elite units, such as the 5th Battalion and the rifle companies of the 6th and 7th battalions of the 60th Regiment of Foot. The rifle was also supplied to, or privately purchased by,

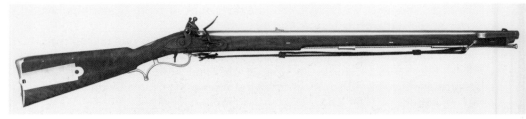

The Baker rifle.

numerous volunteer and militia units. It is recorded that the British army still issued Baker rifles in 1841, three years after its production had ceased.

The mixing of rifle troops and muskets proved so effective that eventually line battalion light companies were replaced with rifle companies. The line battalions found themselves in several different theatres, including the West Indies. The first rifle battalion was soon joined by a second and they found themselves in the Peninsula with Wellington's army, serving alongside the 95th Rifles and the King's German Legion Rifle units. A 7th Battalion was eventually raised as a rifle battalion specifically for service in the American War of 1812. Their uniform was of green jackets with red facings.

After the Napoleonic Wars the Great Powers assembled in Vienna to restore the European state system. It was a delicate balance between the various major and minor powers that restrained aggression by the mighty and upheld the rights of the weak. It was hoped that, by suppressing revolutionary republics and up-holding stable, orderly monarchies, it could build a permanent peace. Despite the conflicting aims and ambitions of Russia, Prussia, Austria, Britain and France, a compromise was created.

The regiment received a new title: firstly, in 1815, its name was changed to The Duke of York's Own Rifle Corps and then, in 1830, to the King's Royal Rifle Corps (KRRC). In 1858 the Rifle Depot at Winchester was made their head-quarters. During the rest of the 1800s, the unit was active in Afghanistan, China, Canada, India, Burma and South Africa.

The Boer War
The regiment was deployed during the Second Boer War after playing a key role in the first war against the Boers. The Battle of Talana Hill, also known as the Battle of Glencoe, was the first major clash of the Second Boer War. Supported by artillery, a frontal attack by British infantry drove the Boers from a hilltop position, but the British suffered heavy casualties in the process, including their Major General Sir William Penn Symons KCB (*c.*1843–99).

Before dawn on 20 October 1899, Boer forces from the independent South African Republic, each numbering 4,000 men, closed in on the coal-mining town of Dundee, situated in a valley of the Biggarsberg Mountains in KwaZulu-Natal, South Africa. Boer farmers established Dundee in 1882 after the discovery of coal close to the surface. Boer General 'Maroela' Erasmus's force occupied the Impati

British Soldiers in the Boer War.

Mountain north of Dundee. They had dragged several German-manufactured Krupp field guns to the top of the hill, but these guns opened fire ineffectually upon the British.

British General Lukas Meyer's men occupied the low Talana Hill east of the town and the 16th and 69th Field Batteries galloped within range and returned fire.

Leaving the 1st Battalion Leicestershire Regiment and the 67th Field Battery to guard the camp, the British Infantry, led by the 2nd Battalion Royal Dublin Fusiliers and supported in succession by the 1st Battalion King's Royal Rifle Corps and the 1st Battalion Royal Irish Fusiliers, moved forward to the foot of the hill, where it was planned that they would advance through a small wood. However, they were pinned down by heavy rifle fire from the top of Talana Hill.

Major General Penn Symons was in command and went forward to urge them on, but was wounded in the stomach. He was able to mount his horse and ride back into Dundee where he later died. Although his forces won the battle, they had to abandon their position and fall back to Ladysmith. A monument to Penn Symons' valour was raised in Victoria Park, Saltash, Cornwall, the county of his birth.

British and Indian Officers in the Boer War.

Symons' successor was Brigadier General James Herbert Yule and under his command the King's Royal Rifle Corps managed to reach a small stone wall at the foot of Talana Hill. The Dublin Fusiliers were pinned down by Boer fire, but with the Royal Artillery laying down accurate fire on the summit, the King's Royal Rifle Corps, supported by the Royal Irish Fusiliers, were able to proceed up the hill. When they reached the top of the hill and were suffering casualties from their own supporting artillery, the Boers abandoned their positions on the hill. General Lukas Meyer's forces mounted their ponies and made off. Despite the British artillery being repositioned to harass the Boer retreat, they declined to fire because of the worry that they might hit their own troops again.

A squadron of the 18th Hussars and the British mounted infantry tried to cut off the Boer retreat, but most of the British horsemen had strayed onto the slopes of Impati. General Erasmus's men, who had so far played no part in the battle due to Impati being shrouded in fog, surrounded the British mounted detachment and forced them to surrender.

Yule's men had been unable to contemplate attacking Impati Mountain because it held Dundee's water supply. They marched and countermarched beneath it for two days under intermittent shellfire. Other Boer forces had cut the British line of supply and retreat. Finally the British force retreated across country at night. After an arduous four-day march of 64 miles (103km), they reached Ladysmith, where they reinforced the garrison. The British won a tactical victory but at a very high cost.

Two officers from the regiment were awarded the Victoria Cross. The Hon. Lieutenant Frederick Hugh Sherston Roberts entered the King's Royal Rifle Corps on 10 June 1891 and during the following four years was on active service on the North-West Frontier of India, including Chitral. He received the Medal and Clasp and was Mentioned in Dispatches. He served in the Boer War of 1899–1902, and lost his life at the Battle of Colenso in an attempt to save the guns of the 14th and 66th batteries. There is a memorial to him in Winchester Cathedral and in the chapel at the Royal Military College, Sandhurst.

Major General Llewelyn Alberic Emilius Price-Davies VC, CB, CMG, DSO was 23 years old and a lieutenant in the King's Royal Rifle Corps. During the Second Boer War, the following deed took place at Blood River Poort for which he was awarded the VC, as reported by the *London Gazette* on 29 November 1901:

> At Blood River Poort, on the 17th September, 1901, when the Boers had overwhelmed the right of the British Column, and some 400 of them were galloping round the flank and rear of the guns, riding up to the drivers (who were trying to get the guns away) and calling upon them to surrender, Lieutenant Price Davies, hearing an order to fire upon the charging Boers, at once drew his revolver and dashed in among them, firing at them in a most gallant and desperate attempt to rescue the guns. He was immediately shot and knocked off his horse, but was not mortally wounded, although he had ridden to what seemed to be almost certain death without a moment's hesitation.

He later achieved the rank of major general. His grave and memorial are at St Andrew's churchyard in Sonning, Berkshire. His Victoria Cross is displayed at the Royal Green Jackets Museum in Winchester, England.

The Great War

When the Great War started in 1914, the King's Royal Rifle Corps expanded to twenty-two battalions. The regiment on the Western Front, Macedonia and Italy saw a great deal of action with sixty battle honours awarded.

An extract from a rifleman's diary for a week in Ypres during July 1915 reads:

> 1st Thursday. Battalion remains in Ypres. There is some shelling. Rifleman Barnes killed and one man wounded. Both are from the Machine Gun section.
>
> 2nd Friday. Battalion remains in Ypres. Fatigue parties sent to clear up the roads.
>
> 3rd Saturday. Battalion remains in Ypres. Heavy shelling of Ecole and firing opened up at Sally Port. One shell exploded in a shelter in which A Coy were cooking their tea: 3 killed 15 wounded of which two died later.

4th Sunday. Battalion remains in Ypres. Stretcher carrying parties every night. Battalion also constructs Dugouts. (7 wounded very slightly). Sergeant Hughes is poisoned from drinking from a bottle found in the town.

5th Monday. Battalion remains in Ypres. New method of spraying smoke helmets carried out. Bomb throwers under Danville go to trenches in the morning. Rifleman Hutchins and Rifleman Freeman Machine Gunners killed by shell. Rifleman Andrews and Rifleman Fletcher wounded.

6th Tuesday. Battalion remains in Ypres. Rifleman Terry and Rifleman Hawkin C Company killed on carrying party. Six wounded. Rifleman Hodges and Rifleman Harris subsequently.

7th Wednesday. Battalion remains in Ypres. Very quiet day as regard to shells. Two sick men taken to hospital. Several houses fell down owing to the wind and the roads had to be cleared. Major Crum slightly wounded. The Prime Minister, Lord Kitchener and a large party visit YPRES.

Thousands of men willing to fight for their country were wounded or killed. Although the following men were not in the 16th (Service) Battalion The King's Royal Rifle Corps, they were in the regiment. In deference to them, here are just a few who fought in Flanders and never returned to their homes and families:

- Rifleman Geoffrey Robinson Abbott R/12727. 18th Battalion King's Royal Rifle Corps from Southminster, Essex. He was killed in action 31 July 1917 aged 39.
- Rifleman Frederick Bennett. 17th Battalion King's Royal Rifle Corps from Flecknoe, Warwickshire. He died 22 March 1918.
- Rifleman David Boswell R/3191.10th Battalion, B Company King's Royal Rifle Corps from Warrington, Lancashire. Family folklore is that David Boswell died in a trench collapse 29 February 1916 aged 21. It is not known if this was due to enemy artillery action or a failure of construction. He is buried at La Belle Alliance Cemetery, Ypres.
- Captain Edmond William Bury. 11th Battalion King's Royal Rifle Corps from Westminster, London, married to Ida. He was killed in action in France on 5 December 1915 aged 31. He was awarded the 1914–15 star campaign medal of the British Empire for his service in the Great War. His son David lost his life during the Second World War while flying with 111 Squadron RAF and is also buried in France.
- Rifleman Harry Semmons Donkin R/19574. King's Royal Rifle Corps from West Jesmond, Newcastle. He transferred to the Royal Scots at some point with the service number 302284. He died of his wounds in a hospital in Maidstone, Kent, 17 May 1918 aged 19.
- Rifleman William Evans. 9th Battalion King's Royal Rifle Corps. He had three little girls, the oldest being just 3 when he was killed on 22 October 1917. His letters to his wife (written in pencil) told her to be cheerful and the letters were formally signed with his name. His name is on the Tyne Cot Memorial in Belgium.

- Rifleman Arthur Charles Franklin R/27748. 1st Battalion King's Royal Rifle Corps from Stratford, London. He was killed in action at Arras 3 May 1917.
- Rifleman J. Fry R/45959. King's Royal Rifle Corps from South Shields. He died 12 November 1918 (a day after the Armistice) aged 18. He had been posted to the 1/13th Kensington Battalion, London Regiment and now lies in Cambrai East Military Cemetery.
- Rifleman James Arthur Gardiner R/24410. 18th Battalion King's Royal Rifle Corps from the Old Kent Road, London. He was married to Emma and was killed in action 14 June 1917 aged 30. According to the family, he was on the front line and lay on top of his commanding officer to save his life. He has no known grave and his name appears on the Menin Gate.
- Rifleman John Graves R/31567. 8th Battalion King's Royal Rifle Corps from Dagenham, Essex. Married to Elizabeth, he was killed in action 24 August 1917 aged 24.
- Lance Corporal George Hatcher 10686. 1st Battalion King's Royal Rifle Corps from Eastbourne, East Sussex. He was killed in action 10 March 1915. He has no known grave and is remembered on the Le Touret Memorial in the Military Cemetery at the village in Flanders.
- Rifleman Edwin Heywood R/15073. 9th Battalion King's Royal Rifle Corps from Tyldesley, Manchester. He was killed in action on the first day of the Arras Offensive 9 April 1917 aged 32. He is buried in Beaurains Cemetery, a short distance from his brother.
- Rifleman Joe Willie Holdsworth C/6237. 18th Battalion King's Royal Rifle Corps from Netherton, near Huddersfield. He was killed in action 20 September 1917 aged 33. His name is on the Memorial Wall at Tyne Cot in Belgium.
- Lance Corporal Wilfred Arthur Hutchins A/3191. 8th Battalion King's Royal Rifle Corps from Birmingham. He was killed in action 4 July 1915 aged 22. Note: there is reference to a Billy Hutchins in The National Archives War Diaries that he died the day after the one stated on the Menin Gate. It shows he was a machine-gunner and was killed by a shell.
- Rifleman James William Keen R/21293. 21st Battalion King's Royal Rifle Corps from Camberwell, London. He died of his wounds 14 Aug 1917 aged 20. His grave is at the Godewaersvelde British Cemetery.
- Rifleman George Law R/10954. 1st Battalion King's Royal Rifle Corps from Clavering, Essex. He was killed in action 31 October 1915 aged 23. Commemorated in Woburn Abbey Cemetery, Cuincy, Pas de Calais, France.
- Rifleman Harry Lee R/11731. 7th Battalion King's Royal Rifle Corps from Ashton-under-Lyne. He was killed instantly 11 May 1917. He died with two other men when a shell landed close to the battalion HQ while they were on parade. He is remembered at London Cemetery Wancourt Road No. 2 Memorial Panel 3.
- Rifleman Frederick William London R/7541. 3rd Battalion King's Royal Rifle Corps from St Pancras, London. He was killed in action 4 May 1915

aged 39. He was married to Georgina and had three children. He is remembered at the Ypres Menin Gate Memorial Panels 51 and 53.

- Rifleman John George McRoy C/12908. 21st Battalion King's Royal Rifle Corps from Monkwearmouth, Sunderland. He died from his wounds 17 June 1917 aged 21. He is buried in Lijssenthoek Military Cemetery in Belgium. John's brother James was killed on 27 August 1917, two months after John. James does not have a resting place as his body has never been found but his name is on the plaque at Tyne Cot Cemetery.
- Rifleman James Arthur Quarmby R/14357. 7th Battalion King's Royal Rifle Corps from Stalybridge, Cheshire. He died from his wounds 15 September 1916 aged 19.
- Lance Corporal Joseph Robson 9654. 4th Battalion King's Royal Rifle Corps from Sunderland. He was killed in action 10 May 1915 aged 22. His name is listed on the Ypres Menin Gate Memorial.
- Rifleman Joseph Sedgwick R/7141. 7th Battalion King's Royal Rifle Corps from Bedworth, Warwick. He was killed in action 6 July 1915 aged 20.
- Sergeant Ben Smales 2631. 2nd Battalion King's Royal Rifle Corps from Leeds, married to Esther. He was killed in action 17 September 1914 aged 35. He was killed by German artillery during the First Battle of the Aisne and has no known grave. His name is carved on the Memorial at La Ferte sous Jouarre.

[There were many Smiths serving in the regiment; they can be identified by their service number and place of residence.]

- Rifleman Albert Smith R/40042. King's Royal Rifle Corps from Larne, County Antrim, died of his wounds 20 November 1917 aged 32.
- Rifleman Albert Arthur Smith A/202204. King's Royal Rifle Corps from Shoreditch, Middlesex. He died at his home 7 November 1918.
- Rifleman Alfred Victor Smith R/39009. King's Royal Rifle Corps from Stratford, Essex. He was killed in action 9 August 1918.
- Rifleman Arthur Smith C/6286. King's Royal Rifle Corps from Derby. He was killed in action 15 September 1916.
- Rifleman Albert (Bert) E. Stephens R/32158. King's Royal Rifle Corps from Southwark, Surrey. He was killed in action 10 October 1917.
- Rifleman John Sutton R/1656. King's Royal Rifle Corps from Birmingham, was killed in action 8 August 1916.
- Lance Corporal Ira William Turner. 2nd Battalion King's Royal Rifle Corps from Newark-on-Trent. He died of his wounds 10 September 1918 aged 27. He is buried at the Abbeville Communal Cemetery.
- Rifleman Francis Albert Vose. 9th Battalion King's Royal Rifle Corps from London. He was at Ypres and was in the trenches at Passchendaele. He went 'over the top' three times. It is understood that when the trench was overrun by German troops, a captured and wounded German officer in the dugout saved Francis from being killed on the spot. His family was notified that he

was missing between 21–27 March 1918 and then, on 31 May 1918, they were notified that he was a POW at Limburg. He spent time unloading scrap from railway wagons. He escaped with another lad and with help from Belgian and French people, they made their way to Calais.

- Rifleman Cecil Wiles. 21st Battalion King's Royal Rifles Corps. Was not called up as, being the eldest son of a farmer, he was in a 'protected occupation'. However, one Sunday morning outside the village church in West Pinchbeck a woman from the village thrust three white feathers into his breast pocket. He resolved to join up and left his wife of three months. He was killed six months later on 8 July 1916.

During the Great War 12,840 men of the King's Royal Rifle Corps were killed, seven members received the Victoria Cross and over 2,000 further decorations were awarded.

After 1918, the unit returned to garrison duties in India, Palestine and Ireland. In 1922, the regiment was reduced from four to two battalions with the third and fourth being disbanded. In 1926, the regiment was reorganized as one of the first mechanized infantry regiments. In 1948, for administrative purposes, the King's Royal Rifle Corps was brigaded with the Oxfordshire & Buckinghamshire Light Infantry and the Rifle Brigade to form the Green Jackets Brigade.

In 1958, the regiment was retitled the 2nd Green Jackets, The King's Royal Rifle Corps (the two other regiments of the Green Jackets Brigade were retitled 1st and 3rd Green Jackets respectively).

In 1966, the three regiments were amalgamated to form the three battalions of the Royal Green Jackets (RGJ) Regiment.

In 1992, the 1st Battalion Royal Green Jackets was disbanded and the King's Royal Rifle Corps were renumbered the 1st Battalion, with the 3rd Battalion (former Rifle Brigade) becoming the 2nd Battalion.

In 2007, the two-battalion Royal Green Jackets Regiment was amalgamated with the remaining light infantry regiments to form the five regular and two territorial battalions of The Rifles.

The 2nd Battalion The Rifles, which is a redesignation of the 1st Battalion Royal Green Jackets, preserves the regiment's traditions. The origins of the Royal Green Jackets (Rifles) Museum at Winchester date back to the aftermath of the Great War.

The National War Museum
In 1917, before the war had ended, the British government decided that a National War Museum should be set up to collect and display material relating to the Great War. The interest taken by the Dominion governments led to the museum being given the title of the Imperial War Museum. Established by an Act of Parliament, the museum was opened in the Crystal Palace on 9 June by King George V. The creation of the museum was the catalyst for many regiments in the British army to start accumulating their own collections of war artefacts and archival material. The King's Royal Rifle Corps (KRRC) and the Rifle Brigade

The Green Jackets Museum, Winchester.

(RB) both did so during the 1920s. It is these collections that now form a substantial part of the material on display in the museum today.

For many years the King's Royal Rifle Corps and the Rifle Brigade collections were housed wherever space could be found for them in the buildings at the Rifle Depot, Winchester. It was not until after the rebuild of the Peninsula Barracks in 1964 that a semi-permanent home for the collections was established on the first floor of the Depot Headquarters Building, the building now occupied by the museum.

Since the King's Royal Rifle Corps was raised on Christmas Day 1755, the evidence of the continued brotherhood of Riflemen is provided by the popularity of its Regimental Association. The continued strength of the Association establishes that once having served as a Rifleman, that distinction stays with its members for the rest of their lives.

If I had covered the complete history of this incorruptible regiment, it would have taken up the whole of this book. Needless to say, the strength and quality of the men who fought in the King's Royal Rifle Corps was, without doubt, exemplary in every respect. The King's Royal Rifle Corps served for more than 200 years throughout the British Empire and the Commonwealth.

The nickname of the regiment is '60th Rifles'. Its motto is *Celer et Audax* (Swift and Bold). The regiment's memorial is in Winchester Cathedral.

Not by the power of Commerce, Art or Pen,
Shall our great Empire stand, nor has it stood;
But by the noble deeds of noble men,
Heroic lives and Heroes outpoured blood.

Chapter Two

The Brigade in Times of War

Fight the good fight with all thy might,
Christ is thy Strength and Christ thy Right;
lay hold on life, and it shall be
thy joy and crown eternally.

Run the straight race, through God's good grace,
lift up thine eyes and seek His face;
life with its way before us lies,
Christ is the Path and Christ the Prize.

Cast care aside, upon thy Guide
lean and his mercy will provide;
trust, and thy trusting soul shall prove
Christ is its Life and Christ its Love.

Faint not nor fear, His arms are near;
He changeth not, and thou art dear;
only believe, and thou shalt see
that Christ is all in all to thee.

Words by John Samuel Bewley Monsell, 1863, Vicar of Egham, near Windsor 1853–70.
Rector of St Nicolas' Church, Guildford and Chaplain to Queen Victoria 1870–75.

Walter Mallock Gee was Secretary to the Junior Division of the Church of England Temperance Society based at Church House, Westminster. Having been introduced to the Boys' Brigade and with the assistance of the CETS, on 11 November 1891 (St Martin's Day), the inaugural meeting of the Church Lads' Brigade took place at St Andrew's Church, Fulham, an area in the London Borough of Hammersmith and Fulham, SW6. This company became known as the 'Pioneer' company of the brigade.

Walter wanted the Church Lads' Brigade to be a complete part of the Anglican Church rather than interdenominational like the Boys' Brigade. He intended that the Church Lads' Brigade would be for the purposes of promoting charity, reverence, patriotism, discipline, self-respect and Christian manliness to the male youth of all classes.

Forming such a brigade was not an easy matter. For the whole of January 1892 the headquarters of the Church Lads' Brigade was the dressing room in Walter's home at Edith Villas, West Kensington. It was the beginning of February before the brigade could move into a third-floor back room at Church House. From 1893 Walter was the colonel of the Church Lads' Brigade.

Walter Mallock Gee.

Lord Robert Baden-Powell.

Further meetings had to be held in London between Walter Mallock Gee's 'Church Lads' Brigade' and the 'London Diocesan Council for the Welfare of Lads'. Everard A. Ford led the meetings and it was agreed that the Church Lads' Brigade should amalgamate with the Gordon Boys' Brigade. Before very long Church Lads' Brigade companies were springing up all over Great Britain.

The Church Lads' Brigade was the first uniformed organization to take up scouting and, in May 1901, began using Baden-Powell's book *Aids to Scouting* to advise Church Lads' Brigade officers as to how they could adopt it to suit their own training scheme.

Additionally, *Hints from Baden-Powell: A Book for Brigade Boys* was a book by the Reverend R.L. Bellamy, vicar of Silkstone near Barnsley, Yorkshire and was published in 1900 after the Relief of Mafeking during the Boer War. The Reverend Bellamy compared the life of a lone scout in enemy territory with the dilemmas faced by a Christian boy in the 'sinful society' of the day.

The brigade's first governor and commandant was Lord Chelmsford and its president was His Royal Highness the Duke of Connaught, who was later to fulfil the same role in scouting. Queen Victoria inspected a parade of the Church Lads' Brigade in August 1896 at Osborne House on the Isle of Wight. After that the Church Lads' Brigade grew quickly and was given Royal Patronage in 1902.

The Church of England cadets came under the County Territorial associations and the CLB units were not badged or affiliated to parent units, but kept their own traditions. This was because the CLB was a centralized body like its sponsor, the Church of England.

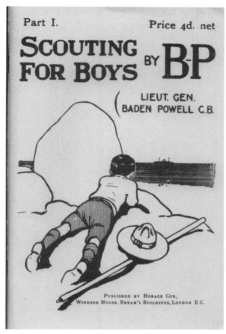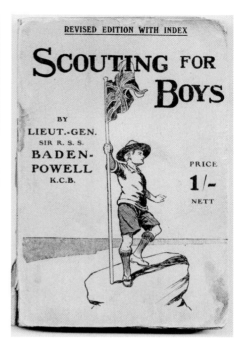

Scouting for Boys.

Lads who were members of the Church Lads' Brigade were disciplined in rifle drills and various military-style exercises. In 1911, the somewhat small movement became recognized by the War Office as part of the Territorial Cadet Force.

The Church Lads' Brigade took its symbols from St Paul's description of Christian armour in a letter to the Ephesians, in which he described a shield, a helmet, a sword, a girdle and a breastplate.

An extract from the *Uxbridge Record*, autumn 2005, by Terry Hissey reads:

Walter Gee was a creature of habit. Every morning he would attend the Eucharist at St Cuthbert's at Philbeach Gardens, Earls Court. It was said of him that he was a 'red hot enthusiast who eats, drinks, sleeps and talks CLB'. To all who knew him he exhibited a magnetic personality with a transparent faith. He had a heart full of love, in fact he was described as 'the most lovable of men', which conquered all of the problems facing the organisation. He was seemingly tireless in his enthusiasm, for instance visiting Canada and Newfoundland and spending three months crossing the Dominion and along the way forming 'Old Comrades Lodges'. Absolute unselfishness was the very keynote of his life. He had a self-effacing attitude and deeply hated publicity and advertisement. Only while he was away in Canada in 1912 did a photograph appear of him in 'The Brigade', his devotion being equalled only by his modesty. It was also said that, 'He never tired, he never grew stale; he never ceased to be a lad at heart.'

Lord Chelmsford.

Walter Gee died at his home on 23 December 1916, after a short illness. The 109th Reserve Battalion (19th) King's Royal Rifle Corps, formerly members of the Church Lads' Brigade, escorted the cortege to the cemetery. The coffin was borne through a guard of troops, with reversed rifles, by six Sergeants of the original 16th (Service) Battalion the King's Royal Rifle Corps, who were trained at Denham. Walter was buried at Hillingdon Cemetery, Uxbridge.

In *The Brigade* magazine of February 1917, Field Marshal Lord Methuen, late governor and commandant of the CLB said, 'No man has done more for the youth of England than Mr Gee.'

The immediate cause of the Great War
On 28 June 1914 the heir to the throne of Austria and Hungary, the Archduke Franz Ferdinand and his wife Sophie, Duchess of Hohenberg, were assassinated at Sarajevo, the capital of Bosnia and Herzegovina. A 19-year-old Serbian student

The Duke of Connaught.

A CLB cadet and badge.

named Gavrilo Princip fired the gun and Austria received very little satisfaction from Serbia on the apprehension of the culprit and those behind his act. This seemed to be an intentional disregard of the situation by Serbia and an insult to Austria. Thirty-seven days later, it was seized upon by Austria and Germany as a reason to declare war.

Every attempt was made to mislead the otherwise peaceful powers as to the aim of the German states. Germany's Kaiser William II (grandson of Britain's Queen Victoria) thought that France couldn't fight because of her bad financial position and lack of heavy artillery. After consultation with his military and naval advisers, 'Kaiser Bill' decided to make preparations for war. He considered the British army to be of little consequence, calling it 'a small contemptible army'. It was due to this remark that the British Expeditionary Force that landed in France in 1914 was nicknamed the 'Old Contemptibles'.

On 1 August 1914, the invading German troops violated the neutrality of Luxemburg. This was considered to be an act of war as France and Britain had guaranteed the Grand Duchy that it would remain neutral.

On 2 August 1914, Germany delivered an ultimatum to Brussels. They wanted to move German troops through Belgium under the false pretext that the French had planned an invasion of Belgian territory.

On 3 August 1914, Germany declared war on France.

On 4 August 1914, Great Britain declared war on Germany, the Great War broke out in the Western world and things were never to be the same again.

King George V was on the British throne at the time. The entry in his diary for the day that war was declared was as follows:

4 August 1914 – Warm, showers and windy. At work all day. Winston Churchill came to report at 1.00 that at the meeting of the Cabinet this morning we had sent an ultimatum to Germany that if by midnight tonight she did not give a satisfactory answer about her troops passing through Belgium, Goschen would ask for his passports. Held a Council at 4.00 ... I held a Council at 10.45 to declare War with Germany, it is a terrible catastrophe but it is not our fault ... When they heard that War had been declared the excitement [of the crowds outside the Palace] increased and it was a never to be forgotten sight when May and I with David [the Prince of Wales] went onto the balcony, the cheering was terrific. Please God it may soon be over and that he will protect dear Bertie's life ...

Report from the *Daily News* newspaper on 4 August 1914 reads:

In London, the people's enthusiasm culminated outside Buckingham Palace when it became known that war had been declared. The news was received with tremendous cheering, which grew to a deafening roar when King George, Queen Mary and the Prince of Wales appeared.

Westminster, Charing Cross and the main thoroughfares round Westminster were thronged all last night with excited crowds. Union Jacks were everywhere to be seen and the air was filled with the sound of patriotic songs. Trafalgar Square was almost impassible. A hostile crowd assembled outside the German embassy and smashed the windows.

Events moved rapidly. Britain had not really expected to be involved in a full-scale war. When Britain did become involved, there was no system of conscrip-

Barton-upon-Humber CLB, 1909.

Proud lads of the CLB.

The man who started the Great War: Gavrilo Princip is seated front row centre.

Kaiser Wilhelm II, German Emperor.

tion in place; nevertheless there was an immediate loyal flocking to the Colours. Patriotic fervour gripped the nation and thousands of teenage lads lied about their age in order to become part of this new adventure. Any young lad who was a member of the Church Lads' Brigade would have had very little conception of the sort of war that awaited him in the trenches.

Few, if any, of the recruitment officers had time to check the age of the volunteers. The rule of thumb seemed to be perfectly simple: if the volunteer wanted to

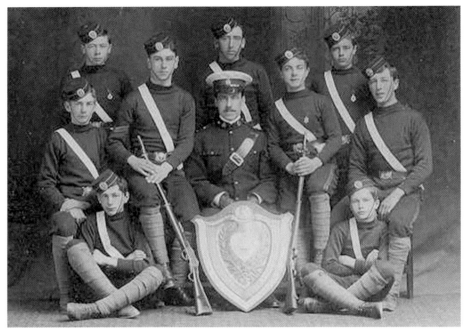

CLB cadets ready for war, puttees and all.

CLB Wakefield Football Club 1913–14, Willie Chappell circled.

Guarding the
Old Flag!

Great War poster: guarding the old flag.

fight for his country and was physically fit enough to do so, why stop him? It is thought that as many as 250,000 'boy soldiers' were recruited and fought in the Great War.

All over the country many members of the church brigades, who were already in the Reserves or Territorials, went off to their military or naval units. When the call to arms came in the summer of 1914, the 16th (Service) Battalion (Church Lads' Brigade) of the King's Royal Rifle Corps was formed under Field Marshal Lord Grenfell at Denham in Buckinghamshire. A battalion was the basic tactical unit of the infantry of the British army in the Great War. A full establishment consisted of 1,000 men, of whom thirty were officers.

Lord Grenfell offered his organization for military service to the Crown. He asked and obtained permission from the British War Office to form an infantry regiment of serving and former members of the Church Lads' Brigade. The regiment became attached to the pre-existing King's Royal Rifle Corps, served as the 16th (Service) Battalion and was sponsored by the Church Lads' Brigade. Later on the 19th (Service) Battalion was formed, also sponsored by the Church Lads' Brigade.

At home, lads of the CLB were involved in all kinds of work to help the war effort. They guarded reservoirs and pipelines, collected old newspapers or blew bugles after the 'all clear' had sounded following Zeppelin air-raids. The CLB 9th County of London Battalion (St Pancras), County of London Regiment (Territorial Force) Headquarters in London suffered bomb damage: ten people were killed and many buildings damaged when the bomb hit.

In 1917, in recognition of the sacrifices of British soldiers of the 16th (Service) Battalion who fought on the Somme, the Church Lads' Brigade affiliated en masse to the King's Royal Rifle Corps as the KRRC Cadets. As part of the British army the cadets and former cadets of the CLB in England were issued the Pattern 1907 Service Dress uniform. This was khaki in colour and consisted of a tunic, trousers, puttees and a cloth forage cap. The practical colour of khaki succeeded the traditions of the green jackets and red coats of peacetime. Both the uniform tunic and cap were adorned with brass buttons. Although general service brass buttons were in existence, many regiments adopted buttons specific to them. The 16th Battalion transferred their CLB uniform buttons to the Pattern 1907 Service

British soldiers waiting to embark.

Dress. The buttons of the 16th Battalion, as with the buttons of all the battalions of the King's Royal Rifle Corps, were blackened to conform to dress regulations specifying that the buttons and badges of all rifle regiments were to be treated in this way.

Francis Wallace Grenfell (*c.*1841–1925) was educated at Milton Abbas School, Dorset, but left school early and passed the army entrance examination. He purchased his commission into the 3rd Battalion of the 60th Rifles in 1859. His early service was uneventful and advancement was slow. On 1 November 1871, following opposition in the House of Lords to a Bill designed to abolish military purchases, a Royal Warrant was issued abolishing all regulations relating to the sale of commissions. He actually purchased his commission of captain in 1871 in the last list of government appointments in which the purchase of British army commissions was allowed. After years of army service and being rewarded with the GCMG, Grenfell was appointed deputy adjutant general for reserve forces at the War Office. It was a post that involved the supervision of reserves, militia, yeomanry and volunteers.

In 1894, he was raised to the position of inspector general. During 1896 he was dispatched to Moscow to attend the coronation festivities of the young Tsar Nicholas II and in 1897 figured prominently at the celebration of Queen

Lord Grenfell.

Victoria's diamond jubilee. In January 1899, he was appointed governor and commander-in-chief of Malta. There he proved to be most successful by displaying much interest in the antiquities of the island and in the methods of any cultivation being used.

At the coronation of King Edward VII in 1902, he was raised to the peerage as Baron Grenfell of Kilvey. In 1903, he was selected for the command of the newly-created Fourth Army Corps and, on promotion to full general in 1904, was appointed commander-in-chief in Ireland, a post that he held until 1908 when he was promoted to field marshal.

Every regiment in the kingdom, Regular or Territorial, had its quota of the nation's lads from the church brigades. It is estimated that around 50,000 brigade lads served in the Great War, during which many honours and distinctions were awarded. The two service battalions of the King's Royal Rifle Corps, contributed by the CLB, were composed entirely of past and present members of the Church Lads' Brigade. The Council of the Football Association formed footballers' battalions from the 7,000 players in England's professional football teams and five sportsmen's battalions were also raised in Britain.

In local recruiting drives, Lord Derby promoted the idea of groups of men from towns and villages enlisting and serving together with their family and friends. The idea was that they would then be able to fight alongside one another. These battalions became known as the 'Pals' battalions (the word 'pal' meaning 'friend' in British English). They were very popular with the ordinary lads of Britain and the well-known poster campaign featuring Lord Kitchener enticed them in droves into the enlistment offices up and down the country. The lads in each of the Pals battalions always stuck together. Never before had there been more groups of happy-go-lucky amateur soldiers, ready to fight and do their bit for their country.

During the first twenty months of the war, 3 million young lads and men volunteered for Kitchener's 'New Army': 144 battalions were raised and paid for by local authorities and from private donations. The cost of the weapons used was not included as this was the responsibility of the army.

The tragic consequences of men of local districts fighting together were realized on 1 July 1916 at the Battle of the Somme, where hundreds of thousands of friends and neighbours were struck down together. Because of the blunders of

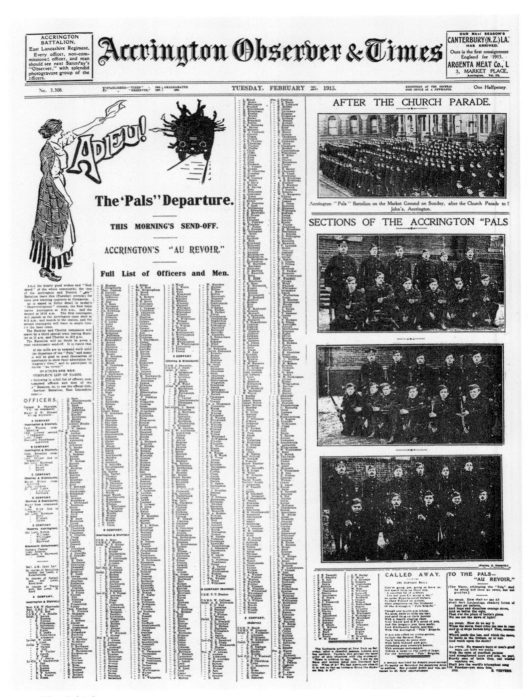

The 'Pals' departure.

the government and their advisors, whole communities were decimated when all of their men were lost.

When the dreadful news from the front reached London, the following speech was made by Francis Grenfell on 26 July 1916 during a House of Lords debate on the military training of the nation:

My Lords, before I say a few words on the question of national training I should like to join with the noble and learned Lord [Lord Parmoor] in his high appreciation of the action of the noble and learned Viscount in the creation of the Officers Training Corps. The movement was welcomed highly in the Army when it was first initiated, and after the war had progressed for about a year I do not know what we could have done to supply officers for the Army had it not been for this corps, which the noble and learned Viscount so wisely formed. Only a few days ago I was at Winchester and inspected a detachment of the Officers Training Corps there. About twenty of these young men were going away to regiments, and were so highly trained that they would require but a very short time before they would be able to join their units at the Front. Winchester has already lost fifteen officers killed and many wounded, and has supplied an extraordinarily large number of officers through this corps.

The most rev. Primate, in his speech on the second day of this debate, referred to a corps with which I am connected and about which I wish to say a few words. As was stated by the noble Viscount, at the age of 14 a boy, as a rule, changes his habits; he breaks away from all moral, social, and very often religious influences, and that is the time when he most requires a guiding hand. I think that the various cadet corps are most useful at that particular period. Of the one with which I am connected, the Church Lads Brigade, I have been governor and commandant for eight years; I was preceded in the commandant-ship by my noble friend Lord Methuen, and before him by Lord Chelmsford; and I may say that now, after twenty years' hard work, the brigade has arrived at a very great state of efficiency. Your Lordships will pardon me if I speak about my own corps, but in doing so I do not wish to depreciate in any way the work of other boys brigades which are doing such excellent work.

In the Church Lads Brigade we have now 60,000 lads in England all under training; and in Australia, Africa, Canada, Newfoundland, and the West Indies we have companies of the brigade. The other day, when I was inspecting a battalion which had been raised from this brigade, I noticed two very dark-looking youths. I asked who they were, and was told that they had paid their passage from the West Indies, they having been members of the Church Lads Brigade there, to come over and join a battalion which was then going out to the Front, which shows the enthusiasm these lads display for the Service. In addition to the 60,000 youths that we are now training as best we can, we have a system of an old comrades association, and when the war broke out I asked Lord Kitchener if he would permit me to raise a

Lord Kitchener.

battalion from those ex-members of the Church Lads Brigade. He said he would be glad if I did so, and I proposed to provide a battalion of 1,100 strong. In a few days I had offers of 2,500. That was at the very beginning of the war. Out of them I was able to form one of the finest battalions of the King's Royal Rifle Corps, which I served in and of which this battalion now forms a part. This battalion, I regret to say, is now very greatly diminished in strength. It lost in one of the attacks during the last week nearly half its strength, and more than half the number of its officers. But I am glad to say that it behaved with the greatest possible gallantry. The colonel, writing to me, wounded as he was, from one of the dressing stations, said — The objective was a trench 1,000 yards distant, with unbroken wire before it, and enfiladed on one flank by the German machine guns, but the battalion was as steady as if on parade; the men behaved splendidly. And he added that there were hardly any officers — only two that he knew of — who had come back unwounded. I do not mention this as anything peculiar, because every battalion of the New Armies has behaved in that gallant way; still it is a great satisfaction to those who have taken an interest in the Church Lads Brigade to know that these men, all drawn from its ranks, should have behaved in such a gallant manner.

I believe that the training which these lads get in the various brigades — especially so in the Church Lads Brigade, because it is connected with religion — is most valuable, and we owe the deepest thanks to the most rev. Primate for his assistance and for the interest he has taken in the movement. But I do not speak of soldiering only. In various walks of life we keep up with these boys; most of them belong to the old comrades association, and in nearly every walk in life we find that the boys who have passed through these brigades — not only our brigade — succeed a great deal better than if they had not passed through the curriculum which we give them. Therefore I am anxious, as a finale to my few remarks, to press upon the Government the great advantages of these cadet corps. At present we get no grant. We do not particularly ask for one, because we do get transport occasionally, and we get bands, and armament, and occasionally munitions. But we hope that this question, after the war, will be taken up seriously in the elementary schools. We know what a great advantage this training is, and we trust that this question will be taken up and cadet corps initiated generally. There are very few at present; in fact, the Church Lads Brigade consists of half of the whole of the cadets in England. We should like to see our brethren growing up round us in greater numbers. And when the question is taken up we hope that the existing corps will be left alone, to a certain extent at least, to manage their own affairs, and that some scheme may be arranged whereby the various new corps may be as similar as possible to the corps which at present exist. I feel sure that the education they get can rightly be considered as part of the training of the nation, and I sincerely hope that this matter will be seriously taken up at the end of the war. Sadly, many of these young men never returned home.

'Boy soldiers' fighting in the Great War – many from Church Brigades – remained a controversial issue throughout the conflict. By the time the war had ended, many thousands of lads, some too young to legally enlist, had been either killed or wounded.

Chapter Three

Eight Good Men and True

At the start of the Great War, the British army held approximately 710,000 men in its active regiments and territorial units. The government, as well as the British public, had been against conscription for more than 100 years. However, it was apparent that the British army was far too small in comparison to the French and German forces, so the Secretary of State for War, Lord Kitchener, saw the need to build an army of at least seventy divisions.

In August 1914 the British government called for an extra 100,000 volunteer soldiers to come forward. By the end of September, 750,000 men had volunteered and by January 1915 more than 1 million had voluntarily joined the armed forces.

When war was declared, conscription in Great Britain wasn't compulsory, so one must wonder what was going through the minds of so many young lads that made them want to leave their homes and join the British army. Was it a chance to change their lives completely; get away from it all; travel and see new

Kitchener's recruitment poster.

things; have an adventure? Whatever the reasons, thousands of brave lads were willing to venture forth from their safe environments to fight for their country on the 'Western Front'. This was the term used to describe the contested armed frontier between lands controlled by Germany to the east and the allies to the west.

Not many people had radios in those days and the only other media coverage at the time was through the newspapers. There were newspaper sellers on almost every street corner, shouting out the headlines, as pedestrians grabbed their daily ha'penny or penny broadsheets.

The British, generally a reserved nation, lived in cities, towns and villages. In August 1914, many people would have been on holiday at the seaside with no thought of what was going on in the outside world. The first few days of that August were rainy and a little chilly, but the rest of the month was warm, dry and sunny. The beach resorts of Great Britain were most probably filled with pleasure-seeking tourists, enjoying the sunshine and sea air. However, the sombre mood in London was reported as 'calm, confident and grim'.

The *Daily Mirror* showed its support for the war as British troops began pre-paring for it. The *Manchester Guardian* (now the *Guardian*) expressed hopes that British military intervention would not be necessary. The *Daily Express* led with the headline on 5 August: 'England expects that every man will do his duty.' That paper also reported that a hostile crowd had demonstrated outside the German Embassy: 'Groaning and hissing were freely indulged in', it said.

The *Daily Mail* left no doubt that it was fully supportive of the government's decision to go to war. 'The proceedings in the House of Commons yesterday were worthy of tremendous occasion. They will fill the nation with fresh courage and confidence,' it said. A patriotic stance was also taken by the *Daily Telegraph*, which reported news of 'enthusiastic troops' at the frontiers and an 'historic scene in the House of Commons'. Literature featured in *The Times* of 4 August with the publication of the first 'war poem' by Henry Newbolt. The paper published war poems almost daily from then on.

Papers that had taken an anti-war stance, such as the *Daily Herald*, plummeted in popularity after 4 August as the public spirit changed and patriotism took hold. Shortly after the British government announced the mobilization of troops, the *Daily Chronicle* warned its readers that the stories it published throughout the war might not give readers the full picture. The *London Gazette*, an official newspaper of record, published a special supplement to its 4 August edition.

This still leaves me wondering why my 'eight good men' (listed below) were so ready to join the fray. Was it because the regimental-styled activities at meetings of the Church Lads' Brigade made them want to join in for real? Or was it the 'stiff upper lip' and British patriotism for king and country that spurred them on? Many of those that joined up were fighting for a state that denied them the vote. Whatever it was, in 1914 they all became soldiers of the 16th (Service) Battalion The King's Royal Rifle Corps.

Five of those lads were members of the Church Lads' Brigade at Tideswell in Derbyshire. Tideswell is a close-knit village and civil parish in the Peak District.

The rush to get to the recruitment office in Whitehall.

CLB Tideswell, 1909.

With a relatively small population in 1914, it is probable that everybody knew each other. This would certainly be the case with the lads who joined the army.

Rifleman Henry (Harry) Barber C428 was born on 24 February 1891 and was christened on 6 March 1891 at Ashover, Derbyshire. Harry was 23 years old when he decided he should 'do his bit' for his country. At that time he lived on the High Street at Tideswell with his mother Annie, his father William and his three brothers and two sisters.

Harry started his army training with the other lads in the 16th (Service) Battalion The King's Royal Rifle Corps at the new army camp at Denham in Buckinghamshire. It must have seemed a million miles away from his home town in Derbyshire. The edited letter below shows that he is not enjoying army life, he dislikes the Territorials and he misses his mother. It also suggests that the lads were billeted in houses until facilities in the camp were ready.

Dear Mother, Father, Sisters Bros.
Just a line or two to let you know I received your most welcome letters and sweetloaf. Dear Mother, the tomato was very badly crushed and the box crushed to atoms. The butter and loaf was all right. You need not send me

Rifleman Harry Barber and his letter from Denham.

any more butter because I have got used to being without it. Do not spend your money on butter for me. I can do without butter. I only want you to send me some fancy bread now and again. Mother, we are having a very wet day here, Wednesday. I have been cooking today and you talk about taking care of myself in the cookhouse. I have been eating all day. I am thinking of sending my washing home this weekend. Only my shirt vest and pants. We are expecting to draw some more money today. Have you got my bit of wage from The Mill when I left Tideswell? If you have not, tell our Fanny to see about it. I do not think we shall be able to come home till Christmas. If all is well Mother, I shall try to save some money to come with.

You know Dear Mother, the Terries [Territorials] are doing better than we are because if you want some of the people to give you some hot meals, they pull a very long face, so we don't get the same done for us as the Terries do. They are a lot better off than we are. They get the people to cook for them and the people here are very funny. We know we are a very good way from home, further off than the Terries. Well dear Mother I shall be able to eat anything when I come back. The Terries are great fat and red faced. No doubt we would have red faces if we ever got as much drink as they get. I shall not get any, whether I get a red face or not.

Tell them all at Tideswell I wish to be remembered to them all. Dear Mother, no doubt you will have seen H Swarbrick by the time you read this. He went home today and he is very bad. If you want to know what kind of place Denham is get H Swarbrick up some night and ask him what camp life is like, He will tell you a tale. He is fed up with it. It is very quiet.

I don't know if I shall be able to get any dinner for our Don when he comes because it's a hard job to get enough for ourselves, but I shall try anyhow. You know, we have not drawn our £5. We are getting our money very slow. It is about nine weeks till Christmas. Never mind all being well I shall be rich at Christmas.

Your Loving Son, Harry.

Rifleman Joseph Isaac Boller C730 was born on 10 October 1894, the eldest son of Joseph and Mary Boller. He had five sisters and two brothers and the family resided at 62 Aston Brook Street, Aston, Birmingham. He was a member of the Church Lads' Brigade at the Bishop Ryder Memorial Church, Gem Street, Birmingham and his father was an officer in the brigade.

The church was a simple building of red brick and stone designed by Rickman and Hussey in the Gothic style, with a pinnacled tower containing eight bells (dated 1869) by Blews of Birmingham. It was built to commemorate the Reverend Henry Ryder, Bishop of Lichfield, who died in 1836 and was consecrated in 1838.

Barely out of his teens, Joe was 20 when he joined the army in 1914. At that time he was working as a nickel-plater, presumably in Birmingham's jewellery quarter.

Jesse Robert Brightmore C480 was born on 18 April 1894 at Sherwood House, Tideswell, Derbyshire and was christened on 20 May 1894. His father, Robert,

Rifleman Joseph Boller with his mother and father and two of his sisters.

was a builder and stonemason. Jesse went to school in Tideswell at the Church of England Junior School and then at Tideswell Grammar School. After leaving school, he became a Westminster Bank employee.

He was 20 when he joined the 16th (Service) Battalion The King's Royal Rifle Corps in 1914. In 1917 he was wounded and at that time was a sergeant, being promoted to captain during his later service.

Rifleman Matthew Ferguson C1647 was born in April 1893 at Mickley Square, Northumberland. In the *Mickley Parish Magazine* of January 1916 it appears that pals E. Ridley and Matthew Ferguson had joined up together and left at the beginning of December 1915 for initial training in Andover. They were both members of the church choir. Then, in the same magazine dated August 1916 (just eight months later), an item states that both boys had been wounded and were doing well in a hospital in England.

Rifleman Sydney Goodwin C432 was born on 6 November 1892 at Tideswell, Derbyshire. He was christened on 24 December 1892. Sydney was one of five sons and five daughters of John Thomas and Ada Goodwin.

John Thomas Goodwin worked as a carpenter and joiner. In 1911, three of his children were still at school, two of the daughters were cotton bobbin winders, two of the boys worked in the limestone quarries and at the age of 18, Sydney and another brother were farm labourers. Sydney was 22 when he joined the army in 1914.

Rifleman Henry Thomas Gwinnell C1316 was born in April 1897 at Eton, Buckinghamshire. He was the only son of Henry and Hester and had two older sisters. After he left school, it is possible he helped his father, who was a cattleman and farmer. Henry was only 17 in 1914 when he joined the army, and while stationed at Uxbridge, he met his future wife.

Rifleman Reginald Lomas C423 was born in Tideswell, Derbyshire on 14 June 1892. In 1901 his father was a publican at the Peacock Inn in Tideswell. In 1911, at the age of 19, Reginald was working as a clerk in the cotton factory.

He joined the army at the age of 22 and was one of my 'Eight Good Men' of the 16th (Service) Battalion The King's Royal Rifle Corps who didn't come home. He died in France on 26 October 1918 (less than a month before the Armistice), and is buried in Awoingt British Cemetery, Nord, France. Strangely, the grave is one of the few without some sort of cross on it. Awoingt was used to bury men from nearby casualty clearing stations, although some graves were established after the Armistice. Along the side wall, there is a row of German graves. Reginald Lomas is buried next to a lieutenant colonel, the Hon. Harold Ritchie.

Reginald's brother, Private Norman Lomas C1818, 1/6th Battalion Prince of Wales's North Staffordshire Regiment (formerly 954, Notts & Derbyshire Regiment), also from Tideswell, was two years older than Reginald. When he was 20, he lodged at Burgh le Marsh, Lincolnshire, and worked as a postman. He returned to Tideswell to enlist in 1914. He fought in the Western European theatre in France and was killed in action on 13 October 1915.

Rifleman Sydney Goodwin.

Rifleman R. Lomas's grave (*left*) and Tideswell War Memorial (*right*) .

Both Robert and Mary Lomas's sons are commemorated on the war memorial in Tideswell's Market Square.

Lance Corporal John Henry Norman C657 was born in July 1893 at Worksop, Nottinghamshire. His father was a railway worker. At the age of 17, John was living with his uncle, Thomas Brightmore, in Tideswell, who is listed as being a stonemason. When he enlisted in the army in 1914, he was working as a jeweller's apprentice with his cousin Wilfred in Tideswell.

When these lads went off to war, none of them was married. Sweaty and covered in mud, they fought for their lives with bayonets, knives and even with their bare hands. Seven of them were wounded and shipped back home to recover.

The wounded lads required evacuation from the battlefields as quickly as possible for their injuries to be treated. However, evacuation could take a long time, as high numbers of casualties often overwhelmed medical teams and the level of fighting made it too dangerous for stretcher-bearers to retrieve the wounded. Basic field dressings, often dirty and contaminated, covered wounds, while the injured were carried to a regimental aid post. Morphine injections managed pain and splints were used for badly-damaged limbs. Fortunately, the widespread introduction of hypodermic needles massively improved the administration of painkillers.

The wounded were then transported to an advanced dressing station 5 miles from the battlefield, most likely by horse-drawn cart or a wheeled handcart. Injuries and conditions were assessed and if possible re-dressed. From here, stretcher-bearers would take them to a field hospital, several miles further back from the front, where severe injuries were treated.

Journeys to field hospitals regularly took between a day and a week. This, combined with a lack of sterile dressings and the fact that antibiotics had not yet been discovered, meant that many injured men died or started to develop severe infections from which they would not recover by the time they had reached a main

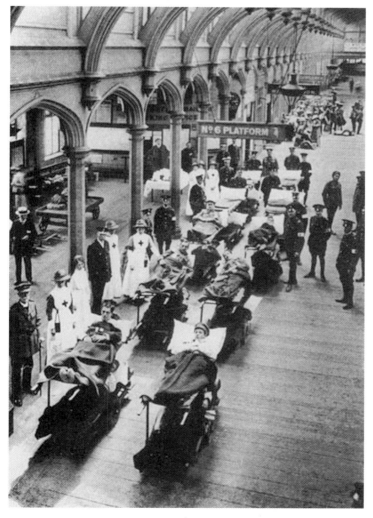

Wounded soldiers returning home.

Medical treatment in the trenches.

field hospital. Dedicated teams of doctors, nurses and women volunteers worked together to help the sick and injured.

Figures suggest that nearly 40 per cent of the men who had gangrene amputations died within two days of reaching the field hospital. Burns treatment of the time generally favoured the application of chemicals, often in the form of coagulants, which had some benefits for smaller-scale wounds by preventing contamination and reducing the chances of infection. However, due to the high mortality rate from serious burn injuries, their benefits were not very obvious.

Hospital ships

The ships that brought the wounded lads back to England were generally painted white with a green line and red crosses running along the sides. With the rough swelling and rolling of the sea, the journey home proved to be torturous for many of the men. Neither was it always safe to be transported back on one of these ships. Germany declared her reasons for sinking hospital ships, announced to the world in the following terms:

> The German Government can no longer suffer that the British Government should forward troops and munitions to the main theatre of war under cover of the Red Cross, and it therefore declares that from now on no enemy

Voluntary Aid Detachment
(VAD) nurses poster.

hospital ship will be allowed in the sea zone comprised between a line drawn from Flamborough Head to Terschelling on the one hand and Ushant and Land's End on the other. If in this sea zone after the expiry of the stated time any enemy hospital ship is encountered, it will be considered as a vessel of war, and it will be attacked without further ceremony.

In 1916 the German press seized opportunities for spreading this slander. When the British hospital ship *Britannic* was sunk in the Aegean Sea with 1,100 wounded on board, about fifty lives were lost. It was at first considered doubtful whether the cause was a torpedo or a mine, but an inspired statement at once appeared in the German *Kieler Zeitung* newspaper to the effect that the *Britannic* had been torpedoed: 'The Britannic was transporting fresh troops for our enemies. If she had not been doing so, our submarines would never of course, have torpedoed her.'

HMHS *Britannic.*

This was answered by an announcement from the British Admiralty on 3 December 1916:

> German wireless messages to the Embassy, Washington, are again promul-gating mendacious reports, purporting to come from Rotterdam, that the hospital ship *Britannic*, recently sunk, had troops on board. A complete statement of all persons carried on board that ship was published on November 14th.
>
> As has been officially stated on several previous occasions, British hospital ships are employed solely in the conditions set forth in the Geneva and Hague Conventions and they carry neither personnel nor material other than that authorised by those Conventions.

The threat against hospital ships contained in the subsequent declaration of unrestricted submarine warfare was answered by the British Foreign Office on 31 January 1917:

> The German Government announce that they have conclusive proof that in several instances enemy hospital ships have often been misused for the transport of munitions and troops. They also state that they have placed these proofs through diplomatic channels before the British and French Governments, and have at the same time declared that the traffic of hospital ships on the military routes for the forces fighting in France and Belgium within a line drawn between Flamborough Head and Terschelling on the one hand, and from Ushant to Land's End on the other, will no longer be tolerated.

His Majesty's Government have received no such communication, through diplomatic channels or other wise, from the German Government as is alleged, and they most emphatically deny that British hospital ships have been used for the transport of munitions and troops, or in any way contrary to the Hague Convention for the adaptation on the principles of the Geneva Convention to maritime war. Under the Convention belligerents have the right to search hospital ships, and the German Government have therefore an obvious remedy in case of suspicion, a remedy which they have never utilised.

From the German Government's statement that hospital ships will no longer be tolerated within the limits mentioned only one conclusion can be drawn, namely, that it is the intention of the German Government to add yet another and more unspeakable crime against law and humanity to the long list which disgraces their record.

In these circumstances, His Majesty's Government have requested the United States Government to inform the German Government that His Majesty's Government have decided that if the threat is carried out reprisals will immediately be taken by the British authorities concerned.

Germany proceeded from threats to deeds. The hospital ship *Asturias*, which had been attacked unsuccessfully by a German submarine as early as 1 February 1915, was torpedoed and sunk on the night of 20/21 March 1917 with all of her crew and staff on board. The British Admiralty announced the outrage a week later:

The British hospital ship *Asturias*, whilst steaming with all navigation lights and with all the proper distinguishing Red Cross signs brilliantly illuminated, was torpedoed without warning on the night March 20/21. The following casualties occurred:

Medical Services	**Crew**
Dead 11.	Dead 20.
Missing, 3 (including 1 female staff nurse).	Missing, 9 (including 1 stewardess).
Injured 17.	Injured 22.

The torpedoing of this hospital ship is included in the list of achievements claimed by U-boats as reported in the German Wireless Press message yesterday.

Another announcement followed on 14 April, making public the sinking of the hospital ships *Gloucester Castle* and *Saita*:

The British hospital ship *Gloucester Castle* was torpedoed without warning in mid-Channel during the night. All of the wounded were successfully removed from the ship. The Berlin Official Wireless of 11 April announced that a U-boat, which left no possible doubt in the matter, torpedoed her.

On the 10 April the British hospital ship *Saita* struck a mine in the Channel during very bad weather and sank. There were no wounded on board, but 5 RAMC Medical Officers, 9 Nursing Sisters and 38 RAMC Personnel were missing and presumed drowned.

Hospital ships sunk by German submarines

Name	Date	Lives Lost
Portugal	17 March 1916	85
Vperiod	8 July 1916	7
Britannic	21 Nov 1916	50
Braemar Castle	22 Nov 1916	1
Asturias	20 March 1917	43
Gloucester Castle	30 March 1917	3
Donegal	17 April 1917	41
Lanfranc	17 April 1917	34
Dover Castle	27 May 1917	6
Rewa	4 Jan 1918	3
Glenart Castle	26 Feb 1918	15

Military hospitals

Several military hospitals in Great Britain existed before the Great War, some even pre-dating the Boer War and going back as far as the Crimean War. Large numbers of public and private buildings (often large houses) were turned over for use as small hospitals, most of which operated as annexes to nearby larger hospitals. Some smaller hospitals became specialist units dealing with mental problems. Other specialist hospitals were developed into units for limbless men, orthopaedic units, cardiac units, typhoid units and those for the treatment of venereal diseases.

As the demand for hospital beds increased, one of the actions taken by the government to provide more capacity was to turn over existing pre-war asylums for military use. Military hospitals became established at hutted army camps. Land, either on existing army bases or acquired nearby for the purpose, was used for construction of major hospitals.

Sir Alfred Keogh, Director of Army Medical Services, was most concerned about the availability of beds in British hospitals. In order to address this problem he established four large convalescent camps at Blackpool, Epsom, Dartford and Eastbourne. Early in 1916 it was decided to further refine the system by creating command depots (military convalescent camps) for the rehabilitative training of soldiers too fit for convalescent camp but not yet fit enough to be returned to their units.

Thousands of wounded lads were shipped back to the British Isles, but that would be no consolation for many more thousands of families that had lost their loved ones in such a terrible war. Every Sunday, for four whole years and beyond, services of remembrance were held in churches for those who did not come home.

Joseph Boller (back row, second left) at army convalescent home.

Listed below are some of those lost lads of the Church Lads' Brigade, 16th (Service) Battalion The King's Royal Rifle Corps – the 'Churchmen's Battalion' – also, 'all good men and true':

- Rifleman Henry Frederick Bowman R29430, 16th (Service) Battalion The King's Royal Rifle Corps. Henry was from Essex and was a member of Hertfordshire and Essex Flying Club. He died of his wounds in France on 23 April 1917 and he is commemorated on the Arras Memorial. Rifleman Albert Clarence Bedson C1239, 16th (Service) Battalion The King's Royal Rifle Corps from Brixton, London. He died of his wounds on 20 May 1917, aged 19. Rifleman Felix John Brinn R/14103, 16th (Service) Battalion The King's Royal Rifle Corps from Acton, Middlesex. He died near Ypres from his wounds on 17 April 1918, aged 21. He had married Gladys Allen the year before in Barnet. His body was never found and his name is on the Tyne Cot memorial.
- Corporal William Chappell C/402, 16th (Service) Battalion The King's Royal Rifle Corp from Ossett, Wakefield, Yorkshire. He died of his wounds on 31 January 1916, aged 20. Willie had joined the Church Lads' Brigade at the age of 13 in 1909. Despite being only 17 years of age, he left his family and travelled to London's King's Cross before going on to Denham. Willie wrote to his mother as soon as he arrived in Denham, on a postcard he bought at the Swan Hotel on the Village Road: 'Dear Mother, Arrived

London 2pm. Came straight here. Can't say where or what we shall do. This place Denham is near Webridge [*sic*]. Don't worry shall be all right. Don't know my address yet. Love from Willie.' He adds one more line: 'Am in this hotel on the photo while writing.'

Willie spent the next six months at Denham undertaking training and guard duties at local bridges and reservoirs, and a further two months in Rayleigh, Essex. They returned to Denham and in June 1915 the lads were moved to Clipstone Camp in Mansfield. Later that summer he moved on to Perham Down, a village near Salisbury Plain and Andover. In November the division received a warning order to prepare to sail for France and the brigade moved by train to Southampton with a

Corporal Willie Chappell.

total contingent of 30 officers and 994 other ranks, 64 horses and mules, 19 vehicles and 9 bicycles.

Willie and the 16th (Service) Battalion The King's Royal Rifle Corps ended their journey into war with a night Channel crossing and landed on 17 November in the Haute-Normandie region of France at Le Havre.

Willie Chappell's medal record.

It was at or shortly after a battle at Béthune that the 19-year-old William Chappell was wounded and died of his injuries. He was buried on 31 January 1916 in Béthune Town Cemetery, Pas-de-Calais. A headstone marks his burial place.

- Rifleman William Hampshire C/1176, 16th (Service) Battalion The King's Royal Rifle Corps from Rochester, Kent. He was killed in action on 28 January 1916, aged 21. His grave is in Cambrin Churchyard Extension, France.
- Rifleman Arthur Sellars G6062, 18th (Service) Battalion The King's Royal Rifle Corps from Buxton, Derbyshire. Died on 15 September 1916 from wounds received at the Battle of the Somme, aged 18.

Written by a schoolgirl about her trip to the war graves in 2002:

I went on a school trip to Belgium to visit the war graves. Those rows of graves and names on walls really illustrated the huge numbers of people killed and showed us the real lives that had been affected. Our bus driver played the bagpipes whilst our teacher read out the names of our ancestors that had been killed in the war. It was very moving and everyone was crying by the end, because although we were only 14, we had respect for these people who had to cope with unimaginable horrors and we were and still are grateful for the lives we live today.

Chapter Four

Becoming one of the King's Men

The principles and details of the training required to be a soldier in the British army were laid down in the Field Service Regulations and in army publications such as *Infantry Training 1914*. Training started with basic physical fitness, drill, marching discipline, essential field craft and so on. As the soldier progressed and specialized, he received courses of instruction relevant to the role he would eventually take. The British army was made up of the following units:

SQUAD   = 9 to 10 men
PLATOON   = 16 to 44 men
COMPANY   = 62 to 190 men
BATTALION = 300 to 1,000 men
BRIGADE   = 3,000 to 5,000 men
DIVISION   = 10,000 to 15,000 men
CORPS   = 20,000 to 45,000 men
ARMY   = 50,000+ men

Every soldier in the Great War had to take an oath of allegiance upon joining the army. Those who wished to swear by God used the following words:

> I [soldier's name], swear by Almighty God that I will be faithful and bear true allegiance to His Majesty King George V, his heirs and successors and that I will as in duty bound honestly and faithfully defend His Majesty, his heirs and successors in person, crown and dignity against all enemies and will observe and obey all orders of His Majesty, his heirs and successors and of the generals and officers set over me.

This process is known as attestation and is a declaration that the soldier is a dependable man of rank and honour.

A soldier's rate of pay for each day of service

	Foot Guards	Infantry of the Line
Sergeant Major	5s 2d	5s 0d
Quartermaster Sergeant	4s 2d	4s 0d
Company Sergeant Major	4s 2d	4s 0d
Company Quartermaster Sergeant	3s 8d	3s 6d
Colour Sergeant	3s 8d	3s 6d
Sergeant	2s 6d	2s 4d
Corporal	1s 9d	1s 8d
Private	1s 1d	1s 0d

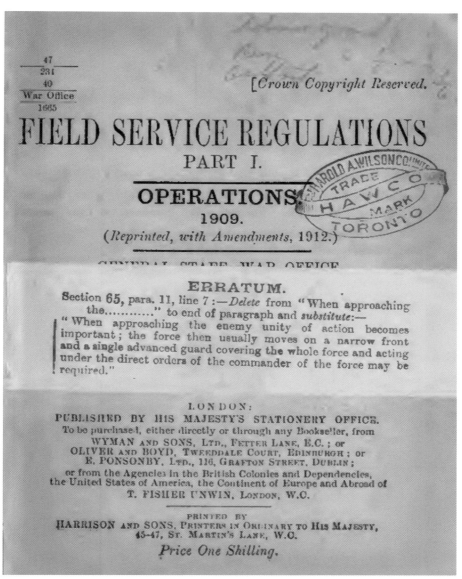

Field Service Regulations.

Additional proficiency pay was payable if a soldier fulfilled conditions as to service and qualification at rates of 3*d* or 6*d* per day, according to his proficiency.

Since 1908 the British army had offered four forms of recruitment. A man could join up as a professional soldier of the regular army or as a part-time member of the Territorial Force (TF). There was also the opportunity to join the Special Reserve (SR) or the National Reserve (NR). Politicians and military men had already had a long-running battle between them about whether Britain should have a system of national conscripted service. By 1914 this had not come about and Britain's army was entirely voluntary.

Recruitment rules were simple. To enlist and fight abroad, a lad had to be aged 19 or over. No one could join the army under the age of 18. One could enlist if aged 18 but had to remain in Great Britain until reaching the age of 19 before being allowed to be posted abroad. The recruit had to be taller than 5 feet 3 inches and aged between 18 and 38. A lad wishing to join the army could do so providing he passed certain physical tests and was willing to enlist for a number of years.

However, these rules were written before the Great War was declared and any previously-held agreements on how a war should be fought. Wars had always brought out the patriotic side of a nation, with the same being seen in Germany as well as in Great Britain. Almost every man from every nation in the world wanted to help defend his homeland.

British lads could join at a regimental depot or at one of the normal recruiting offices, with a choice over the regiment he was assigned to. The terms for the infantry were that he would join for a period of seven years full-time service with the colours, to be followed by another five years in the Army Reserve. For the artillery it was an initial six years, plus another six.

When war was declared there were 350,000 former soldiers on the Army Reserve list, ready to be called back to fill the establishment of their regiments.

Reforming the system
The Haldane Reforms were a series of far-ranging reforms of the British army made from 1906 to 1912 and named after Secretary of State for War Richard Burdon Haldane. They were the first major reforms since the Childers Reforms of the early 1880s and were made in the light of lessons learned from the Second Boer War.

The major element of the reforms was the creation of an Expeditionary Force, specifically prepared and trained for intervening in a major war. This had existed before, but it had not been prepared at all well for overseas service. The newly-organized force would have a permanent peacetime organization and a full complement of supporting troops.

At the same time, the reserve forces were restructured and expanded to ensure that the overseas forces could be efficiently reinforced and supplied with new recruits. To ensure that home defences would not suffer because of sending the regular forces overseas, the militia formed the Special Reserve and the Volunteer Force and the yeomanry were reorganized into a new Territorial Force. The latter two reforms were grouped together into the Territorial and Reserve Forces Act 1907.

To encourage the development of military skills, an Officer Training Corps was established in public schools and universities. Military strategy was revitalized by a new Imperial General Staff. It would ensure principle, political beliefs and common strategic aims among the various military forces of the British Empire, including the Dominions and British India. Finally, the regular army itself would be reformed by the development of a new operational and training doctrine as laid down in Douglas Haig's new *Field Service Pocket Book*.

The Reservists

The Special Reserve provided a form of part-time military service. It was introduced in 1908 as a means of building up a pool of trained reservists in addition to those of the regular Army Reserve. Special Reservists enlisted for six years and had to accept the possibility of being called up in the event of a general mobilization and undergo all the same conditions as men of the Army Reserve. This meant that it differed from the Territorial Force in that the men could be sent overseas. Their period as an SR started with six months of full-time preliminary training (paid the same as a regular) with three to four weeks' training per year thereafter. A man could extend his SR service by up to four years, but could not serve beyond the age of 40. A former regular soldier whose period of Army Reserve obligation had been completed could also re-enlist as an SR and serve up to the age of 42.

All regiments had a unit (or more) dedicated to the administration and training of the Special Reservists. For example, in most infantry regiments it was the 3rd (Reserve) Battalion. In all there were 101 reserve battalions in existence in August 1914. Their job was to provide reinforcement drafts for the active service battalions. Staffed by regular soldiers, each SR battalion had a complement of 8 officers, 1 regimental sergeant major, 38 non-commissioned officers, 10 drummers and 40 privates of the regular army. The official establishment when all reservists were on duty was a little over 600, smaller than a full-scale serving battalion.

The SR men were mobilized in early August 1914. The army also maintained a list of officers on active reserve with many also being mobilized in 1914. It was not very easy to spot an Army or Special Reservist just from the details given on their medal index cards, as the numbers on them resembled those of men in the regular army. However, if they had a number prefixed by SR or 3, then they were a Special Reservist. Between them and the Army Reservists, they represented a large proportion of the original divisions of the BEF that went to France in 1914.

Army Reserve

This was a pool of men who had already completed a term of service with the regular army. It was organized into three sections as follows:

- **Section A Reserve** was for men who had completed their service in the regular army and who undertook to rejoin (if required) in an emergency that did not require general mobilization. A man could serve no more than two years in Section A. Pay was 7 shillings a week in addition to the reservist's earnings as a civilian. He had to attend twelve training days per year.
- **Section B Reserve** was the most common form of Army Reserve service for men who had completed their service in the regular army and were serving

their normal period (typically five years) on reserve. Section B reservists could only be called upon in the event of general mobilization. Pay was 3 shillings and 6 pence a week and a man had to attend twelve training days per year.

- **Section D Reserve** was for men who had completed their time in Section B Reserve. They could choose to extend for another four years and were placed in Section D Reserve. Terms, pay and training were the same as in Section B.

The Army Reservists were mobilized in early August 1914 with many of them filling up the ranks of the regular army units to their war establishment. Those surplus to the immediate needs of the regular army battalions were posted to the Special Reserve. Thus the (usually) 3rd Battalion of each regiment was massively and very rapidly expanded. Very large numbers of men passed through the SR battalions before being posted to the regular units.

The Territorial Force
The Territorial Force was created in 1908 as a form of part-time volunteer soldiering. Its original purpose was to provide a force for home defence and men were not obliged to serve overseas. Territorial Force troops undertook to serve full-time in the event of general mobilization.

Most TF units had struggled to attract sufficient men to fill their designed establishment and in consequence the reserves were well under strength in 1914. Theoretically the TF Reserve should have been one-third the size of the whole TF, but by August 1914 it numbered only 2,000 men.

The National Reserve
The National Reserve was, in essence, a register maintained by Territorial Force County Associations of all those who had military experience but who had no other reserve obligation. It was divided into three classes: Class I for those aged under 42; Class II for officers and senior ranks under 55 and junior ranks under 50 for home service only; Class III for those who were not medically fit for Classes I and II. Its strength at 1 October 1913 was 215,000 all ranks.

In October 1914 the National Reserve was formed into Protection Companies, which were attached to existing TF battalions for the guarding of railways and other vulnerable points in Britain. By November 1914, all Class I and II men were ordered to present themselves for enlistment. In March 1915 the Protection Companies were redesignated as Supernumerary Companies TF. By July 1915 there was a wide-scale trawl of these companies to identify men capable of marching 10 miles with a rifle and 150 rounds of ammunition. Those who were classified as medical Category A went to service battalions, while Category Cs were posted to provisional battalions. Category B men were formed into the 18th to 24th battalions of the Rifle Brigade. These battalions were sent to Egypt and India at the end of 1915 to replace TF units committed to Gallipoli and Mesopotamia. Those left in Britain eventually formed the 25th Battalion Rifle Brigade

TF and served as a garrison battalion at Falmouth. As for the Supernumerary Companies, they were eventually formed into the Royal Defence Corps.

The outbreak of the Great War saw the bulk of these changes put to the test. The Expeditionary Force was quickly sent to the Continent, while the Territorial Force and Reserves were mobilized, as planned, to provide a second line. It gave an opportunity for men to join the army on a part-time basis. Territorial units of most infantry regiments and of each of the corps (artillery, engineers, medical, service and ordnance) were formed. For example, most county regiments of the infantry formed two Territorial battalions. These units were recruited locally and became more recognized and supported by the local community than the regulars. Recruits had a choice of regiment, but naturally the local nature of the TF meant that in general each man joined his home unit. The TF County Associations and the administration of the local TF were planned to be a medium by which the army could be expanded in wartime. Men trained at weekends or in the evenings and went away to a summer camp.

Territorials were not obliged to serve overseas but were enlisted on the basis that in the event of war they could be called upon for full-time service. The physical criteria for joining the TF were the same as for the regular army but the lower age limit was 17.

In August 1914, in addition to the 247,500 serving troops who were in the current regular army, there were two forms of reserves for men below commissioned rank. The Army Reserve was 145,350 strong and the Special Reserve had another 64,000 men.

New types of reserves created during the Great War

Class W Reserve and its Territorial Force equivalent Class W(T) were introduced in June 1916 by Army Order 203/16. They were for 'all of those soldiers whose services are deemed to be more valuable to the country in civil rather than military employment'. Men in these classes were to receive no salaries from army funds and would not wear army uniform. However, they were liable, at any time, to be recalled to the colours. From the time a man was transferred to Class W until being recalled to the colours, he would not be subject to military discipline.

In October, Army Order 355 of 1916 introduced Class T Reserve. There was no Territorial equivalent. Class T consisted of men in about thirty specific skilled trades (almost all industrial or munitions-related) who would otherwise have been transferred to Class W. Terms and conditions were as for Class W.

Class P Reserve and Class P(T) were introduced by the same army order. These classes consisted of men 'whose services are deemed to be temporarily of more value to the country in civil life rather than in the Army'. They could not be lower than medical grade C iii and as a result of having served in the army or TF would, if discharged, be eligible for a pension on the grounds of disability or length of service. Men in Classes P and P(T) were, for the purposes of pay, allowances, gratuity and pension, treated as if they been discharged on the date of their transfer to Class P or P(T) and that they did receive money from the army. Other terms and conditions were as for Class W.

The Reserve

The British army of 1914–18 used the word 'reserve' in many different contexts. The forces at home, whether they were of men going through basic training, manning the home defences or awaiting posting overseas, were 'The Reserve'. Units and formations overseas that were not actually at the fighting front were also 'The Reserve'. A battalion, on coming out of the line for rest, might say it was now in 'Brigade Reserve'. A whole brigade, moving to the rear for training, might be in 'Divisional Reserve'; a division, also going further back, might be in 'Corps Reserve'; and so on.

When an attack was made, a certain number of troops were held ready as a second wave to exploit any gains made by the first troops to go in. These were also known as 'reserves'. Commander-in-Chief Sir John French lost his job in late 1915 after controversy about his poor handling of the divisions held in reserve at the Battle of Loos.

The creation of an army

On the day that war against Germany was declared, it needed amazing strength and know-how to expand the small professional force of the British army to the number of men needed to fight. It had to be an army capable of defeating one of the world's most formidable military machines.

It was generally believed in Britain that the war would be over in about four months and the men would be home in time for Christmas or, if not, for the start of the new term at Oxford.

Horatio Herbert Kitchener (*c.*1850–1916), 1st Earl Kitchener of Khartoum, was born in Listowel, County Kerry, Ireland. He was educated at the Royal Military Academy, Woolwich. Kitchener was commissioned in the Royal Engineers and from 1874 served in the Middle East. In 1886 he was appointed governor of the British Red Sea territories and, subsequently, was assigned to Egypt as adjutant general in Cairo.

His energy and thoroughness led to his appointment as commander-in-chief of the Egyptian army in 1892. His reputation in Great Britain was enhanced by his firm, tactful and successful handling of the explosive Fashoda Incident. Created Baron Kitchener in 1898 and then Viscount Kitchener in 1902, he was sent as commander-in-chief to India. He quarrelled with the Viceroy of India, Lord Curzon, over control of the army in India. The British Cabinet upheld Kitchener and Curzon resigned.

Remaining in India until 1909, Kitchener was bitterly disappointed at not being appointed viceroy. In September 1911 he accepted the post of consul general (acting administrator) of Egypt and, until August 1914, ruled that country and the Sudan.

He was on leave in England when the Great War broke out and had just received an earldom and another viscountcy and barony. Reluctantly, he accepted an appointment to the Cabinet as Secretary of State for War and was promoted to Field Marshal. Shortly after the declaration of war, Kitchener issued a call for volunteers to increase the size of the army. He did not believe that the Territorial Force was an appropriate structure for doing this. The public response to his appeal was rapid and overwhelming, but died down to average only 100,000 men per month. He warned his colleagues that the conflict would be decided by the last 1,000,000 men that Great Britain could find to go into battle. Addressing the British Expeditionary Force in August 1914, he said: 'Do your duty bravely. Fear God and honour the King.'

As one of the few who believed that the war would last several years and cause heavy losses, he needed more men. Steps had to be taken to encourage further enlistment. One of his first actions was a massive recruitment campaign to dramatically expand the British army. Soon a distinctive poster featuring his face appeared all over Britain, encouraging a vast army of British citizens to enlist, which was a most extraordinary national achievement. With great speed, he enlisted a large number of volunteers and had them trained as professional soldiers for a succession of entirely new armies. Dubbed the 'New Army', Kitchener's efforts represented the first time that Britain had fully committed its manpower to building up its land forces. By the end of 1915 he was convinced of the need for military conscription but, in deference to Prime Minister Herbert H. Asquith's belief that conscription was not yet politically practicable, he never publicly advocated it.

Kitchener was handicapped by British governmental processes and by his own distaste for teamwork and the delegation of responsibility. Initially, he directed Britain's overall war strategy as well as overseeing recruitment and munitions acquisitions. His Cabinet associates, who did not share in the public idolatry of Kitchener, relieved him of his responsibility in the planning of industrial mobilization and later strategy, but he refused to quit the War Cabinet.

Lord Kitchener sailed from Scrabster to Scapa Flow on 5 June 1916 aboard HMS *Oak* before transferring to the armoured cruiser HMS *Hampshire* for a diplomatic mission to Russia. During a Force 9 gale, while en route to the Russian port of Arkhangelsk, the *Hampshire* struck a mine laid by the newly-launched German U-boat *U-75* commanded by Curt Beitzen. Shortly before 19:30 hours, the ship sank west of the Orkney Islands. Kitchener, his staff and 643 of a crew of 655 were drowned or died of exposure.

The 16th (Service) Battalion (Church Lads' Brigade) was formed on 19 September 1914 and began its training at Denham, Buckinghamshire. Lieutenant Colonel C. Kindersley-Porcher (of the Coldstream Guards) was in command, Major C. Wyld (of the Coldstream Guards) was second-in-command and Major F. Sitwell (of the Durham Light Infantry) was adjutant.

The officers and men were billeted in Denham and Uxbridge until the camp huts were completed. The hutted accommodation was completed in November and Denham became an army training and transit camp, placed to take advantage of the adjacent Denham Golf Club railway station. It was sited, in what is now known as Higher Denham, by the GWR/GC Joint Railway (now the Chiltern Line).

HMS *Hampshire*.

CLB at Denham.

16th Battalion, C Company, 11th Platoon, KRRC.

Church Army cartoon.

Denham Railway Station.

In the issue of the *Middlesex Advertiser and Gazette* (Uxbridge edition) dated 27 December 1919 there was a lengthy article titled 'Uxbridge and the War'. It attempted to outline the town's contribution to the war effort. One section ran as follows:

THE DENHAM CAMP

During October 1914 the Church Lads' Brigade began to send large numbers of recruits from all over the country to the temporary quarters fixed up for them in the parish of Denham, the headquarters being the golf links clubhouse, and the field and farmhouse of Mr Lipscombe, below the railway. This centre was fixed upon, we believe, through the instrumentality of Major Wyld of the Tilehouse, who became the second in command. Various other billets were found in the farm buildings of the parish, and Mercer's Mill near Uxbridge also made one of the 'barracks'. The young fellows took to their rough quarters with right good humour and, showing the splendid utility of the moral training their organisation had given them, proved themselves to be an exceptionally nice body of men, so that Uxbridge and the surrounding villages in Bucks did well to take them to their hearts in the thorough and hospitable manner in which the men were received throughout their period of training in the district. Subsequently huts were built for the men, and a YMCA hut was provided, thanks to the hard work of the late Dr Walker. Facilities for recreation for the young men were provided at St Margaret's parish room, and other schoolrooms of local churches and scores of homes in the neighbourhood entertained the men on Sundays. The departure from Denham was quite an event about the middle of March 1915, and on behalf of the town Mr W.J. Hutchings wrote to the battalion a letter of goodwill and wishes of success, and to this the Commanding Officer replied warmly, thanking Uxbridge people for their kindness to the boys.

Training went on systematically, perhaps helped by the knowledge of drill and discipline gained in the Church Lads' Brigade. Progress was rapid as the recruits undertook basic training and guard duties at local bridges and reservoirs. When the time came for the men to take their shooting course, they proved to be remarkably proficient and reached the highest average in the division.

In January 1915, together with Lord Grenfell, the Archbishop of Canterbury inspected the battalion. The Primate addressed the lads as, 'the only exclusive Churchman's Battalion in the British Army and the first of its kind since the days of Crecy and Agincourt'. He also congratulated the men on their smartness, even though the uniform was blue and temporary, as the khaki was not yet available. The blue uniform was unpopular with the men, as they felt it made them look more like postmen than soldiers. They also had to use poles to drill as rifles were in short supply. Great delays in obtaining equipment, telephones, transport, material and even the most necessary clothing for the men added greatly to the discomfort of the troops and the difficulty of training them for war.

In March 1915 the 16th (Service) Battalion The King's Royal Rifle Corps was transported to Rayleigh in Essex for eight weeks as part of its training. The

Harry Barber and pals waiting for their uniforms to arrive.

soldiers were billeted around town and the horses were stabled near the centre of town. However, despite the willingness of the townspeople to take soldiers into their homes, there was not enough room. Every schoolhouse, parish room and public building had to be requisitioned and was filled to overflowing because of the numbers of so many men of the various units.

Special training exercises in trench-digging and night operations were also held in the nearby town of Thundersley. Spells of trench-digging, at which each of the infantry brigades took a turn, made an almost welcome break from the monotony of general life. Yet the men remained invincibly cheerful and were prepared to extract some fun out of every trifling incident.

It wasn't until the battalion was at Rayleigh that they received the issue of their 'drab-brown' (khaki) uniforms. When the time came for the lads to leave Rayleigh, nearly all the inhabitants turned out to show their respect for the officers and men. Many firm and lasting friendships had been forged and letters of appreciation were sent to the battalion:

The Rectory, Rayleigh, Essex.
1st June, 1915.
I am sure it will be a pleasure to you to hear how excellent has been the conduct of the men of the Battn. K.R.R.(C.L.B.) during the time they have been here in this parish. The inhabitants upon whom they have been billeted

The 16th KRRC in Rayleigh.

have nothing but words of praise for them, and from my personal observation and inquiry I can state that the town has been as quiet and free from
drunkenness during their presence here as when no troops are with us. Their
attachment to their Church has been to me most pleasant to see, a very large
number of men being always present at our Sunday evening services, and
many regular communicants. Their Chaplain (Rev. J. Duncan) took the
greatest interest in the social and spiritual welfare of the men, and it was very
evident that they, on their side, much appreciated this. It is with real regret
we saw them leave for Denham a fortnight ago.

   A.G. Fryer, Rector

The Rectory, Thundersley, Essex.
10th July, 1915.
I have been intending to write to you for some time past, but in addition to
being a bad correspondent, I have been an invalid, so that must be my
excuse. I have wanted to thank you for raising such a splendid battalion of
the K.R.R.s. I can speak from experience, for their sojourn amongst us gave
universal pleasure, and true were the regrets when the K.R.R.s moved elsewhere. Their conduct was beyond praise; it sounds possibly exaggerated, but
I speak but the truth. As a congregation they were exemplary, and they made
for me the service a delight, and I shall remember their stay with gratifica-
tion, for they proved, if proof were needed, that a spiritual training makes
men helpful, chivalrous, and manly. We mention the officers and men of the
K.R.R. in our regular prayers for those who are at the front now or who have
offered themselves to go, and shall continue to do so. I personally consider it
was a great privilege to minister to such men whilst they were staying here.
May God bless and prosper them and the Church Lads' Brigade.

   J.N. Talfourd Major, Rector.

On leaving Rayleigh, the battalion returned to Denham for another month.
   Before the Depot Company moved from Denham there was a celebration of
the Holy Communion which, in many respects, was unique. The altar and
furniture had previously been removed from the hut that had served as the camp
church, so a table borrowed from the hospital served as an altar. A simple cross
was fashioned by one of the riflemen and flowers were borrowed from another
hut.
   Out of the 200 men in the camp, 160 attended for their Communion. Reverence and earnestness marked the whole service with many kneeling in prayer
throughout the proceedings. The words of one of the chosen hymns rang out:

   The King of Love my Shepherd is,
   Whose goodness faileth never
   I nothing lack if I am His,
   And He is mine for ever.

The British army deals fairly with all religions and during the Great War treated
the different denominations with much sympathy and consideration. Most of the

lads at the front had an opportunity of attending services much the same as those they had been used to in their own home town.

Every brigade has a Church of England, Roman Catholic and Nonconformist chaplain, with an extra chaplain for any other denomination most strongly represented. It does not often happen that all the men in a battalion profess the same faith, but the 16th (Service) Battalion The King's Royal Rifle Corps claimed that every man was a member of the Church of England.

Known as the 'Churchman's Battalion', religion was the mainspring of its patriotism, courage and devotion. About 75 per cent of the lads were communicants, who knew their faith and were not ashamed to confess it.

On the battalion's departure from Denham, the Uxbridge Urban District Council passed a resolution of goodwill to them and placed on record their appreciation of the character, courtesy and conduct of the men during the whole of their stay in the district.

> The Mount, Harefield Road, Uxbridge.
> 22nd March, 1915.
> To the Officer Commanding
> Battalion K.R.R.C.
> I am urged to send a message of greeting and goodwill from the townsfolk of Uxbridge to the splendid fellows under your command who have lately been stationed at Denham Camp. Many (very many) have been the expressions of satisfaction with the general good conduct of the men of the K.R.R. and their smart military bearing.
>
> On behalf of the inhabitants of Uxbridge and the district it gives me considerable pleasure in sending this letter, conveying to the officers and men the warmest of farewell greeting, with best wishes for all needful health and strength to carry forward to a successful issue whatever experience they may have in future days.
>
> With a personal God-speed, Believe me,
> Yours sincerely,
> (Signed) W. J. Hutchings,
> Chairman, Urban District Council.

In June 1915 the lads moved to Clipstone Camp in Mansfield and became attached to the 33rd Division of the 100th Brigade. Each camp line could now hold a complete battalion. The lines were self-sufficient and contained sleeping quarters, mess rooms, cook-houses, parade grounds and a guardhouse to keep the lads in check should they go astray. Each hut was heated and had electricity and water provided by Mansfield Corporation.

The first troops arrived at Clipstone in driving rain following a march from Edwinstowe. Questions were raised in Parliament about the poor quality of the food. The Member of Parliament for Mid-Derbyshire enquired with the Secretary of State for War about 'the scarcity and inferiority of the food and the conduct of some of the officers'. Presumably the men had complained about

Clipstone Camp: huts as far as the eye could see. The roads between the huts were known as 'lines'.

the food and had been robustly dealt with by their superiors. No further action was taken and the arrangements were deemed to be of an acceptable standard.

With the opening of three YMCA huts, conditions at the camp improved. Men could watch concerts, write letters, listen to lectures and obtain refreshments. The largest hut contained a 97-foot-long concert hall and a further garrison theatre was provided. On the other side of the camp, the NACB (Navy and Army Combined Board) made use of the newly-constructed colliery workshops to cater for the troops. The NACB was the Great War equivalent of the NAAFI and included a bakery and grocery store. Additional recreational activities included swimming in nearby Vicars Pond and in the spa pools to the north-west of the camp.

To some of the lads, who had never been away from home before, it was all very similar to having a jolly good time at a holiday camp. Local legend suggests that the Duke of Portland was so offended by seeing nude soldiers bathing in the spa pools that they were drained to deter such activities. The lads could visit the nearby town of Mansfield to mingle with the local population and local businesses boomed. Early doubts about the impact of the camp and so many soldiers roaming around the town were largely unfounded.

The religious needs of the lads were also considered. The Bishop of Southwell successfully appealed for funds and a temporary hut was built to accommodate a congregation of over 900. Other denominations and religions had similar facilities and huts were organized for Roman Catholic, Wesleyan and Jewish soldiers. St Mary's, the local church, was prominent in the life of the camp and its inhabitants.

With the camp now in full swing, up to 30,000 soldiers could be accommodated and the serious business of training for war became its primary purpose. The first tenants of the camp had been busy at work in the area to the south of the camp that formed part of Sherwood Pines. Rifle, pistol and machine-gun ranges were dug and some still exist to this day.

During the summer Lieutenant Colonel Kindersley-Porcher had to resign on account of ill health and Major Wyld was given command of the battalion. On 3 August 1915, the battalion departed for Perham Down, a village near Salisbury Plain and Andover. The final training was eventually completed and all the arrangements were made for the lads to depart to France.

Look out Kaiser Bill, here we come!
It was a damp morning in November 1915, muddy underfoot and with a cold, biting wind. The lads marched with little or no conversation. Only the rhythm of marching feet echoed through the darkness. The long training was over and soon the ultimate test would be upon them all. It was three or four hours after midnight and a train was waiting to take over 1,000 men to Southampton. A few friends were there to say 'Goodbye' and wish them all good luck.

Were they excited at the prospect of soon being within the fray of what was happening in France? Was the anticipation almost too overwhelming? It is impossible to speculate about what any young lad was visualizing at that period in British history.

Arriving at their destination, they were relieved of their packs with orders not to leave the dockside. Hot tea and food was provided and it is possible that it made the cold, dark place they were in seem a little brighter. There was a twelve-hour wait before the call came for the lads to muster. The whole battalion was drawn up into one of the big dockyard sheds ready to march off to the waiting ship.

Hoarse commands of non-commissioned officers had just ceased when, without warning, the clear-cut notes of a cornet rang out with the tune of *Keep the Home Fires Burning*. It was played with a delicacy and sympathy that touched the hearts of everyone listening to it. The men joined in and the chorus was sung with a strong and reverent feeling.

> Keep the Home-fires burning,
> While your hearts are yearning,
> Though your lads are far away
> They dream of Home;
> There's a silver lining
> Through the dark cloud shining,
> Turn the dark cloud inside out,
> Till the boys come Home.

The ship they sailed on could have been the SS *Mona's Queen*. Together with other Steam Packet vessels, *Mona's Queen* had a most distinguished record during the First World War. She was chartered in 1915 and used as a troop carrier. The necessary work to fit her out was undertaken by the Steam Packet Company's own workshops at Douglas, Isle of Man. Once completed her initial task was to ferry troops, mainly between Southampton and the main port serving the British Expeditionary Force at Le Havre.

As they mounted the gangplank, each man was given a lifebelt in case it was needed. A last look at England, as the ship skirted around the north-east coast of the Isle of Wight, was required before the 126 nautical mile journey got under way. Some of the lads slept and some talked in whispers under the stars that twinkled in the clear sky overhead. Others, not being good sailors, were retching their hearts out over the side. Dawn was breaking when the engines slowed down and the ship finally drew up alongside the quay at Le Havre.

There was an almost party-like atmosphere as the 16th (Service) Battalion The King's Royal Rifle Corps marched through the streets of France for the first time. They belted out the old refrain with gusto for the benefit of the friendly allies who greeted them with cheers and welcoming smiles as they went by:

We are some of the K.R.R.,
We are some of the boys,
Mind all our manners,
Spend all our tanners,
We are respected wherever we go.

When we're marching through the street,
Doors and windows open wide,
All the girls begin to cry,
The K.R.R. are passing by.
We are some of the boys.

The first months in France
Eventually the rest camp was reached. Washed and fed, the weariness had almost vanished and never did bedding down in a tent seem so comfortable. The lads began foraging for themselves and discovered a YMCA hut that sold food supplies and cigarettes, etc.

The next morning it was time to move on again. At the railway station a train of considerable length was placed at their disposal, but there were not enough carriages to go round because most of the train was made up of commodious cattle trucks. Between thirty and forty lads scrambled into each empty space with much laughing and joking, as they heaved their packs on board. Although it was all a joke at first, the joke had lost its full flavour before the journey was finished.

All that day and right through the night the train crawled along at a snail's pace. Whenever it stopped, the lads got out to stretch their legs, exchange views, drink cocoa and eat whatever had been provided. Sometimes they did not return

British troops arrive at Le Havre.

to the cattle trucks immediately but ran alongside the train, only taking their places again when their blood was circulating more freely in their veins. For twenty-three hours they sat, stood, slept and shivered. Eventually, tired, cold and stiff but more than pleased, they arrived at their destination.

Outside the railway station the battalion was drawn up, then left to itself for an hour or so. They looked around at the flat, rather desolate countryside and speculated on many things. In the distance they could hear the booming of heavy artillery and wondered how long it would be before they had to go into the trenches. Then there was more stir and movement, as orders were shouted out here and there. On the march once again, they were able to stretch their cramped limbs and were buoyed up by the thought of a comfortable billet, food and a bed.

The officers were billeted in the houses and the lads in barns, stables, lofts, cottages, schools and any other available habitable place. In time everyone was settled. The villagers were hospitable and provided a liberal supply of straw for those in the barns and lofts, etc. A straw bed with a blanket over them and one underneath, four good walls and a roof to keep out the rain and cold made a comfortable sleeping-place.

During the next eight weeks they were billeted in many different villages, all of which bore strong family resemblances. For the most part the people were hospitable and ready to make friends. One might have thought the language would have troubled the lads, but in a way that was all their own, they made their needs known and generally got what they wanted.

It was a huge job finding the necessary accommodation for a whole battalion. In addition to the men, suitable places had to be found for the transport, the quartermaster's stores, the doctor, the orderly room, guard room, officers' mess, and so on. Two officers generally shared a modest bedroom; more often than not with only a single bed, in which case the floor served as a sleeping-place for one of them.

Billeted in a French village, life went on with as much normality as possible, especially if the men were 'resting', i.e. out of the trenches after a long spell and were some miles behind the firing line. Life went on pretty much as it did in England. Parades, guard duty, lectures, rifle practice, route marches and so forth.

There was much to remind the men of home. Every day the postman – the most popular man in the battalion, with the possible exception of the cooks – brought heaps and heaps of letters and parcels.

Embroidered silk postcards were first made in 1900 for the Paris Exposition, but it was during the Great War that these postcards reached their peak of popularity. The women of France and Belgium did the embroidery onto strips of silk mesh, initially by hand, then subsequently on home machines and later in factories. Once completed, the multiple image strips were sent to the factories for cutting and mounting onto postcards. There were two principal formats: the panel-style with a rectangle of embroidered mesh fixed to the card, and the envelope-style in which the panel could be opened to reveal a small card insert. Many subjects were embroidered: romantic images of hearts and flowers, military regiment badges, flags and patriotic images, images of statesmen and military leaders, Christmas greetings, year numbers, and so on. All subjects are now much collected with the regimental badge cards being in greatest demand. Thousands of designs were produced and, as a thing of beauty in such a harsh war environment, they became popular for the soldiers to send home as keepsakes for their much-loved wives, sweethearts and families.

'Pa-per! Eng-leesh pa-per!' Small French boys and girls piped out the cry in every village and sold all of the London daily newspapers a day after publication. For the halfpenny papers the lads paid one penny and tuppence for those that sold at home for a penny. Every week the British government provided free cigarettes from reputable English tobacco companies, so the men smoked their cigarettes and read their newspapers just as they had done so regularly in England during the pre-war days.

All through the first eight weeks of the 16th (Service) Battalion The King's Royal Rifle Corps' French tour, there were many other things to prevent the lads from becoming dull. Theatres, well within earshot of the guns, were full to capacity night after night. Boxing contests, concerts, etc formed the regular recreation for the men back from the firing line. Exciting football matches were played with more shouting when a goal was scored than when a German aeroplane was brought down. Concerts were held whenever a suitable building could be found. Unfortunately, that was not an easy matter.

Silk postcard from France.

Christmas Day 1915

The battalion rested in a French village. The padre found a schoolmistress who spoke English very well. She said she had learned it as a child in England itself. When asked if her school could be borrowed for the day, she remarked that she had liked England and said: 'Are not the soldiers fighting to protect my beloved France?' She placed the schoolroom at the disposal of the lads, who found that she had decorated it and written in English on the blackboard 'A Happy Christmas'.

At midnight the first Communion was celebrated and over 100 British lads, far away from home, began that Christmas Day by giving welcome to 'Him' whose birthday it was.

During the day there were three more celebrations of the Holy Communion, as well as a parade service. Some 400 men made their Communion, while the French schoolchildren looked in through the windows and wondered about the big English soldiers who had squeezed themselves into their small seats. A memorable Christmas Day of 1915 was spent in billets at the Western Front.

A present from the palace

Previously, in November 1914, an advertisement had been placed in the national press inviting monetary contributions to a 'Sailors & Soldiers Christmas Fund'. Its purpose was to provide everyone wearing the king's uniform and serving over-seas on Christmas Day 1914 with 'a gift from the nation'.

Our Gift from Princess Mary and the Donors to her fund. XMAS. 1914.

A message from the king and queen.

Created by Princess Mary, the 17-year-old daughter of King George V and Queen Mary, the response to the appeal was truly overwhelming. It was decided to spend the money on an embossed brass box, based on a design by Messrs Adshead and Ramsey, containing seasonal 'comforts' for those serving.

The 'tin' itself was approximately 5 inches long by 3¼ inches wide by 1¼ inches deep with a double-skinned hinged lid. The surface of the lid depicted the head of Princess Mary in the centre, surrounded by a laurel wreath and flanked on either side by the letter 'M' monogram. At the top was a decorative cartouche containing the words 'Imperium Britannicum' with a sword and scabbard either side.

The contents varied considerably. Officers and men on active service afloat or at the front received a box containing a combination of pipe, lighter, 1oz of tobacco and twenty cigarettes in distinctive yellow monogrammed wrappers. Non-smokers and boys received a bullet pencil and a packet of sweets instead. Indian troops were often sent sweets and spices, and nurses were treated to chocolate. Many of these items were dispatched separately from the tins themselves, as once the standard issue of tobacco and cigarettes was placed in the container there was little room for much else apart from the greetings card.

Great efforts were made to distribute the gifts in time for Christmas and huge demands were made on an already stretched postal service. More than 355,000 were successfully delivered, but as time pressed on, a shortage of brass meant that many entitled personnel did not receive their gift until as late as the summer of

Princess Mary's gift box.

1916 and in January 1919 it was reported that 'considerable' numbers had still not been distributed. Orders for brass strip were placed with the United States (who were not yet involved in the war) and a large consignment was lost with the sinking of the ship *Lusitania*. As so much brass was being consumed in the production of weapons and munitions, the quality of the boxes that were manufactured later on was rather poor, comprising an inferior plated alloy rather than the earlier pure raised brass examples.

What a journey those boxes must have made across the Channel and then on to the men fighting day and night in icy cold and muddy trenches, so far away from their families at Christmas. When the fund eventually closed in 1920 it had the remarkable sum of £160,000, with the surplus going to the Princess's charity for the families of servicemen.

A few days before the 16th (Service) Battalion went into the trenches for the first time, they arrived at a large French town. A theatre capable of holding over 1,000 people was filled to its utmost capacity every night with the soldiers. The movie showing was a Charlie Chaplin film. What a time the men had as the full house rocked with laughter. Less than 5 miles away were the German trenches and from them came the dull roar of the big guns in action.

News came that the first platoon was to go into the trenches for instructional purposes. They were to be followed by the rest of the platoons in turn, until all had been initiated into the mysteries of the firing line. Danger and death had to be faced and it was natural that some of the lads wanted to make their

Communion before leaving. The altar, with its simple ornaments, was set up again and those who were going to the trenches the following morning flocked into barns and stables or whatever modest building was available where services were being held.

The whole battalion completed the instructional training without mishap and the men made their next Communion a Holy Thanksgiving for their safe return from the front.

In the firing line
On the first Sunday morning of the New Year (1916), the Churchman's Battalion was drawn up in full marching order. This band of brave warriors – their average age was less than 21 – standing in the pale light of dawn and waiting for orders to move, faced the most critical day in the lives of so many of them. There was a tense feeling as the lads marched away. They were going into the firing line for eight long days. They whistled and sang and there was some light-hearted chaff, a joke or two and ringing laughter. An Englishman does not wear his heart on his sleeve when he goes into battle, knowing there is a job to be done as he marches forward.

Onward, Christian soldiers, marching as to war,
with the cross of Jesus going on before.
Christ, the royal Master, leads against the foe;
forward into battle see his banners go!
Onward, Christian soldiers, marching as to war,
with the cross of Jesus going on before.

At the sign of triumph Satan's host doth flee;
on then, Christian soldiers, on to victory!
Hell's foundations quiver at the shout of praise;
brothers, lift your voices, loud your anthems raise.

Like a mighty army moves the church of God;
brothers, we are treading where the saints have trod.
We are not divided, all one body we,
one in hope and doctrine, one in charity.

Crowns and thrones may perish, kingdoms rise and wane,
but the church of Jesus constant will remain.
Gates of hell can never gainst that church prevail;
we have Christ's own promise, and that cannot fail.

Onward then, ye people, join our happy throng,
blend with ours your voices in the triumph song.
Glory, laud, and honor unto Christ the King,
this through countless ages men and angels sing.

Words by Sabine Baring-Gould (1834–1924); music by Arthur Sullivan (1842–1900).

They stopped for a few minutes to rest. They were no more than 2 miles from the trenches when the intense screeching and bursting of shells could be heard. How-

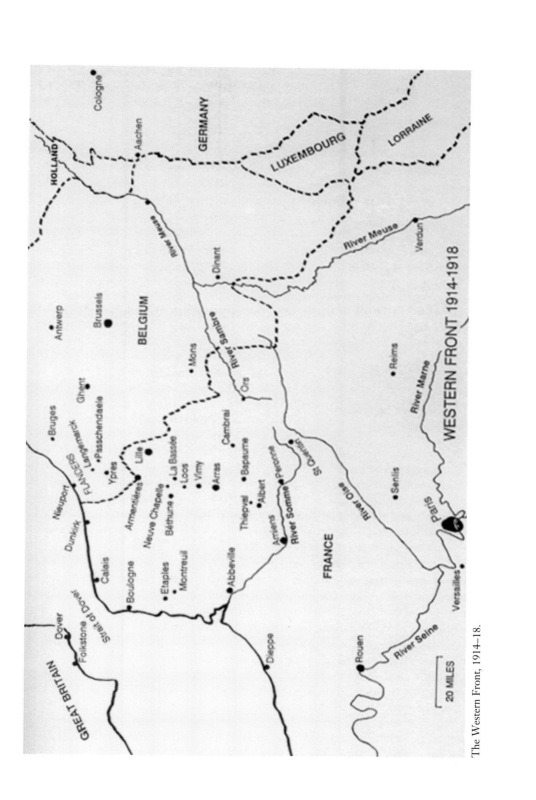

The Western Front, 1914–18.

ever, they were much more interested in the small boys and girls who had baskets containing all sorts of good things: chocolate, oranges, apples, cakes, cigarettes. The little vendors each cried out their wares in turn, oblivious to the noise going on around them. The lads bought freely and were not too critical over the change they received.

With a shout of 'Quick March!' they were off along the road again. There were not so many people about and here and there were houses with all their windows broken and gaping holes in roofs and walls. The Boche had scored heavily. At one house a father and mother had been killed and their children made orphans and homeless. Every day, just a few hundred yards from the trenches, German shells swept and almost decimated vast areas. Villages full of men, women and children tried to live their ordinary lives and do their usual work. Although they realized the danger they were in, for the most part they scorned it.

There was another halt before the trenches were reached. The artillery was hard at work with guns flashing and shells exploding. The men were not sorry to go off to the cover of the communication trenches. These were narrow and muddy and it was difficult to get through them with a full pack. If two persons met, it was almost impossible for them to pass each other, but for the most part the trenches were well made with miles and miles of mazes in which the lads burrowed like rabbits, giving battle to the foe they could not even see. One or two companies reached the support trenches and stayed there. The rest went steadily on until suddenly they found themselves in the front-line trenches. The firing line, in appearance, was not much different from the other trenches they had passed and more often than not was a little less dangerous.

The trenches were quite businesslike, with the rifles in position for instant use and periscopes that revealed to watchful eyes the doings of the Boche across the expanse of no man's land. The warning when gas attacks were coming was usually a hooter or a gong, in which case helmets had to be put on without delay. Protection was the PHG (Phenate Hexamine Goggle) helmet that had to be carried at all times. Commanders organized practice alerts at some of the most inconvenient moments. Sentries were always on guard at specific locations.

The dugouts were deep and spacious and, all things considered, surprisingly comfortable. A front-line trench was quiet and peaceful one minute and raging like an erupting volcano the next. It was as much like hell as anything in the real world could be. The men did not have time to settle down in their new surroundings or even get their bearings before there would be a series of terrific explosions. The earth would tremble violently before being blown into the air with a roar that could be heard miles away. The falling earth and everything else around it rained down everywhere for many minutes. There were great gaping holes in the ground from where the Germans had exploded two or three land mines at a time.

Perhaps 100 or more brave lads would have been wounded, killed or buried in the debris. Feverish digging parties worked like mad and many who had fallen were got out just in time. The stretcher-bearers, ever 'Friends of the Wounded',

In the trenches.

would dash forward to assist the injured and convey them through the narrow trenches to the dressing station. Those who escaped with only badly shaken nerves seized their rifles again and were prepared to attack the Germans, should they try to occupy the crater.

Hour after hour it went on, with screaming shells falling on all sides: in the trenches, out of the trenches, on open roads, behind the lines, on peaceful villages, on innocent children and civilians alike. Hand grenades, trench mortars, bombs, rifles and machine guns also played their part in the campaign of destruction. However, it was not one-sided as the British replied effectively, using similar weapons and, on the whole, more of them (although the weapons used by the British did not reach or fall on German soil).

The lads in the trenches fought against tremendous odds, stubbornly and persistently cheering one another on. They cared for the wounded, reverently removing the dead, listening to instructions and carrying out orders. Their thoughts were always for their comrades who needed help or guidance, while concentrating on the main task of repelling the Germans.

At last, when the fury of the combat had died down and everything became comparatively quiet again, tired and worn as they were, there was no rest yet for the lads at the front. Trenches had to be rebuilt in places and damaged structures repaired. There were lots of jobs to be done as a result of the long and fierce

Unofficial Christmas truce with the Germans.

conflict, but the worst was over and the lads marvelled that they were alive to tell the story of that first full day of responsibility in the firing line. However, few could have guessed the horrors it would bring before the sun set again in that winter sky. A day of sacred and peaceful associations was turned into a day of bloodshed and destruction. It was a duel between life and death that had raged all day long, and that day was a Sunday. War didn't allow for a Sabbath of rest and piousness.

The casualties of war
The Royal Army Medical Corps arrangements were adequate and quite wonderful. From the firing line to the base, many miles behind the trenches, was a great chain of dressing stations and hospitals. The sick and wounded were passed from one to the other by means of a system that worked smoothly and brought fruitful results. Young lads, battered and broken in the war, merited the most tender and thorough treatment. As far as was humanly possible, they received it out in Flanders.

The wounded appreciated the roomy, well-ventilated wards of a hospital. Fresh cut flowers were placed beside their beds and there was a bright array of pictures on the walls. There was no lack of books, magazines, cigarettes and good food. Alas, not all recovered and death was busy in the hospitals nearest the

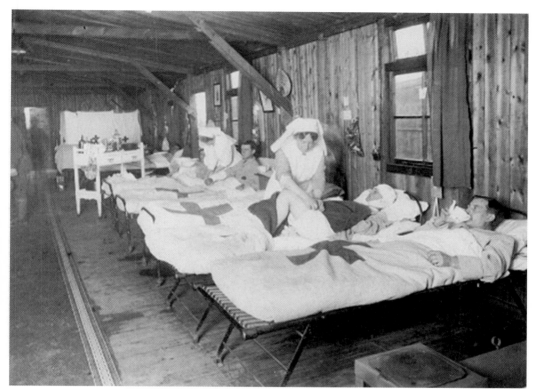

A field hospital.

trenches. Doctors and chaplains alike had to watch the last moments of those who died. In their own different ways, they did what they could to strengthen and comfort a soldier in his final struggle.

Afterwards there would follow one of the saddest things to be seen at the front: the burial of the dead. Simplicity marked the service throughout. There was little or no ceremony, but much solemnity and real respect for the comrade who had given up his life at the call of duty. Burials took place at night in the cemeteries just behind the trenches for those who were killed in battle. No light was shown for fear of attracting the enemy's fire. Everything was done as quietly as possible. One might think that ground consecrated to the heroic dead would escape wanton destruction, but it was not so. Wherever possible, a lad would be buried by a chaplain of the church to which he belonged. Men from the same battalion were generally present and joined in the sad last rites. Nothing could exceed their reverence and care for their fallen comrades. For the lads who had died under such tragic circumstances, no pain or effort was spared to enable them to be buried in a 'Soldiers' Cemetery' and with the recognized funeral service.

At risk of their own lives, many British lads ventured over the parapet into no man's land to bring back the body of a pal and, no matter how weary and tired they might have been, they would have dug a grave and tended it afterwards. Young lads walked miles just to see the grave of one they had known, facing shells and possible death, to pay their last respects at his burial.

One of the most heart-rending deeds performed by many chaplains at the front was writing letters of condolence and sympathy to the families of those lost in the Great War. The heroism of our lads at the front was matched by the heroism of the women at home, especially the mothers, wives, sisters and sweethearts who had no hope of ever seeing their loved ones again. To all mourners, the words of Baring Gould's popular hymn came with renewed and uplifting power:

> Through the night of doubt and sorrow
> Onward goes the pilgrim band,
> Singing songs of expectation,
> Marching to the Promised Land.
>
> Soon shall come the great awaking,
> Soon the rending of the tomb
> Then the scattering of all shadows,
> And the end of toil and gloom.

English soldiers' cemeteries are to be found in many parts of France and Belgium. It is clear that they are well looked after and, indeed, everything possible is done to make them worthy of the great and faithful dead who died in order that Great Britain might live. The symbol of the victory of Life over Death and the eternal triumph of the Risen Christ is on every cross that bears the name, number, regiment and date of death of the man who sleeps beneath that hallowed soil. The whole scene is suggestive of peace and confidence and surely brought solace to those hearts that bled for husbands, sons, brothers and sweethearts.

After that first Sunday

Less than a month later, the battalion had returned from their first long spell in the trenches and many gallant comrades had been left behind.

Those who were there would never forget the services of Easter Day 1916. The first Easter celebration of the Holy Communion took place in a loft, moderately large but not nearly large enough to accommodate all those who wanted to attend. It was necessary for the lads to make their Communion and then pass along to give room to the many communicants standing outside. Later in the morning there was a parade service in a theatre capable of holding 1,000 soldiers and it was almost full. This was followed by Holy Communion, when nearly 300 soldiers made their act of faith. Some of the lads who were there had been confirmed in that room only a few days previously. They were now able to make their first Communion in a theatre that was mainly used for the entertainment of those at the front. Between 500 and 600 officers and men of the 16th (Service) Battalion The King's Royal Rifle Corps made their Easter Communion while the guns roared and thundered only a mile or two away. The 16th can truly claim to be a battalion of 'Soldier-Churchmen' in more than name only.

Acres and acres of war graves.

Credit for this must largely go to the Church Lads' Brigade that had trained them in the critical years of their youth. The brigade had kept them honest and true until early manhood, before bringing them together for service to their country. Nowhere has it been better served nor its ideals more clearly expressed than among those first thousand men who made up the now familiar 'Church-men's Battalion'.

The following is an account from records of the 16th Battalion:

In November the Division received a warning order to prepare to sail for France, and the Brigade moved by train to Southampton with a total contingent of 30 officers and 994 other ranks, 64 horses and mules, 19 vehicles and 9 bicycles. The 16th Battalion (Church Lads' Brigade) of the King's Royal Rifle Corps ended their journey into war with a night Channel crossing and landed on 17 November 1915 in the Haute-Normandie region of France at Le Havre.

From Le Havre, the battalion moves first by train via Abbeville to Thienne on 19 November and then after a few days in Boesegham it marches on to Annezin by the 30 November. Various course and training continue while different parts of the battalion are giving some trench familiarisation in rotation. Others are attached to the 180th Tunnelling Company RE, as working parties for mining activities. They move to St.Hilaire on the 12 December, where they remain until the 28 December. Christmas day 1915 passes without any special note and 28-29 December they move to billets in Bethune. The Battalion gets the bath house on New Year's day, but there is no clean kit available.

On 2 January 1916, the first Sunday of the New Year, the battalion moves into the firing line for eight days in trenches near Bethune. The battalion's position comes under an intense bombardment that lasts for hours. As the firing and shelling dies down, the damage has to be repaired. This work, together with digging out the buried men, goes on for the next few days while the enemy continue to snipe, shell and machine gun. The battalion is relieved on the 10 January. Their losses for that first Sunday alone were 9 killed and 27 wounded.

Chapter Five

1915: The 33rd Division

It wasn't until November 1915 that the 33rd Division made its way to France. It had adopted an insignia of the 'double-three' from a set of dominoes.

Its final training and firing practice had been completed on Salisbury Plain, but the original artillery wasn't able to accompany it. Instead, it received the artillery that had been raised for and trained with the 54th (East Anglian) Division.

As the war progressed there appeared to be total confusion between the organization and numbering of the regular, Territorial and New Army brigades, with batteries being moved from one brigade to another.

On 10 December 1914 the War Office had authorized the formation of a Fifth New Army.

In April 1915 the original Fourth New Army was broken up and its units converted for training and draft-finding purposes. With this taking place, the newly-formed Fifth New Army was redesignated to become the Fourth New Army. Its divisions were renumbered 30th to 35th. The original 40th Division was re-numbered, becoming the 33rd Division. There were many other changes before things finally began to settle down.

Movement of the division across the English Channel began on 12 November and by 21 November 1915 all units had reached the concentration area near Morbecque, a small town in the department of Nord of the French region Nord-Pas-de-Calais, which is located in the township of Hazebrouck-Sud, part of the district of Dunkerque.

Soon after its arrival the division was considerably strengthened by the exchange of 98th Brigade for the experienced 19th Brigade from 2nd Division, and there were also other changes. So it wasn't until 1916 that the 33rd Division actually found itself in the midst of the fighting.

The 100th Brigade was raised as part of Kitchener's New Army and its notable commanders were Major General Herman James Shelley Landon and Major General Sir Reginald John Pinney. It was made up of the following battalions:

- The 13th Battalion Essex Regiment (West Ham), formed 27 December 1914 by the mayor and borough. May 1915: moved to Brentwood. August 1915: moved to Clipstone Camp and came under the orders of 100th Brigade in 33rd Division. 17 November 1915: landed at Boulogne. 22 December 1915: transferred to 6th Brigade, 2nd Division. 22 December 1915: left the brigade.
- 16th (Service) Battalion Middlesex Regiment (Public Schools). 1 September 1914: formed in London by Lieutenant Colonel J.J. Mackay. Moved to Kempton Park racecourse, then on to Warlingham in December. July 1915:

moved to Clipstone Camp and came under command of 100th Brigade in
33rd Division. Moved in August to Perham Down. 17 November 1915:
landed at Boulogne. 25 February 1916: left division and transferred to GHQ
Troops. 25 April 1916: transferred to 86th Brigade in 29th Division.
11 February 1918: disbanded near Poperinghe in Belgium.

- 17th (Service) Battalion Middlesex Regiment (1st Footballers). 12 December
  1914: formed in London by W. Joynson Hicks MP. April 1915: moved to
  White City, then on to Cranleigh. July 1915: moved to Clipstone Camp and
  came under command of 100th Brigade in 33rd Division. In August moved
  to Perham Down. 18 November 1915: landed at Boulogne. 8 December
  1915: transferred to 6th Brigade in 2nd Division. 10 February 1918: disbanded in France.

- 16th (Service) Battalion The King's Royal Rifle Corps (Church Lads'
  Brigade). 19 September 1914: formed from current and previous members
  of that organization at Denham, Buckinghamshire by Field Marshal Lord
  Grenfell, Commandant of the Church Lads' Brigade. March 1915: moved to
  Rayleigh in Essex but returned to Denham in May. June 1915: moved to
  Clipstone Camp and came under orders of 100th Brigade in 33rd Division.
  August 1915: moved on to Perham Down. 17 November 1915: landed at Le
  Havre.

- 1st Battalion The Queen's Regiment. August 1914: based at Bordon Camp
  under the command of 3rd Brigade, 1st Division. 13 August 1914: landed
  at Le Havre. 8 November 1914: transferred to No. I Corps. 21 July 1915:
  transferred to 5th Brigade, 2nd Division. 15 December 1915: transferred to
  100th Brigade, 33rd Division. 5 February 1918: transferred to 19th Brigade,
  33rd Division.

- 2nd Battalion Worcestershire Regiment. August 1914: based at Aldershot as
  part of 5th Brigade in 2nd Division. 14 August 1914: landed at Boulogne.
  20 December 1915: transferred to 100th Brigade in 33rd Division.

- 1/6th Battalion Cameronians. August 1914: based at Muirhall in Hamilton
  as part of Scottish Rifle Brigade, Lowland Division. March 1915: left the
  division and moved to France. 21 March 1915: landed at Le Havre. 24 March
  1915: transferred to 23rd Brigade in 8th Division. 2 June 1915: transferred
  to 154th Brigade in 51st (Highland) Division. 12 January 1916: became
  Divisional Troops training as Pioneers. 25 February 1916: transferred to
  100th Brigade, 33rd Division. 29 May 1916: merged with 1/6th Battalion to
  become 5/6th Battalion.

- 100th Machine Gun Company was formed in Grantham, Lincs. 28 April
  1916: moved to France and joined 33rd Division. 19 February 1918: moved
  into No 33 Battalion, MGC. 7–25 September 1918: attached to 58th Division. 2–15 October 1918: attached to 25th Division.

- 1/9th Battalion Glasgow Highland Light Infantry. August 1914: formed at
  Greendyke Street, Glasgow as part of Highland Light Infantry Brigade in
  Lowland Division. Moved on mobilization to Dunfermline. 5 November
  1914: left the division and landed in France. 23 November 1914: joined

5th Brigade in 2nd Division. 30 January 1916: left the division and became GHQ Troops. 29 May 1916: the battalion joined 100th Brigade in 33rd Division.
• The 100th Trench Mortar Battery was formed on 13 June 1916.

Commanding the division at the outset was Major General Herman James Shelley Landon, CB, CMG (*c.*1859–1948). Landon was born in August 1859, the son of James Landon and Mary Maria Landon. The family was comfortably well off, living in the respectable area of Paddington, London. Educated at Harrow from 1874 to 1876, he left school just before his seventeenth birthday. He attended the Royal Military College at Sandhurst, passing out in 1879 and taking a commission in the 6th Regiment of Foot.

Serving in the Sudan in 1898, he saw action at the Battle of Atbara and the Battle of Omdurman and was Mentioned in Dispatches. In 1900, he returned to the Boer War and took temporary command of the 2nd Royal Warwickshire Regiment. Again Mentioned in Dispatches, he was promoted to lieutenant colonel although not receiving the appropriate pay. From there he was sent to India where he joined the 1st Battalion of the Royal Warwickshires. In 1902, Landon was promoted to substantive lieutenant colonel and given command of the battalion.

In 1904 he received a brevet promotion to colonel and remained in command until 1906. From February to October 1906 he was on half-pay and in October was appointed Inspector of Gymnasia in India. In 1907 he was promoted to substantive colonel. In 1910, he returned to active command when he was made brigadier general and given command of the 3rd Brigade.

October 1914 saw him promoted to major general. The 3rd Brigade was part of the 1st Infantry Division and was mobilized with the British Expeditionary Force that was sent to France at the outbreak of the Great War. Landon was its commander during the retreat from Mons, the Battle of the Marne and the Battle of the Aisne.

During the First Battle of Ypres, Divisional Commander Major General Samuel Lomax was killed in action and Landon took acting command. By the end of the battle in November 1914, he himself was invalided home and was relieved as divisional commander by Major General David Henderson. On 13 November 1914 Lieutenant Colonel Richard Butler formally replaced Landon in command of the brigade.

On his recovery in December, Landon was appointed Inspector of Infantry and, early in 1915, was appointed to command the 9th (Scottish) Division of the New Army. He accompanied it to France but, due to ill health, was replaced in September 1915 before the division saw combat at the Battle of Loos. Returning in October 1915, he took command of the 33rd Division and remained with it when it went into combat at the Battle of the Somme in July 1916.

On 9 July 1916, the 33rd Division arrived at Saleux on the south-western outskirts of Amiens. Placed under the 15th Corps, Fourth Army, it spent its first couple of days in reserve. Over the next three days the division passed through

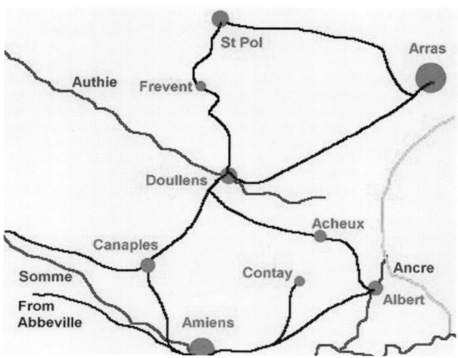

Amiens, 1916 (Somme railways).

St Sauveur (north-west of Amiens), Vecqemont (east of Amiens) and Morlancourt (south of Albert). On 12 July it reached its reserve positions at Bécordel-Bécourt on the eastern fringes of Albert and entered the Somme Offensive. Two days later on 14 July 1916, moving eastwards to Flatiron Copse on the edge of a valley north of Fricourt, an attack commenced at Bazentin Ridge.

The 33rd Division was largely composed of local units often known as 'Pals' units that were raised from the Church Lads' Brigade, the Boy Scouts, the Boys' Brigade, public schools, footballers and other sports associations. Did the lads realize, when they signed up, that the 'Poor Bloody Infantry' had the deadliest role of all and shouldered so much of the burden of carrying and the labouring work?

On 15 July 1916, one company of the 16th (Service) Battalion The King's Royal Rifle Corps (the Church Lads' Brigade Pals Battalion) had been given the task of 'clearing' the wood they had been fighting in to prepare for a further advance. However, of the 200 lads who went in, only 67 came out. The division was engaged there until 17 July.

Before the end of the month the 33rd Division saw further action at High Wood. It was then withdrawn from the line until 25 October, when a series of actions carried out until 7 November brought about the capture of the Dewdrop and Boritska trench systems.

Before the battles

At the front, the British were always near the French army and many times had received help from their artillery. Throughout the autumn and winter of 1915 a frequent exchange of visits and hospitality took place between the British and the French generals and their staffs. Most of Britain's officers and staffs could speak French, so it came about that a great deal of the French military was to be seen.

The chefs in the kitchens of the British and the French were made to pull out their utmost efforts to create some merry dinners for such visits. Although generally the French cooks left the British far behind, there was one dish at which Britain excelled. It was the soldiers' suet and currant pudding which, when perfectly cooked, masqueraded as 'Duff aux Soldats'. It was always welcomed and completely demolished by the French dinner guests. Many warm friendships grew and the most cordial of relations existed between everyone.

Gas masks

By the spring of 1915, gas masks had become a standard feature of British army kit. At first they were like a crude sanitary pad soaked in what were supposedly gas-absorbing chemicals and had to be strapped over the nose and mouth. Later in the year the 'smoke helmet' made an appearance, which was a chemically-treated cloth hood with eyepieces and a rubber mouth valve that fitted over the entire head and neck.

In 1916 the Small Box Respirator (SBR) put in an appearance. This was a waterproof mask fitted with eyepieces. The wearer breathed through a tin cylinder filled with filtering chemicals. It was a less than pleasant experience if the mask had to be worn for prolonged periods but preferable to the alternative of breathing in various gases.

A new style of fighting known as 'trench warfare' pitted the two armies in mortal combat. It was trench against trench and the distance between them was so short that they could yell to each other across the lines. However, soldiers rarely ventured into the area between the two trenches commonly referred to as 'no man's land' for fear of being gunned down, and in the ground between the trenches there was nowhere to hide from land mines. As a result of trench warfare, battles would often settle into a stalemate situation.

In August 1914, the French army was the first to employ the use of gas. They used 26mm grenades filled with tear gas. The small quantities of gas were delivered by firing 19cm cartridges that were not even detected by the Germans. The stocks were rapidly consumed and by November a new order was placed by the French military. It was an act of desperation as opposed to a premeditated act that all but went against the 'rules' of war. However, while the French were the first to use gas against an enemy, the Germans had been giving a great deal of thought to the use of poison gas as a way of inflicting a major defeat on any enemy. Chemical agents such as mustard gas became a way of breaking the uneasy deadlock of trench warfare.

Germany's first attempt at using chemical weapons came in 1915 at the Battle of Ypres in Belgium in the form of chlorine gas. The gas cleared large sections of

Wearing a gas mask while trying to fire at the enemy.

soldiers from the front lines, who fled once exposed and ultimately it killed 5,000 of the enemy's opposing troops. Chlorine gas burns the throats of its victims and causes death by asphyxiation, much like the smoke that kills people during a house fire.

Trench fever

In August 1914, with so much fervent talk and reports in the newspapers, it was no wonder that some of the lads felt the need to be part of the ongoing excitement that promised travel and new adventures. Maybe the idea of wearing a smart new uniform appealed? They couldn't possibly have foreseen, or even heard about, the many disagreeable maladies they might suffer from spending days on end in the wet and pest-ridden trenches.

By 1915, many British soldiers had encountered 'Chatts', which may have been derived from 'chattel': 'Something personal, carried around. Every Conceivable Shade Supplied ... most clinging, and will live anywhere. Once you have them you will never be without.' A joke, perhaps, but it was no laughing matter for the troops in the trenches who had to live with them. For almost every man who served in the trenches during the Great War, millions of lice were their constant companions. Neither side was immune to them.

Eric Partridge, a British infantryman and famous academic, wrote: 'Chatts were not fleas or bugs; they did not jump, but crept.' Usually they were pale fawn in colour and would leave red blotchy marks where they had bitten, but it was the itching caused by their crawling that drove the lads mad. Once the chatts had found a 'host', they rapidly multiplied.

Partridge also said that one way to get rid of the parasites was by 'searching uniforms and underwear, especially along the seams, and treatment meant cracking the lice between the thumbnails. They squelched blood, but not their own!' When the weather was good, he wrote, 'groups of men could be seen with their shirts or trousers or tunics laid over their knees, cracking lice and jokes together.'

A French soldier wrote: 'The lice feared solitude and had a profound sense of family . . . lice have a very warm, very soft bedroom, where the table is always laid. There, in their numerous moments of leisure, they followed the counsels of their creator: they multiplied.'

Lice infestation not only caused frenzied scratching but also the transmission of a disease known as trench fever. It started with shooting pains in the legs, followed by a high fever. It was not fatal, but a course of treatment could take between six to twelve weeks.

The problem of lice infestation became so acute that, at one stage, a War Office 'boffin' suggested spraying the troops' underwear with a chemical that

Fighting fleas in Flanders.

would kill any tiny creatures with which it came into contact. It was sprayed on the underwear of a party of kilted volunteers, who were deliberately infected with lice and the volunteers then sent on daytime marches. Later the officer in charge said:

> After a mile or two some of the men began to complain of an itching of the skin ... often I had to permit the more frenzied to remove their underclothes and march carrying these in their hands ... Apart from their marches they lived a carefree life...They all put on weight, their physiques and appetites improved; the same applied unfortunately to the lice.

Numerous stories and jokes about trench lice circulated among the men at the front. The soldier poet, Robert Graves, remembered one session when a certain Private Bumford came up to him and said:

> We were just having an argument as to whether it's best to kill the old ones or the young ones, Sir. Morgan here says that if you kill the old ones, the young ones die of grief; but Parry here, Sir, says that the young ones are easier to kill and you can catch the old ones when they go to the funeral ... You've been to college, Sir, haven't you?

The only positive and effective remedy, after living in the same clothes for days on end, was a bath and a change of clothes at a delousing station. However, opportunities to do this did not happen very frequently, so 'chatting' became a normal routine during quiet times and rest periods.

Trench foot

For young soldiers, especially those that had been in the army since 1914, life in the trenches had become almost intolerable. Rats bred in enormous numbers, chiefly fed on the corpses of dead soldiers but also with an eye for anything left in a dugout.

If trench fever, transmitted by the lice, hadn't affected our young lads, it was probable that some other disease or ailment would bring them down. Trench foot was a particular problem in the early stages of the war. For example, during the winter of 1914–15 over 20,000 men in the British army were treated for trench foot.

Boots worn with puttees were intended to keep small stones and suchlike from causing problems while marching. However, when standing for hours on end in a trench more than ankle-deep in water, the skin takes on the effect that one sees if keeping the hands submerged in water for a long time. It eventually causes the skin to break down, fall away and exposes the muscles underneath.

Trench foot was a medical condition caused by prolonged exposure of the feet to damp, unsanitary and cold conditions as experienced in severe wet weather. The affected feet often became numb, turning red or even blue as a result of poor vascular supply. The lads' feet sometimes began to have a decaying odour, due to possible early-stage necrosis setting in. As the condition worsened, their feet also began to swell.

Trench foot inspection.

Advanced trench foot often involved blisters. If left untreated, open sores would lead to fungal infections and usually resulted in gangrene, causing the need for amputation. As with other cold-related injuries, trench foot left its sufferers more susceptible to it in the future. Trench foot doesn't necessarily need freezing conditions (unlike frostbite) and can occur even in quite warm climates. It was the combination of cold and wet that was the danger, with trench foot setting in after only ten to twelve hours if conditions for it were suitable. If the complaint was treated properly, complete recovery was usual, although marked by severe short-term pain when feeling to the feet returned.

Trench foot was a serious problem for both sides in the conflict. Conditions in the trenches of the Great War were perfect for the disease, as troops could be standing in water for hours or even days on end. One soldier on the Somme recalled that 'the water from two hillsides had come into the valley and filled our trench, in some places, waist deep. In order to keep the trench from being absolutely waterlogged, we had to pump continuously with the four pumps with which we had been supplied.'

Trench foot poster.

By the end of 1915 British soldiers in the trenches had to have three pairs of socks with them and were under strict orders to change their socks at least twice a day. This was a regimen of common sense, hygiene and strict military discipline. As well as drying their feet, soldiers were told to cover them with a grease made from whale oil. It has been estimated that a battalion at the front would use 10 gallons of whale oil every day.

Brigadier General Frank Percy Crozier argued that 'The fight against the condition known as trench-feet had been incessant and an uphill game.' Officers tried to solve the problem by instructing that 'Socks are changed and dried in the line. Thigh boots are worn and are dried every four days when we come out.'

Two new pieces of equipment were issued during this period. The first was the 'thigh gum boot'. A few pairs were distributed among battalions in the line for trials and reports. The gumboot was a real boon to men who had to stand for hours in mud and water, providing they were able to get into a dry place from time to time and ventilate their feet. Casualties from trench foot dwindled to quite small proportions, thanks to the precautions recommended and enforced.

Tin Hats

The other new weapon of defence was the steel helmet. At first only a few were issued to sentries, officers and NCOs on duty, but their benefit was so apparent that they were soon a regular part of the fighting man's equipment, despite the unfavourable report on them by a senior officer on the grounds that they were 'unbecoming'.

Shellshock

Apart from the most terrible and maiming wounds to the bodies of the lads, Combat Stress Reaction (CSR) is a term used within the military to describe acute behavioural disorganization. Seen by medical personnel as a direct result of the trauma of war, it is historically linked to shellshock. It is an acute reaction that includes a range of behaviours resulting from the stress of battle that decrease the combatant's fighting efficiency. In the Great War, shellshock was considered a psychiatric illness resulting from injury to the nerves during combat. The horrors of trench warfare meant that about 10 per cent of the fighting soldiers were killed and the total proportion of troops who became casualties (killed or wounded) was 56 per cent.

Whether a shellshock sufferer was considered 'wounded' or 'sick' depended on the circumstances. During the early stages of the war, soldiers from the British Expeditionary Force began to report medical symptoms after combat including tinnitus, amnesia, headache, dizziness, tremor and hypersensitivity to noise. While these symptoms resembled those that would be expected after a physical wound to the brain, many of those reporting sick showed no signs of head wounds.

By December 1914 as many as 10 per cent of British officers and 4 per cent of enlisted men were suffering from 'nervous and mental shock'. The term 'shellshock' came into use to reflect an assumed link between the symptoms and the

Showing off the new Brodie helmets (1916).

effects of explosions from artillery shells. Charles Myers first published the term in an article in *The Lancet* in 1915.

The number of shellshock cases grew during 1915 and 1916, but it remained poorly-understood both medically and psychologically. Some doctors held the view that it was a result of hidden physical damage to the brain, with the shock waves from bursting shells creating a cerebral lesion that caused the symptoms and could potentially prove fatal.

Another explanation was that shellshock resulted from poisoning by the carbon monoxide formed by explosions. At the same time an alternative view described shellshock as an emotional rather than a physical injury. Evidence for this point of view was provided by the fact that an increasing proportion of men suffering shellshock symptoms had not been exposed to artillery fire. Since the symptoms appeared in men who had had no proximity to an exploding shell, the physical explanation was clearly unsatisfactory. In spite of this evidence, the British army continued to try to differentiate between those whose symptoms followed explosive exposure from others.

The war poets Wilfred Owen and Siegfried Sassoon were both diagnosed as suffering from neurasthenia or shellshock and met when they were recovering at Craiglockhart War Hospital in Edinburgh.

With these developments going on, it is hard to imagine what the members of the Church Lads' Brigade were wondering. Nevertheless, there were battles to be fought and the 33rd had to 'straighten up and show that stiff British upper lip'.

Battles of the 33rd Division
The Battle of Albert, 1–13 July 1916, is the official name for the British efforts during the first two weeks fighting of the First Battle of the Somme. It had been intended to be a big Anglo-French assault on the centre of the German lines, but the original plan had been somewhat disrupted by the German attack at Verdun on 21 February that had pulled in an ever-increasing number of French troops. By the time the Battle of Albert had begun, it had turned into a largely British affair with support from the French Sixth Army already on the Somme itself.

The Battle of Bazentin Ridge, 14–17 July 1916, comprised part of the second phase of the Somme Offensive and was launched primarily by the Reserve Army (twelve battalions). Rawlinson's Fourth Army provided a further battalion on a front extending from Longueval to Bazentin-le-Petit Wood.

The attacks on High Wood were scheduled for 20 July 1916. In visiting one of the strongpoints under his command, war poet Robert Graves made his way along a road illuminated by bright moonlight. He came across a dead German sergeant major, wearing full equipment including his pack, lying in the middle of the road with his arms stretched out wide. Further along, Graves discovered small hollows that contained the bodies of men of the 2nd Battalion Gordon Highlanders. It appeared they had crawled in to escape enemy fire during a German counter-attack and sadly had subsequently died from their wounds.

On that very same day, Robert Graves was badly wounded while fighting from the trenches in Bazentin cemetery. From there he was carried from the Regimental Aid Post (located in the quarry just behind the cemetery) along the short distance into Mametz Wood, where use was being made of a German dressing station that had been captured on 12 July during an attack by the 38th (Welsh) Division. So bad were his wounds that his condition was thought to be hopeless and he was placed upon a stretcher to wait for death.

However, the next morning, while clearing away the dead for burial, an orderly noticed that Graves was breathing. Immediately he was placed in an ambulance and taken to No. 36 Casualty Clearing Station at Heilly (about 5 miles from Albert) and then by ambulance train to No. 8 Hospital at Rouen. Later he was considered fit enough to make the long journey home to Queen Alexandra's Hospital in Highgate, London, where he eventually, physically if not mentally, recovered from his wounds.

The battalion's commanding officer (Lieutenant Colonel Crawshay) had previously seen the badly-wounded Graves and was informed that there was no hope that he would live. Accordingly, he wrote a letter of condolence to Robert's mother. *The Times* newspaper reported the death and Graves became the proud possessor of a letter of apology from that newspaper's advertising manager indicating that no charge would be made for the announcement that Graves had not died of his wounds!

As well as his major wounds, he also suffered a cut above his eye possibly caused by a chip of marble from one of the headstones there. Graves records the incidents fully in his autobiography, *Goodbye to All That*.

There was more action at High Wood and then the 33rd Division was withdrawn from the line until 25 October. On Sunday, 29 October there was another dawn attack, this time by 1st Cameronians (Scottish Rifles), while the 5/6th Scottish Rifles 19th Brigade attempted to extend their hold on Boritska Trench. They were stopped by machine-gun fire. On 1 November at 05:45 hours, another attempt was made. Some of The Rifles entered the trench, but were driven out. At 13.30, the 100th Brigade tried again with 1/9th Highland Light Infantry and the 2nd Worcesters in conjunction with a French attack. They were stopped by mud and machine-gun fire from Le Transloy cemetery.

On Friday, 3 November 1916 the 7th Lincolns repelled a further attack on Zenith Trench. Pockets of Germans were discovered in the trench in the evening and were cleared by the bombers of the 7th Green Howards.

On Saturday, 4 November, together with the 1st Battalion, Queen's Regiment, the 98th Brigade 33rd Division attempted to take the ridge east of Dewdrop Trench without success.

The next day, the 33rd Division attacked at 11.10 with the 2nd Worcesters and the 16th (Service) Battalion, The King's Royal Rifle Corps, both from the 100th Brigade, and the 2nd Royal West Kents' 19th Brigade. The Worcesters took Boritska, while the King's Royal Rifle Corps took Mirage Trench. The West Kents tried to push on to the Lesboeufs-Le Transloy road but failed.

The 33rd Division was involved in a great deal of action around Lesboeufs. On 6/7 November 1916 the 100th Brigade (33rd Division) was relieved by the 24th Brigade (8th Division) when a series of actions had brought about the capture of the Dewdrop and Boritska trench systems.

On 8 November 1916, the 8th Division relieved the remainder of the 33rd Division.

During 1917 the 33rd Division was very much involved in the Arras Offensive. From 9 April to 16 May 1917, British, Canadian, New Zealand, Newfoundland and Australian troops attacked German defences near the French city of Arras. The First Battle of the Scarpe, the Second Battle of the Scarpe, the actions on the Hindenburg Line and operations on the Flanders coast (Operation HUSH) were all part of the campaign. The Hindenburg Line battles were the Battle of the Epehy, the Battle of the St Quentin Canal, the Battle of the Beaurevoir Line and the Battle of Cambrai.

The 33rd Division also took part in phases of the Third Battles of Ypres 1918. The different phases of the Battle of the Lys 1918 were the Battle of Messines, the Battle of Hazebrouck, the Battle of Bailleul, the defence of Neuve Église, the First Battle for Kemmel Ridge and the fighting for and recapture of Ridge Wood. The final advance in Picardy was the pursuit to the Selle, ending with the Battle of the Selle.

When Rawlinson's Fourth Army reached the River Selle in October 1918, they were faced with three problems: crossing the river itself, crossing the railway

Albert railway station in ruins.

embankment on the far side and the ridge above the embankment. The decision was made to commence the assault at night and, as the river was not so very wide at this point, planks would be used for the soldiers to cross in single file. Later, pontoons would be required for the artillery to cross the river. The attack took place during the night of 17 October and continued until 20 October.

After crossing the river in fog, the battle developed into a dogfight. In the morning the three brigades were thoroughly mixed up. Commander Walter Braithwaite had left the organizing to his divisional commanders: E.P. Strickland (1st Division), T.O. Marden (6th Division) and G.F. Boyd (46th Division).

Of these three commanders, Gerald Boyd stands out as being different. He had joined the Devonshire Regiment in 1895 as a private soldier, was commissioned into the East Yorkshire Regiment in 1900, began the Great War as brigade major in Hunter-Weston's 11th Brigade and was finally promoted GOC 46th Division in September 1918.

In the night attack Boyd was instructed to carry out 'Chinese' deception manoeuvres, meaning lots of movement and shelling but not actually taking part in the battle. Unlike earlier battles, when time would have been lost while men were sorted back into their original brigades, these three brigade commanders carried on directing the battle, each instructing the battalions closest to their command posts. This was a far better organizational method than the one that existed in the German lines where time was lost in reorganizing the men.

Englefontaine was captured by the 18th and 33rd divisions on 26 October 1918 and, that night, was relieved by the 38th (Welsh) Division. After a period of rest at Troisvilles, the 33rd Division re-entered the line on 5 November, advancing through the Forêt de Mormal. By 7 November advances had been made on a line

Englefontaine British Cemetery.

Tuileries British Cemetery.

to the east of the Avesnes-Maubeuge road. Once again it was relieved by the 38th (Welsh) Division and moved to the Sambre Valley near Leval.

In November 1918 the Englefontaine British Cemetery was created by the burial officer of the 38th (Welsh) Division and men of the 33rd Division. It was enlarged after the Armistice by the concentration of graves from Les Tuileries British Cemetery. There are now more than 150 1914–18 war casualties commemorated on this site. Of these, ten are unidentified. It contains the graves of fifty-five soldiers from the United Kingdom. The cemetery covers an area of 586 square metres and is enclosed by a low rubble wall. Les Tuileries British Cemetery, Englefontaine was behind the garden of a house, on the north side of the road to Salesches, at a hamlet called Les Tuileries.

The 33rd Division was still in the Sambre Valley when the Armistice was signed. The division remained on the Western Front right up until the end of the war.

By 4 December 1918, the 33rd had moved to Montigny, where King George V inspected it. By 17 December 1918 it had moved on to Hornoy. Demobilization continued throughout the first months of 1919. Divisional HQ moved to Le Havre on 28 February and on 30 June 1919 the division ceased to exist.

The Great War had cost 33rd Division 37,404 men killed, wounded or missing. There is no memorial plaque at the Somme for the 33rd Division.

Chapter Six

1916: The Battle of the Somme

On 27 January 1916, conscription into the armed forces of Great Britain was made compulsory.

For almost the next three years, dozens of battles were fought simultaneously. Hundreds of paths were crossed by thousands of allied troops attempting to destroy their enemy.

> Before action
> By all the glories of the day
> And the cool evening's benison,
> By that last sunset touch that lay
> Upon the hills where day was done,
> By beauty lavishly outpoured
> And blessings carelessly received,
> By all the days that I have lived
> Make me a soldier, Lord.
>
> By all of man's hopes and fears,
> And all the wonders poets sing,
> The laughter of unclouded years,
> And every sad and lovely thing;
> By the romantic ages stored
> With high endeavour that was his,
> By all his mad catastrophes
> Make me a man, O Lord.
>
> I, that on my familiar hill
> Saw with uncomprehending eyes
> A hundred of Thy sunsets spill
> Their fresh and sanguine sacrifice,
> Ere the sun swings his noonday sword
> Must say goodbye to all of this;
> By all delights that I shall miss,
> Help me to die, O Lord.
>
> W.N. Hodgson (1893–1916).

Serving with the 9th Battalion The Devonshire Regiment, Lieutenant Hodgson was preparing for the Battle of the Somme. The scheduled date for the start of the battle was originally to be in August 1916, but had been brought forward to 29 June. Owing to bad weather during the week leading up to the battle, the date of the attack, now planned for 11:00 hours on 28 June, was moved once again to the morning of 1 July 1916. It is believed that Noel Hodgson wrote the poem on 29 June 1916.

The 16th (Service) Battalion (Church Lads' Brigade) came under orders of 100th Brigade in 33rd Division that fought in the Battle of Albert, the Battle of Bazentin, the attacks on High Wood and the capture of Boritska and Dewdrop trenches, which were all phases of the Battles of the Somme.

The first day of the Somme attack was the most costly day in British military history and has stained Britain's image of the Great War ever since.

The battle commenced on 1 July 1916 and continued until November 1916. It was preceded by a week-long artillery bombardment of the German lines: 1,738,000 shells were fired at the Germans, the logic being that the artillery guns would destroy the enemy's front-line trenches and the barricade of barbed wire that protected them.

Field Marshal Haig heavily supported the use of artillery fire, but the Germans had very deep dugouts and all they had to do when the bombardment started was to move their men into the relative safety of those trenches. When the bombardment ended, the Germans knew that this was the signal for the British infantry to advance. They then moved from the safety of their dugouts and manned their machine guns to face the oncoming British and French forces.

By this time the lads were far removed from the loyal churchgoers they had been back at home. Gone were memories of halcyon days, green fields and peaceful villages. Nothing could possibly compare with the strenuousness, the wonderful heroism, the appalling discomfort and weariness experienced at that time by allied soldiers. British battalions went into battle fit, strong and full of confidence to take their part in the great offensive. Several days later, just a handful of the men that had gone into battle fresh and clean came out covered in mud and exhausted, with many of their dead comrades left behind. All their religious virtue had been abandoned during their two years already served in the British army.

The 16th (Service) Battalion became known as the 'Black Button Bastards' of the 100th Brigade due to their use of bad language. Their chaplain, Reverend J. Dunean, said that he always knew the part of the trenches where his lads were to be found by their excessive use of inappropriate language. Nevertheless, the lads were proud of the traditions of their adopted regiment and their quick march of 140 steps a minute. Wherever they marched and no matter how arduous the journey, their voices rang out in song:

Pack up your troubles in your old kit-bag,
And smile, smile, smile,
While you've a lucifer to light your fag,
Smile, boys, that's the style.
What's the use of worrying?
It never was worth while, so
Pack up your troubles in your old kit-bag,
And smile, smile, smile.

The 'lucifer' was a popular make of match and a 'fag' still remains British slang for a cigarette. A kit-bag (also known as a duffle bag) is a large cylindrical canvas or heavy-duty cotton bag with a flat base and punched holes round the other end for tying with a drawstring. It is generally carried balanced on one shoulder, with a hand held up to steady it. It was the traditional means of carrying personal equipment (bedding, clothing, etc) in both the army and the navy. *Pack Up Your Troubles in Your Old Kit-Bag, and Smile, Smile, Smile* is the full name of a marching song of the Great War, published in London in 1915.

Written by George Henry Powell under the pseudonym of George Asaf, it was set to music by his brother Felix Powell. A play presented by the National Theatre recounts how music-hall stars rescued the song from their rejects pile and re-scored it to win a wartime competition for a marching song. It became very popular, boosting British morale despite the horrors of that war. It was one of a large number of music-hall songs aimed at maintaining morale, recruiting for the forces, or defending Britain's war aims.

The Battle of the Somme was the conflict that best symbolized the horrors of the bloodiest of warfare in the Great War. This single battle had the most marked effect on overall casualty figures and epitomized the futility of the stalemate of trench warfare. The Somme was the British army's major offensive on the Western Front in 1916 and included thousands of confident British volunteers, keen to take part in what was expected to be a great victory.

Between January and July 1916, the strength of the British armies on the Western Front in bayonets and sabres increased from 450,000 to 660,000. With such a large number of forces in the field from almost every British regiment, the control exercised by a commander-in-chief was restricted to general guidance and devolved into the responsibility of each army commander. Those responsibilities were entrusted to Generals Sir Henry Rawlinson and Sir Hubert Gough, commanding respectively the Fourth and Fifth Armies. For five months (July to November 1916) they controlled the operations of a huge force in one of the greatest wartime struggles ever to take place.

The preliminary artillery bombardment began seven days before the infantry was due to go in, but the effect was not as expected and large portions of the German front line remained intact. The German lines on the Somme contained a large number of deep concrete bunkers that protected their forces from the British bombardment, allowing them to emerge once it was over. Worse still, along most of the British front the bombardment failed to destroy the German barbed-wire defences.

The choice of front for the allied offensive was governed by the consideration that neither the British nor the French alone were deemed strong enough to undertake such aggressive action on such an immense scale. It was therefore considered necessary to deliver a combined attack.

The whole town of Montreuil had been taken over as the general headquarters of the British army. The 3,000 civilians who still lived there were outnumbered by the military and needed the authority of the British to travel in or out of it.

Official War Diary, 16th Battalion KRRC, 1 and 2 January 1916.

Official War Diary, 16th Battalion KRRC, 29 and 30 January 1916.

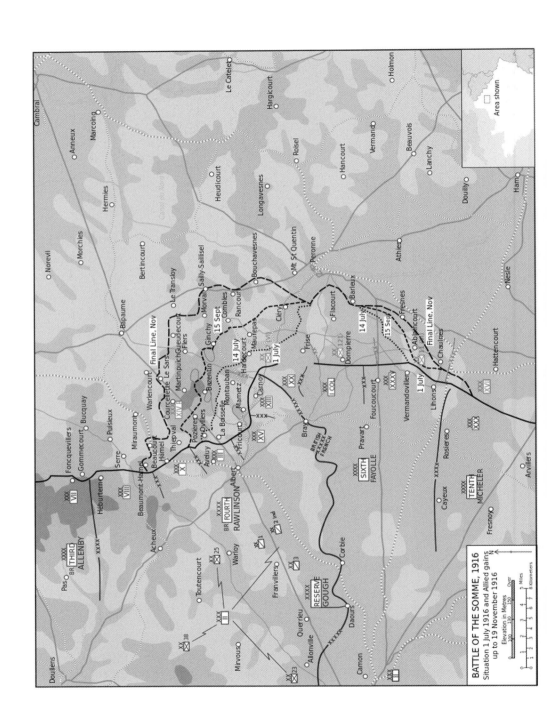

BATTLE OF THE SOMME, 1916
Situation 1 July 1916 and Allied gains
up to 19 November 1916

Elevation in Metres

| 90 | 130 | 150 | Over |

Area shown

Manning the guns.

The troops earned the nickname of 'geraniums' because of the red hatbands worn by the staff officers.

General Sir Douglas Haig (commander of the BEF) moved to Advanced Head-quarters, a château that had been prepared for him 15 miles behind the battle line at Beauquesne.

On the morning of the day before the long-planned campaign, General Haig, a devoutly religious man, attended a service that was held in a modest wooden barrack. The 'church' was the Church of Scotland and a flag with the blue and white cross of St Andrew fluttered from the flagpole above the entrance. There was the distant sound of a bombardment going on some 70 miles away. Across those 70 miles, church services were being held for the troops encamped there and about to go into battle.

It had rained for the past week but on 30 June 1916 conditions had improved, although it was still overcast and there was a high wind. General Rawlinson noted in his War Diary that the total number of men involved at the start of the battle was about 500,000. There were 1,500 guns, of which 450 were of a large calibre. Some 150,000 rounds of ammunition had been fired that day and 50,000 fired into the enemy front lines during the night.

Loading 2-inch British trench mortars.

The first day

When the allied attack began at 07.30 on Saturday 1 July, a hazy mist had lifted to a clear sky and the first 100,000 soldiers went 'over the top'. The offensive was a combined Franco-British effort on a 25-mile front both north and south of the Somme. The French attacked towards Péronne, reaching the outskirts of

Douglas Haig with Major General C.C. Monro (commanding 2nd Division), Brigadier General J.E. Gough (Haig's chief of staff), and Major General Sir Edward Perceval (commander of 2nd Division's artillery).

Hardecourt and Curlu, and the British attacked Montauban and Mametz. To the north-west of the Albert-Bapaume road, the British made little progress against the German defences except for a small gain at the Leipzig Redoubt to the south of Thiepval. On that day was recorded the highest number of casualties the British army had ever suffered. There were nine Victoria Crosses awarded from that day's fighting alone.

There were very few church parades on the Somme the next morning. Most of the padres had their hands full looking after the wounded, helping out at the aid

'Over the top'.

posts or burying the dead. There were more casualties on 2 July, estimated at about 30,000. Thunderstorms set in and carried on for the rest of the week. Some gains were made by the allies and several more Victoria Crosses awarded, showing to what extent British soldiers were prepared to fight.

Thirteen divisions, along an 18-mile front, made the attack on 1 July 1916 from Montauban to Serre. Field Marshal Haig had the idea that if he could capture the German front line along this entire front, he could then break through their second and third lines before turning left and rolling up the German lines to the sea. This was an overly-optimistic plan that was doomed to fail, and it did. Along the northern two-thirds of the front, virtually no ground was taken.

As the thirteen British divisions walked towards the German lines, machine-gun fire started, the slaughter began and it became a huge baptism of fire for Britain's new volunteer armies. Many Pals battalions – men from the same town who had enlisted together in order to serve together – suffered catastrophic losses. Whole units died together and for weeks after the initial assault, local British newspapers were filled with lists of the dead, wounded and missing.

By the end of that first day, the British had suffered 57,000 casualties, of whom 20,000 were dead: their largest single loss. Some 60 per cent of all officers involved on the first day were killed. Thirteen divisions at full strength contained at least 130,000 men and the British suffered over 40 per cent casualties. The British high command had no idea of the scale of the disaster. Communications back from the front line were almost impossible to understand and it took the best part of a week before the total casualty figures for 1 July 1916 were known. This was the most costly single day in British military history.

Although a few British units managed to reach the German trenches, they could not exploit their gains and were driven back. The Battle of the Somme, intended to be a decisive breakthrough in the war, became a byword for futile and indiscriminate slaughter with General Haig's tactics remaining controversial even to this day.

The French advance was considerably more successful. They had more guns and faced weaker defences, but were unable to exploit their gains without British back-up and had to fall back to their earlier positions.

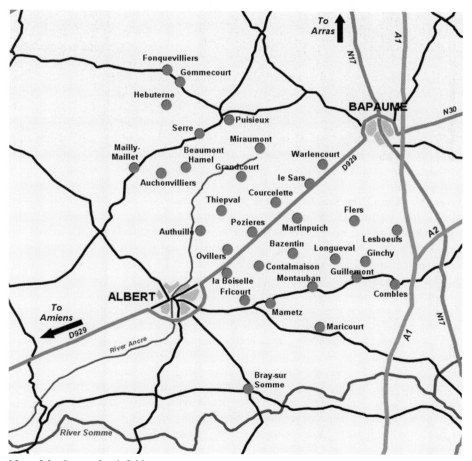

Map of the Somme battlefields.

Haig was encouraged to order a renewal of the assault along the entire front on 2 July 1916. The day began with an unsuccessful German counter-attack at the junction of the British and French armies, where both had advanced from their own front lines. During the day, as the scale of the losses suffered on the previous day became clearer, Haig's planned attack was cancelled corps by corps. Very few brigades remained fit enough to organize another major assault so soon.

The army was still in chaos on 3 July 1916, when an attempt was made to capture Ovillers and Thiepval. La Boiselle, Bernafay Wood and part of Ovillers were captured. The plan of attack was repeatedly changed, partly to allow units longer to prepare and partly in an attempt to save the already limited stocks of artillery ammunition. The German counter-bombardment had destroyed most of the field telephone wires that were connected to various artillery batteries, so the changes in orders often failed to get through in time.

On 6 July, David Lloyd George was appointed Secretary of State for War and Lord Derby as Under Secretary of State for War, and on 9 July E.S. Montagu was appointed Minister of Munitions.

During those first two weeks of fighting in the First Battle of the Somme, the infantry's named objectives were often impossible to recognize in a terrain devoid of distinguishing features. Some of the names given to various positions and German trenches were a credit to the imaginative capabilities of the staff that created them and their poetic variety even prompted later comments by official historians. Questions were even raised in the House as to whether any British irony was intended by names such as Hazy Trench, Rainy and Dewdrop Trenches and Cloudy and Mild Trenches. Comparisons were noted regarding their similarities to wet English summer afternoons and the dreadful realities they posed for the attacking troops. 'The ingenuity of staffs, commanders and others was constantly exercised in finding names for new German trenches' (from the book *Military Operations France and Belgium, 1916* by Captain Wilfrid Miles, 1938). On 10 July the Germans were assembling in Mametz Wood and the fighting was grim. The operational order stated that the division would attack the wood with the aim of 'capturing the whole of it' and the attack was on a larger scale than had ever been attempted before.

The fringe of the wood was soon reached, despite heavy casualties. A number of German machine guns were silenced and some bayonet fighting took place before the wood was entered. Field Marshal Haig visited General Rawlinson, but was informed that the British forces had failed to get into Mametz Wood.

The weather then changed dramatically and, although overcast, it was very hot with no wind and a thick cloudbank. For the next three days the fierce and vicious fighting continued with the Germans not yielding to constant British pressure, as they gave up ground. The 14th (Service) Battalion (Swansea) The Welsh Regiment went into the attack with 676 lads. After a day of hard fighting, almost 400 men had been killed or wounded before being relieved.

By 12 July Mametz Wood was effectively cleared of the enemy. The Welsh Division had lost about 4,000 men killed or wounded in this searing engagement. It would not be used in a massed attack again until 31 July 1917.

The next objective was Trônes Wood. Because of the unsettled weather conditions the attack was delayed for twenty-four hours, but the British penetrated it on 8 July 1916. This is a tear-shaped wood located a further half-mile distant from Bernafay, midway between the German-held village of Guillemont to the east and Montauban to the west. Trônes Wood had been a strongpoint and a fortified artillery position before the assault on 1 July. The position at the 'corner' of the revised line rendered it a formidable defensive position due to the prospect of German artillery fire from guns between the villages and batteries close by to the east and the north at Longueval, Guillemont. The attack was timed for 03:00 hours, but the men were greatly hampered by gas shells and the misting of the eyepieces in their masks in the damp atmosphere. Consequently, their advance across the ground between Bernafay and Trônes Woods took place some three hours after it was planned.

One of the lads wrote:

> We marched to the line during the night and found ourselves in a long communication trench. I reckon it was just before dawn and quite dark when the Germans started to shell us with gas shells. At that time, we had the old gas masks made of grey material with two round pieces of glass to see through, but soon got steamed up and a rubber tube to put in our mouths to breathe. We had the gas mask on quite a long time and, in some cases affected the skin on some of the chaps' faces. Just before day break, I felt a tap on my shoulder. I was given an enamel cup which I was told to drink. To my surprise, it was rum. This was the first time I had tasted alcohol. The Germans must have sent quite a lot of gas shells because we were all thirsty. But the next thing we heard was the whistle for us to go over the top – it was terrible.

Soon after midday, the German artillery began a systematic bombardment of the wood. Crashing timbers, flying splinters and clouds of cordite-ridden dust spewed all over the lads. They stumbled around, seeking any form of cover in this onslaught. The official report states that the battalion was fired on by hostile artillery from the north, north-east and east. The strongest fire came from the north and east and was described as 'terrific'. An officer wrote: 'It seemed as if every gun in the sector had been switched on to this one small area', while a private wrote:

> Somebody had sent me some chocolate and I stood up to hand it out to the others. Just then, a shrapnel shell burst and it hit everybody except one of us. I got shrapnel in my foot. No one was badly wounded. We'd been ever so lucky, but the only chap, who wasn't injured, was too shocked to bandage us up. We started to make our way back through the wood, to a dressing station.

Recognizing the number of casualties and the limited communication and vulnerability from the northern end of the wood, the order was given to withdraw at 15:00. This was carried out along Trônes Alley, retiring to Bernafay Wood.

The Basilica in Albert with the golden virgin on top. The troops believed that when it fell, the war would end.

Regrettably, a group of forty men did not receive the order to withdraw and were left behind to face the prospect of a German counter-attack. The denseness of the wood made it awkward to reorganize the various companies as they were scattered over a distance of about half a mile. It made communication and movement in the fallen timber and thick undergrowth almost impossible.

As the evacuation was carried out, the Germans attacked in force at 14:15 and quickly occupied the entire wood, cutting off the detachments of A and B Companies in the north-west of the wood. The men held out for as long as they possibly could until they were eventually bombed out. A few men tried to escape across the open ground but were cut down by the enemy. None returned. All were either killed or captured. Further south, confusion reigned as groups were left isolated in the wood but the withdrawal was completed by 17:00 hours.

The lads who were killed at Trônes Wood are commemorated at the Thiepval Memorial. Records of injuries for men in the Great War are very limited, as many service records were burned following the bombing of the store at Kew in 1940.

British forces moved on towards High Wood in a continuation of the push through German lines. High Wood is a small forest near Bazentin-le-Petit in the Somme department of northern France. Realizing the best chance of success was

Thiepval Memorial.

to focus on the right of the line where progress had been made, Haig decided to change tactics. This was an awkward area to fight from, cramped and away from the best roads, but elsewhere the German front line was essentially intact. The French General Joffre did not approve of this change of emphasis and even tried to order Haig to attack further north, but this was without success as Haig chose to ignore Joffre's opinion. The rest of the fighting at the Battle of Albert involved a series of attacks on the front, east of the village of La Boisselle, on the Albert-Bapaume road. It slowly pushed the Germans back towards their second position on Bazentin Ridge.

The Battle of Albert, which had begun on 1 July, ended on 13 July. Some of the lads probably hadn't had their clothes off for a couple of weeks and had only been allowed a small ration of water for washing and shaving. Each day, as dawn approached, there would be a period of 'stand to' that lasted about an hour and a half in order to get ready in case of enemy attack. After this the lads 'stood down' and ate breakfast. Army rations eaten in the trenches were far from appealing to the appetite. Trench food consisted of a tinned vegetable stew called Maconochie, corned beef, rissoles, 'hard tack' biscuits, bacon and sausages, tinned pork fat and beans, cheese and bread and jam.

With all the horror of the killing behind them, as they stood down for a 'rest' period the relief of getting away from the front provided an opportunity to get cleaned up. A visit to a barber's shop or, when it was their turn, a hot bath, was a complete luxury. A jolly good rest for the battle-worn lads gave some of them a little mental escape from the shocking and terrible conflict.

Pay had built up while soldiers were at the front, giving them the opportunity to indulge in some spending at local shops, gambling establishments and

Dinner time in the trenches.

brothels. There were restaurants that specialized in good home cooking, and bars in the side streets where the drinks were half-price. Film showings or concerts were provided by divisional concert parties or by such organizations as the Young Men's Christian Association (YMCA).

The Battle of Bazentin Ridge, 14–17 July 1916

The National Day of France is on 14 July, otherwise known as Bastille Day. This was the second since the war had begun and there was hope, even though the Germans were still to be defeated.

For the past fourteen days many battles had raged on with losses and gains on both sides. Under very heavy bombardment and on a wide front, the British attacked and broke through the Germans' second line. The dawn attack was launched on Longueval and other objectives. The Battle of Bazentin Ridge was the start of the second phase of the Battle of the Somme.

Starting on 14 July, Haig's intention was to launch an attack with the 15th and 13th corps against that part of the German second line. General Rawlinson, commander of the Fourth Army, had devised a plan of attack, but Haig did not believe it possible for the inexperienced recruits of the New Army to carry out the complex manoeuvres required in advance of a dawn attack.

However, General Rawlinson persisted with his plan that required the 13th Corps to advance up to half a mile into no man's land on the night of 13/14 July. This was necessary because no man's land was particularly wide at this part of the line. The 15th Corps, on the left of the line, didn't have to make such a dramatic advance, although its right-hand division did need to move forward during the night.

The attack started at 03:25 and was preceded by a five-minute artillery bombardment. This initial attack was successful in gaining ground along most of the line. The short bombardment and the unexpected dawn attack caught the Germans completely by surprise. It became apparent to the British that High Wood itself was deserted and a large gap in the German lines was waiting to be exploited.

A request was dispatched to headquarters at around 09:00, asking for permission to send infantry into the wood. It was decided that this was an ideal scenario for the use of cavalry, who could move far more quickly than the infantry and may even break right through to Bapaume. However, by midday there was no news from headquarters that a cavalry advance had been ordered.

The initial attack captured the German second position along a 6,000-yard front. To the right of the main attack, the 18th Division spent the morning clearing Trônes Wood, preventing the Germans using it to fire into the side of the main attack. By 10:00 and with no German resistance, several British officers had advanced towards the wood without coming under any fire. Major General Watts, commander of the 7th Division, wanted to advance into the woods but he was ordered to wait for the cavalry to come forward as originally planned.

Towards the evening of that day, High Wood came into the reckoning. The British attack originally scheduled for 17:15 was delayed first until 18:15 and then till around 20:00 hours. German defenders were slowly moving back towards the wood, effectively plugging the hole in their lines. They had established sufficient defences and their marksmen were hidden among the poppies that were in full flower in the golden fields of corn. At midnight on 14 July, the Germans counter-attacked in High Wood and the British could not hold on to it. Together with machine-gun crossfire, the enemy was able to decimate the oncoming British.

The 7th Dragoon Guards and the 20th Deccan Horse arrived, but not until the evening. Both regiments had at times served as infantry in the trenches. Delays, confusion and hesitation meant that the British did not attempt to occupy the wood until the evening when, finally, the two regiments of cavalry were sent forward at around 19:00 hours. They reached the woods but then had trouble trying to advance through the trees. They were able to capture the southern part of the woods, but the Germans held on to a line at the northern edge. These two regiments made the only cavalry charge of the battle and withdrew at 03:40. Although the cavalry had gained a foothold and held out until the morning of 15 July, they were unsupported and forced to withdraw. The two regiments suffered 10 dead, 91 wounded and 3 missing; 43 horses were killed outright, 103 were wounded and 15 went missing. The mounted cavalry would play no further part in the Somme battles of 1916. During the hot summer, 18-kilometre uphill marches while carrying full equipment plus 120 rounds of ammunition with only a ten-minute halt allowed in each hour were hard to take. As the men marched, they passed bits and pieces of the bodies of soldiers killed during the weeks before and carcasses of horses that had been shot from beneath their riders; the most horrifying of scenes for any man to see, let alone young lads barely out of their teens. However, they had to carry on: it was their job and it had to be finished once and for all.

Two battalions of the 100th Brigade were ordered to go forward and hold the dangerous gap that now existed in the line between High Wood and Bazentin-le-Petit. The infantry advanced through the wood but met with increasing opposition from a strong German line being prepared, known as the Switch Line, which ran through the northern apex of the wood. The infantry attacks on 14 July that had begun at 03:25 had met with success. Twenty-four hours later the fighting had continued in the north-eastern corner of High Wood and now the Germans held it once again.

On 15 July, a company of the 16th (Service) Battalion The King's Royal Rifle Corps, 33rd Division made the next attempt on the wood, but by this time great numbers of Germans had reoccupied it. Part of the 100th Brigade had been held back and they were glad of a night's rest in the open air. Listening to the massive din of the shelling in front of them at High Wood, the Church Lads' Brigade must have said a few prayers that night as they waited to go 'over the top' in the morning.

The capture of High Wood was essential for further British attacks planned on 15 July. By daylight further troops were thrown in for the attack that was due to start at 09:00, but the bombardment actually began earlier at 08:30. It sounded loud and impressive but had no particular effect as the shells were dropping short

The 20th Deccan Horse drawn up in ranks during the Battle of Bazentin Ridge, 1916.

of their targets. The fighting continued through a raging inferno of shells, rifle and machine-gun fire, but by the evening the Germans were still in control of High Wood. The problem was the Switch Line that was long, deep and heavily manned. It was closely interlinked to the trenches that lay in front of it by a network of fortifications that were almost impregnable. So as long as the Germans held the Switch Line, they would continue to hold High Wood.

It was a clear bright day and amongst the war-torn remnants of the remaining trees, lads of the King's Royal Rifle Corps lay dying. The lucky ones, who had only been wounded, had dragged themselves or been carried off by the stretcher-bearers to the nearest dressing station. Chaos and confusion reigned as the continual flow of the injured waited for ambulances to take them to the casualty clearing stations on the other side of Albert. Spare stretchers were soon used up and critically ill soldiers lay in rows, on the bare earth, without even a blanket to cover them. The walking wounded had an incredibly long wait for treatment. Every orderly, nurse and doctor worked tirelessly around the clock.

Taking place on the right was the Battle of Delville Wood (15 July– 3 September). After two weeks of carnage from the commencement of the Somme Offensive, it had become evident that a breakthrough of either the allied or German line would be most unlikely. The great offensive had gradually degenerated into the capture of small prominent towns, woods or features that offered either side tactical advantages from which to direct artillery fire or to launch further attacks. Delville Wood was one such feature, making it important to both German and allied forces.

As part of a large offensive that had started on 14 July, General Haig intended to secure the British right flank, while the centre advanced to capture the higher-lying areas of High Wood in the centre of his line. In the Battle of Delville Wood the fighting was hell. The British achieved their objective and it was considered a tactical allied victory. However, it was one of the bloodiest confrontations of the Somme, with both sides incurring many casualties. Although a victory, the British advance to the north had made only marginal gains by the end of the battle.

The Battle of Delville Wood is of particular importance to South Africa. It was the first major engagement entered into on the Western Front by the South African 1st Infantry Brigade, which also contained a contingent of Southern Rhodesians. The casualties sustained by this brigade were of catastrophic proportions with losses of 80 per cent, yet they managed to hold the wood as ordered. This feat has been described as 'the bloodiest battle hell of 1916'.

While the Battle of Bazentin Ridge continued for another three days, reinforcements were sent up, including men from the 1/9 Highland Light Infantry (Glasgow Highlanders). From left to right the 9th Division successfully captured most of the village of Longueval, but was unable to clear the Germans out of the northern part of the village. To their left, the 8th Brigade of the 3rd Division was briefly held up by uncut wire, but was able to advance after the German position was outflanked. The 9th Brigade then captured Bazentin-le-Grand, despite encountering machine-gun fire. Next in line the 7th Division attack captured the German front line that had been effectively destroyed by the British artillery.

During this period a number of Germans were seen retreating towards High Wood and the next defensive line (the Switch), but were killed before they could reach it. By 07:30 the division had captured Bazentin-le-Petit. Finally, on the left, the 21st Division captured Bazentin-le-Petit Wood and helped to clear the village.

The fighting had now developed into two separate battles. The last serious British offensive came on 15 July when the 91st Brigade replaced the cavalry in High Wood and made a determined but unsuccessful attempt to clear the woods. That evening the brigade was ordered to retreat back to Bazentin-le-Grand. Further attacks were hampered by a German counter-bombardment which filled the old no man's land with poison gas, making it difficult and dangerous for the lads to move to the new front line.

The battle for High Wood

After the first failed attack on High Wood, the weather was poor for the next few days with overcast skies, cloud and rain on and after 16 July. Now the deep and formerly dry trenches had two or three inches of liquid mud at the bottom. The ground above them, churned up by the passing of troops and supply wagons, was slippery and treacherous. The steady drizzle seeped into the earth and trickled into the shell-holes, turning every old trench and ditch into a water hazard.

During the afternoon of 18 July the enemy developed his expected counter-attack against Delville Wood. By sheer weight of numbers and at a very heavy cost to the Germans, they forced their way through the northern and north-eastern portions of the wood and into the northern half of Longueval, which British troops had cleared only that morning. This further enemy attack on Delville Wood marked the commencement of a long and closely-contested struggle.

Progress was slow and only brought about by the continuation of hard fighting. The 33rd Division, commanded by Major General Landon, attacked yet again. By the time dawn broke, the 33rd Division had managed to establish a footing and the British had captured half of High Wood.

The next attack took place in the early morning of 20 July. A bombardment commenced at 02:55, followed by an infantry attack. The battalions taking part again marched past Crucifix Corner and, in some cases, up to the site of the Bazentin-le-Petit windmill. This was located on a ridge and was used for observation and as a signaller's post. Both the British and the enemy's artillery were very active and, two days later, after severe fighting the northern portion of Longueval and the orchards were cleared of the enemy by the 5th Division.

Crucifix Corner

There was a water dump there, and regimental
Carts came every day to line up and fill full
Those rolling tanks with chlorinated clear mixture;
And curse the mud with vain veritable vexture.
Aveluy across the valley, billets, shacks, ruins,
With time and time a crump there to mark doings.
On New Year's Eve the marsh glowed tremulous
With rosy mist still holding late marvellous
Sun-glow, the air smelt home; the time breathed home.
Noel not put away; new term not yet come,
All things said 'Severn', the air was full of those calm meadows;
Transport rattled somewhere in the southern shadows;
Stars that were not strange ruled the most quiet high
Arch of soft sky, starred and most grave to see, most high.
What should break that but gun-noise or last Trump?
But neither came. At sudden, with light jump
Clarinet sang into 'Hundred Pipers and A',
Aveluy's Scottish answered with pipers true call
'Happy we've been a'together.' When nothing
Stayed of war-weariness or winter's loathing,
Crackers with Christmas stockings hung in the heavens,
Gladness split discipline in sixes and sevens,
Hunger ebb'd magically mixed with strange leavens;
Forgotten, forgotten the hard time's true clothing,
And stars were happy to see Man making Fate plaything.

Ivor Gurney (28 August 1890–26 December 1937).

On 11 November 1985, Gurney was among sixteen Great War poets commemorated on a slate stone unveiled in Westminster Abbey's Poet's Corner.

There were many Crucifix Corners on the Western Front during the First World War. This one, on the Somme battlefield between Bazentin-le-Grand and High Wood, is perhaps the best-known. It was an assembly point for allied troops going up through what was known as Death Valley to attack High Wood.

While the assaults on High Wood continued, the artillery bombardment raged and the infantry crept as close as they could to the wood and the German lines. However, when they advanced to attack, they met with little success in Wood Lane or in High Wood itself. British soldiers did enter the wood, but in several places within the wood German machine-gun emplacements caused heavy losses. The Switch Line was another strongly-held line from which the defenders resisted. When the Germans counter-attacked from the west of the wood, many troops retired and congregated at Crucifix Corner which, being hidden from view from the German positions, must have seemed safer.

For the next two months, High Wood remained a British target throughout the Battle of Pozières Ridge (23 July–3 September 1916). As a result of the cavalry action and because of the hot weather, the stench from the fallen carcasses of the horses was horrendous. Small groups of soldiers wearing gas masks crawled into no man's land in order to dig pits, drag the offending horses into them and cover them over.

The 2nd Royal Welsh Fusiliers were in reserve and it was on their way up to the wood, near Bazentin churchyard, that Robert Graves (mentioned in the previous chapter) was badly wounded. The 1st Battalion Queen's Regiment and the 16th (Service) Battalion The King's Royal Rifle Corps relieved the remaining troops at 01:00 on 21 July. The wood had been taken, but not held.

More attacks achieved no further gains. The Germans reoccupied most of High Wood, until only the southern corner remained in British hands. They also dug a new defensive position known as the 'Intermediate Trench', ahead of the Switch Line to the west of the wood. This meant that taking the wood, which had almost been in British hands twice before, became an even tougher proposition. The remainder of Delville Wood was recovered by the 2nd Division on 27 July.

By the middle of August the wood was almost completely destroyed. Trees were just stumps, having been blasted to death by shellfire, and the churned-up ground was covered with the dead from both sides of the conflict. Frank Richards, in his book *Old Soldiers Never Die*, described the conditions in High Wood at that time. Parts of the parapets of trenches contained the corpses of those killed in earlier attacks and he describes heads, arms and legs sticking out. The survivors had used the bodies of dead men as shields and they had then been covered with earth to build up a parapet. This must account for the fact that so many bodies of dead soldiers were never found.

There had been a terrific number of casualties on both sides. One cannot even begin to imagine the horrible mutilation and violation suffered by so many soldiers during those dark days and nights of continuous warfare. During the operations every branch of the 33rd Division had been taxed to the extreme. The artillery was continuously in action under exhausting conditions. Guns were crowded forward into positions that offered little or no cover and were kept constantly at work, firing at difficult targets or providing hastily-prepared barrages for local operations. Difficulties with transport hit the artillery harder than any other branch of the service.

The weather grew worse and the few forward tracks were almost lost in the general morass of disorderly bogs and marsh. Convoys from batteries and divisional ammunition columns plunged up to their axles in mud over the shell-torn ground that lay between the head of the made-up roads and their gun positions. Before they could get back to their open lines, they had to take their place in the solid train of slow-moving traffic.

Conditions had changed remarkably since 1915. It was many days before a single mule train could get through over the High Wood crest. There were a few minor actions over the next two weeks as the Fourth Army was concentrating on taking Guillemont. The British tried to move their lines closer to the wood. Digging small trenches out from the front line directly ahead and then digging at 90-degree angles to join these created a new front-line trench ahead of the original one. During the night the British moved carefully over no man's land, leaving a section of their front-line trench to rapidly dig another one ahead of the original. By the morning they were safely within it and closer to the German front line.

Hydraulic devices known as 'pipe-pushers' were used to push tin canisters containing ammunition ready to be exploded under the German trenches. There were also flame-throwers, but these were not portable weapons at the time. The British version of the flame-thrower was a large 2-ton machine that had to be carried in parts and then assembled in the front lines. Although both pipe-pushers and flame-throwers were used, neither had any significant impact on the outcome at High Wood.

High Wood is not large but was of tremendous significance during the Battle of the Somme. The name 'High Wood' presumably derives from the fact that the wood was at the top of a slope on slightly higher ground. The elevation is not that great, but in a relatively flat landscape, height and therefore improved vision were a tremendous advantage. The Germans were holding it in July 1916 and were not about to give up these advantages lightly. High Wood was first attacked on 14 July 1916, but the British were unable to take it.

Foureaux Wood was the last of the major woods in the Somme Offensive of 1916 to be captured by the British. On 21 July, General Haig reported to the High Commissioner:

> Between the Leipzig Redoubt and Delville Wood, the Battle continues without intermission. Northwards of the Bazentin-Longueval line the British advance has been pushed forward to Foureaux Wood, from whence the enemy was driven. During the night the enemy counter-attacked, after an intense bombardment with gas shells, and succeeded in effecting an entry in the northern part of the wood, but failed to dislodge us from the southern half. Elsewhere the situation is unchanged.

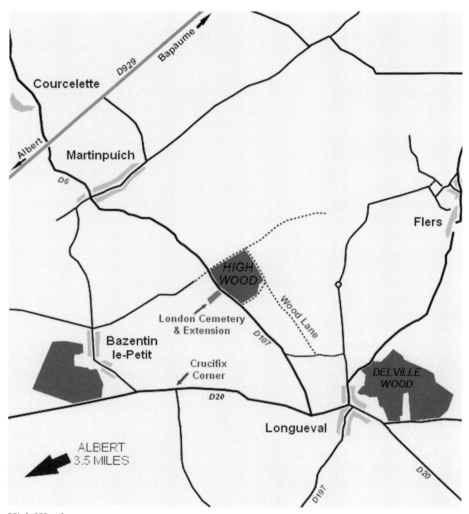

High Wood.

The *Daily Mail*'s correspondent in France reported:

> The German Attack on Longueval was shrewdly conceived, and if successful would have endangered the front where the French and British lines meet. The enemy pretends that only a brigade was engaged, but French experts estimate that there were six divisions (twelve brigades) on a two and a half-mile front. Despite the tremendous odds and the exceptional fury of the Germans, the British magnificently withstood the attack.

Another report by Mr Phillip Gibb from London on 22 July stated: 'German prisoners reveal the grave anxiety reigning behind the German lines, where they do not minimise the greatness of our menace, and are straining every nerve to formidably resist.'

Towards the end of July the fighting heated up, as did the weather. There was heavy fighting at Verdun and on 3 August the French had progressed with the British gaining ground to the west of Pozières.

King George V visited the area on 10 August. During his visit he was the guest of honour at a luncheon party at the Fourth Army Headquarters at Quierrieu. The party included Sir Douglas Haig, General Joffre and senior commanders of the French army. General Rawlinson escorted the king to observe the mine craters at Bois Français. The site is to the right of the wood where the German

Britain's King George V and Belgium's King Albert touring the Western Front, 1916.

Kiel Trench was situated. The king advised Rawlinson of the political ploy against Haig in an effort to curb the current offensive. The king's visit to the Western Front lasted five days and he returned to England on 15 August.

The Kiel Trench is where the author Siegfried Sassoon won his Military Cross. In May 1916, Sassoon had gone out into no man's land and met the wounded Lieutenant Stansfield who was being assisted back to the British lines by two of the raiding party. Sassoon then discovered Corporal O'Brien who was lying badly wounded at the bottom of a 25-feet-deep crater. He returned to the British trenches and came back with some helpers who managed to get a rope around the wounded corporal. With the aid of a stretcher-bearer and others, the wounded man was brought back to safety. Alas, Corporal O'Brien died of his wounds and was later buried behind the lines at Citadel Cemetery Plot 3, Row F, Grave 17.

Despite a whole series of attacks spanning a further two months and various actions leading to the final assault with tanks, High Wood held out until 15 September 1916.

As marked on French maps of today, the real name of High Wood is Bois des Fourcaux. However, during the Great War it was marked on some maps as Bois

British Cabinet minister David Lloyd George (second from left) on a visit to the Western Front on 12 September 1916. Lloyd George became British prime minister in December 1916.

des Foureaux. It was never fully cleared after the war and it is estimated that the remains of around 8,000 British and German soldiers are still buried in High Wood today.

The brave horses

When the war broke out in Western Europe in August 1914, both Great Britain and Germany had a cavalry force that numbered about 100,000 men. Such a number of men would have needed a significant number of horses and most senior military personnel at that time believed in the supremacy of the cavalry attack.

At the beginning of the war the British army owned 25,000 horses. This was not considered enough and during the next two weeks a further 165,000 horses were requisitioned from British civilians. Millions of horses were claimed or given voluntarily to the service, with mounts as diverse as farm ponies and even thoroughbred racehorses. Military vehicles, as with any mechanized vehicles of the time, were relatively new inventions and prone to breakdown problems. In 1914 the British army only owned eighty motor vehicles, therefore they were very dependent on horses for transporting good and supplies. This was especially true of the Western Front where conditions made it very difficult to use motor vehicles. Horses, along with mules, were reliable forms of transport and needed little maintenance compared to a lorry.

Lord Kitchener ordered, at the request of many British children who were concerned about the welfare of their ponies, that no horse under 15 hands (60in or 152cm) should be confiscated. The British Army Remount Service, in an effort to improve the supply of horses for potential military use, provided the services of high-quality stallions to British farmers for breeding their brood mares.

Smaller breeds were used to carry British troopers, while larger horses were used to pull artillery. Riflemen with tall horses suffered more from fatigue, due to the number of times they were required to mount and dismount their animals. Horses over 15.2 hands fared worse than those under that height. Well-built thoroughbreds of 15 hands and under worked well, as did compact horses of other breeds that stood 14.2 to 14.3 hands. Larger crossbred horses were acceptable for regular work with plentiful rations but proved less able to withstand short rations and long journeys.

Horses and mules used for draught work and pulling artillery were found to be more efficient when they were of medium size and with good endurance rather than those that were tall, heavy and long-legged. The British army purchased a large number of mules from the USA. The mule has amazing stamina and was able to endure the terrible conditions in the front line better than the horse. By the end of the war, the British army owned 213,300 mules.

The continued supply of horses was a major issue of the war. Although tractors were also used to pull artillery and supplies, horses performed the bulk of artillery transportation. Every British army detailed organization depended on actual horsepower. This was a logistical challenge in itself, as it required hundreds of tons of fodder each day and extensive veterinary support services. One estimate

British infantry at Morval, 1916.

puts the number of horses that served in the Great War at around 6 million, with a large percentage of them dying from war-related causes.

To meet its need for horses, Britain imported them from Australia, Canada, the US and Argentina. The United States was asked to help with remount efforts even before their formal entry into the war. Between 1914 and 1918, the US sent almost 1 million horses across the sea and another 182,000 were transported together with American troops. This deployment seriously depleted that country's equine population. Only 200 horses returned to the US, 60,000 having been killed outright.

By the middle of 1917, Britain had procured 591,000 horses and 213,000 mules, as well as almost 60,000 camels and oxen. The Army Remount Service spent £67.5 million on purchasing, training and delivering horses and mules to the front. The department became a major multinational business and a leading player in the international horse trade through supplying horses not only to the British army, but also to the armies of Canada, Belgium, Australia, New Zealand, Portugal and even a few to the US.

Shipping horses between the United States and Europe was both costly and dangerous. American Expeditionary Force officials calculated that almost seven times as much room was needed per ton for animals than for average wartime cargo and over 6,500 horses and mules were drowned or killed by shellfire on allied shipping attacked by the Germans. In turn, New Zealand lost around 3 per cent of the estimated 10,000 horses shipped to the front during the war.

No one could have contemplated the shocking horrors of trench warfare, which explains why the cavalry regiments had reigned supreme beforehand. In Great Britain, along with the guards regiments, the cavalry regiments were seen as the senior regiments in the British army and cavalry officers held very many senior army positions. The cavalry used only the best horses and these had to be strong as the average cavalryman's weight was 12 stone (over 76kg) and his equipment, saddle, ammunition, etc usually weighed another 9 stone (over 57kg). Men in the cavalry were instructed to take the weight off their horses as much as they could.

The advent of trench warfare made such charges not only impractical but impossible. A cavalry charge was essentially from a bygone military era and machine guns, trench complexes and barbed wire made such charges all but impossible. However, some cavalry charges did still occur, despite the obvious reasons why they should not.

By the spring of 1918, the war had become more fluid but despite this, in March 1918 the British launched a cavalry charge at the Germans. Out of 150 horses used in the charge, only 4 survived. The rest were cut down by German machine-gun fire.

A horse ambulance.

Although a cavalry charge was no longer a viable military tactic, horses and mules were still invaluable as a way of transporting materials to the front. Army horses died in their hundreds of thousands. They were the hapless victims of land mines, shellfire, machine-gun bullets and gas; not to mention neglect, overwork and exposure to the harsh weather conditions. Horses, during the whole of a hot summer, suffered severely. Gun teams, ration and ammunition wagons were frequently knocked out at night on the shell-swept roads. The scenes on any morning were more than enough to make all horse-lovers fervently hope that any wars of the future would be waged without the aid of horses. They received no rewards and were allowed no 'nervous breakdowns' but it is certain that most of them suffered very acutely from fear and the suffering of shellfire.

The problem at Guillemont

The Battle of Guillemont (3–6 September 1916) was an attack by the Fourth Army on the village of Guillemont. The village is to the east of Combles and south-west of Montauban. Longueval and Delville Wood lie to the north-west and Ginchy to the north-east. The village lay on the right flank of the British sector, near the boundary with the French Sixth Army.

The Fourth Army had advanced close to Guillemont during the Battle of Bazentin Ridge (14–17 July) and the capture of the village was the culmination of British attacks that had begun on 22/23 July to advance on the right flank of the Fourth Army in order to eliminate a salient further north at Delville Wood. German defences ringed the wood and had observation over the French Sixth Army area to the south towards the Somme.

On 30 July 1916 the village of Guillemont and Falfemont Farm to the south-east were attacked. During a subsequent local attack on 8 August 1916, in British

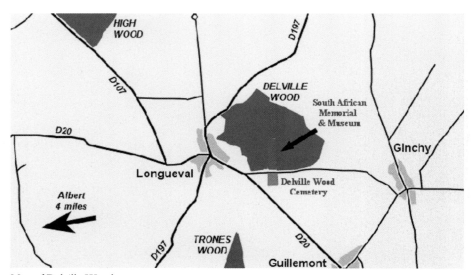

Map of Delville Wood.

conjunction with a French attack north of the Somme, troops again entered Guillemont and, yet again, were compelled to fall back. This was due to the failure of a simultaneous effort against the enemy's trenches on the flanks of the village.

In preparation for a general attack intended for mid-September from the Somme north to Courcelette, the French Sixth Army, the Fourth Army and Reserve Army conducted numerous attacks to capture the rest of the German second line and to gain observation over the German third line. The German defences around Guillemont were based on the remaining parts of the second line and numerous fortified villages and farms north from Hem, Maurepas and Combles to Falfemont Farm, Guillemont, Ginchy, Delville Wood and High Wood, which commanded the ground in-between.

One of the problems in high summer on the Somme was the unending buzz of the bluebottles. They were everywhere and swarmed in black clouds above the men's heads. They fed on the bodies of the dead, infested the trenches and settled in their thousands on the bags containing army rations. Sleep was impossible with interruptions of the flies landing on ears, eyes and noses. The lack of clean water was almost the worst thing to bear and in August all of the troops were suffering from diarrhoea.

Devastation of Delville Wood.

Guillemont taken

Numerous attempts had been made by Joffre, Haig, Foch and the army commanders Rawlinson and Fayolle to coordinate joint attacks. All had failed due to a recovery by the German army from the disorganization caused by the defeats in early July. Disagreements over tactics by Haig and Joffre in July and August were caused by the congestion behind the front and the ever-increasing German artillery fire on targets behind the front line.

Roads and tracks had been obliterated by Anglo-French artillery fire and had become swamps in periods of rainy weather. Inexperience, unreliable machinery, guns and ammunition and an unpredictable flow of supplies from Britain reduced the effectiveness of the British armies. Difficulty in coordinating attacks by the allied armies and the large number of piecemeal attacks resorted to by the British resulted in costly failures. The French Sixth and Tenth armies had similar difficulties, despite the severe strain put on the German Second and First armies, which were forced into a similar piecemeal defence.

Joffre met with Haig on 11 August to press his policy of combined broad-front attacks, proposing an attack on 22 August to advance from the Somme, north through Combles, Ginchy, High Wood and Thiepval. This was to be followed by an attack on 1 September to take Bouchavesnes, Rancourt, Morval, Flers, Martinpuich, Courcelette and Grandcourt. Haig proposed a less ambitious attack from the Somme to High Wood on about 18 August, to which Joffre agreed.

Haig and Foch met on 19 August and arranged plans to capture Guillemont on 24 August, combined with French attacks from the Somme to Maurepas. The British decided upon another attack for 26 or 27 August, from Cléry to Le Forêt by the French and Wedge Wood to Ginchy. Arrangements were made with the French army for a series of combined attacks to be delivered in progressive stages. These should have embraced Maurepas, Falfemont Farm, Guillemont, Leuze Wood and Ginchy.

On 16 August 1916, an attempt to carry out the first stage of a prearranged scheme met with only partial success. Two days later, after a preliminary bombardment that had lasted thirty-six hours, a greater combined attack was undertaken. In spite of a number of enemy counter-attacks valuable progress was made, but the 33rd Division failed to progress at High Wood.

Allied troops established themselves in the outskirts of Guillemont village and occupied Guillemont Station. On 23 August, the 35th Division repulsed a violent counter-attack on the station. The next day, the 33rd and 14th divisions made further important progress on a wide front north and east of Delville Wood. It was on this day that General Rawlinson heard that twelve tanks had arrived.

On 24 August, Haig criticized Fourth Army headquarters for failing to adequately supervise the planning of attacks, which had been too narrow and conducted with insufficient forces. Haig wanted an attack on Guillemont with two and a half divisions to ensure a continuous attack on the whole front and far more scrutiny by Rawlinson of subordinates in the preparation of those attacks. The need to replace divisions opposite Guillemont created difficulties in coordination with the French and several days of rain from 25 August delayed the next attack to 3 September.

In order to organize larger combined attacks and because of postponements due to bad weather, a pause in Anglo-French attacks at the end of August co-incided with the largest counter-attack by the German army in the Battle of the Somme. Joffre, Foch and Haig abandoned attempts to organize large combined attacks in favour of sequenced army attacks and the capture of the German defences from Cléry on the north bank of the Somme to Guillemont.

The ground to the south of Guillemont was dominated by the enemy's positions in and about that village. It was therefore hoped that those positions might be captured first, before an advance to the south of them was pushed further forward in the direction of Falfemont Farm. It was evident that Guillemont could not be captured as an isolated enterprise without very heavy losses.

After taking over from 13th Corps in mid-August, a meeting was held with the divisional commanders to discuss the next attack. It was stressed that it would take place along the entire corps front and that supervision from above would not be inconsistent with granting initiative to subordinates. The corps' General Officer Commanding Royal Artillery (GOCRA) was to decide the lines of barrages, but would liaise with divisions, who would then work out the details.

Divisional plans were coordinated by 14th Corps headquarters rather than them being dictated to them. Discretion by divisional commanders would be retained within the corps plan, especially as command of the artillery reverted to the divisions at zero hour. Observation posts were established with provision for telephone, visual and pigeon communication.

Guillemont was captured and held. German counter-attacks were defeated and the ground consolidated during a rainstorm overnight. Operations against Ginchy from the south and towards Leuze and Bouleaux Woods commenced. Much fierce and obstinate fighting continued during this period on the fronts of the two allied armies. British lines were pushed forward wherever possible by means of local attacks and by bombing and sapping. The enemy was driven out of various forward positions from which he might hamper British progress. By these means many gains were made which, though small in themselves, in the aggregate represented very considerable advances. The enemy's counter-attacks were incessant and frequently of great violence, but they were made in vain and at heavy cost. The fierceness of the fighting can be gathered from the fact that one regiment of the German Guard Reserve Corps, which had been in the Thiepval Salient opposite Mouquet Farm, is known to have lost 1,400 men in fifteen days.

This brought the French Sixth and British Fourth armies onto ground that overlooked the German third position. The first two days of September, on both army fronts, were spent in preparation for a more general attack. The Battle of Delville Wood had ended and also that of Pozières Ridge. The Battle of Guillemont had been won by the British and although Ginchy had been taken, it was lost again. The fighting towards Falfemont Farm and High Wood continued.

The British assault was delivered on 3 September 1916 at 12 noon on a front extending from the extreme right to the enemy trenches on the right bank of the

Ancre, north of Hamel. The French attacked simultaneously, also on the right. For three days the tide of attack and counter-attack swayed backwards and forwards among the ruined houses of the village, with the greater part of it remaining in the enemy's possession.

In order to keep in touch with the French, the assault on Falfemont Farm on 3 September was delivered by the 5th Division three hours before the opening of the main assault. In the impetus of their first rush, British troops reached the farm but could not hold it. Nevertheless, they pushed on to the north of it and on 4 September delivered a series of fresh assaults from the north and west. This strongly-fortified position was occupied piece by piece and by the morning of 5 September, the whole of Falfemont Farm was in allied possession.

Meanwhile, further progress had been made to the north-east of the farm, where the local commanders showed considerable initiative. By the evening of 5 September, allied troops were established strongly in Leuze Wood, which on the following day was finally cleared of the enemy.

The barrier broken: Ginchy

Even though most of Ginchy and High Wood remained in the enemy's hands, very noteworthy progress had been made in the course of those four days' operations, exceeding anything that had been achieved since 14 July. The barrier, which the enemy had maintained for seven weeks against allied further advance, had at last been broken. More than 1,000 prisoners were captured and many machine guns taken or destroyed in the course of the fighting. The French had made great progress on the right, bringing their line forward to Louage Wood, Le Forêt and Cléry-sur-Somme. Rain, congestion and the relief of tired divisions forced a pause in French attacks until 12 September. In the Battle of Ginchy (9 September) the Fourth Army captured the village, ready for the Battle of Flers-Courcelette (15–22 September).

Weaknesses in the allied lines had disappeared and gains made at the front now required operations. Preparations for a further attack upon Ginchy continued without intermission and at 14:45 on 9 September the attack was reopened on the whole of the Fourth Army front. More than 500 prisoners were taken in that operation and during the following days, taking the total since 1 July to over 17,000.

Results achieved

By steady, relentless pressure and fierce struggles, the Germans were worn down and their power of resistance broken. The vigour and determination that British troops pressed to their advantage was often followed by successful night attacks. These awakened the enemy to a fuller realization of their danger. It seemed that they considered their troops, who were already on the spot and secure in their impregnable defences, sufficient to deal with anything thrown at them. The great depth of the enemy's system of fortification gave them time to reorganize their defeated troops and hurry to bring in numerous fresh divisions and more guns.

Despite this, German forces were still pushed back, steadily and continuously. Trench after trench and strongpoint after strongpoint were taken from them.

The enemy had considerably delayed the allied advance, but the effort had cost them dear. Collapse of German resistance during the last few days of the struggle justified the belief that a decisive victory would lie with the allied troops, who had displayed such fine fighting qualities and such indomitable endurance and resolution.

There was also considerable bombardment of the allied troops from the air. Manfred von Richthofen, the future German fighter ace, shot down a British aircraft, but several German aircraft were shot down in retaliation.

After Rawlinson's inspection of the area that was covered with troops, guns, lines and bivouacs, he wrote in his report: 'A German airman could not drop a brick without killing someone.' He described the conditions as appalling and the ground being so completely flattened that the extension of the railways had been made impossible.

The third phase
The progress of the French and British forces was still interdependent. The closest cooperation continued to be necessary in order to gain the further ground required and enable advancement on a sufficiently wide front. To cope with this situation a united command is usually essential, but the cordial good feeling between the allied armies and their earnest desire to assist each other proved to be equally effective and removed any difficulties.

On the right, the French arranged to continue the line of advance, in close cooperation from the Somme to the slopes above Combles, but instead, by directing their main effort northwards and isolating Combles, they opened up the way for their attack upon Sailly-Saillisel. The cavalry had secured a line from High Wood to Longueval.

Under heavy fire, the British tried to establish a line inside the wood in readiness for an attack the following day upon the German forces situated in the northwestern half. Instead, British headquarters decided to launch an attack upon Martinpuich in the north. They had overlooked the fact that the Germans had not yet been fully cleared from High Wood. Midway between Bazentin-le-Petit and Martinpuich there was sited the formidable German Switch Line of defence. By launching an attack upon Martinpuich, the British would find themselves open to a direct line of fire from the wood. Therefore a simultaneous attack from the western side of the wood, directed at the German position, was launched, repeatedly and without success.

For the 33rd Division attacking towards Martinpuich, the consequences were devastating. Later that evening the British were forced to withdraw entirely from High Wood.

On 12 September, a steady methodical bombardment commenced at 06:00 and continued, without interruption, until the moment of attack at 06:20 on 15 September. The infantry assault commenced at 08:40 and thirty-six of the new British tanks were brought into action for the first time.

Introducing 'Little Willie'

The tank was a British invention, but the idea behind its development was too old to effectively combine 'firepower, protection and mobility'. On 20 February 1915 the First Lord of the Admiralty, Winston Churchill, created the 'Landships Committee' to investigate a mechanical solution to the stalemate of trench warfare on the Western Front.

Known as 'Mother', the first successful tank prototype completed its secret trials in early 1916 and the new Mark I tank was used in battle for the first time at Flers-Courcelette on 15 September 1916.

Ruston Hornsby had been developing the caterpillar tractor since 1902 and had built an oil engine-powered crawler to move lifeboats up a beach in 1908. The British army had on several occasions tested Hornsby's tractors as artillery tractors between 1905 and 1910, but they had not been adopted. Hornsby therefore sold his patents to the Holt Tractor Company of California, USA.

In July 1914, Lieutenant Colonel Ernest Swinton, a British Royal Engineers officer and the official war correspondent, learned about Holt tractors and their transportation capabilities in rough terrain, but the information was just passed on and not acted upon. In October 1914, in a letter to Sir Maurice Hankey, Secretary of the Committee of Imperial Defence, Swinton suggested that the British Committee of Imperial Defence should build a power-driven, bulletproof, tracked vehicle that could destroy enemy guns.

On 17 February 1915, Hankey persuaded the lukewarm War Office to undertake trials with a Holt tractor but as the caterpillar bogged down in the mud, the project was abandoned and the War Office gave up any further investigations.

In May 1915, the War Office carried out new tests on a trench-crossing machine. The machine was equipped with large tractor wheels that were 8 feet in diameter. These carried girders on an endless chain, which were lowered above a trench so that the back wheels could roll over it. The machine would then drag the girder behind it until it reached a flat terrain, so that it could reverse over the back wheels and set them back in place in front of the vehicle. The machine proved much too cumbersome and was abandoned.

When Winston Churchill first learned of the armoured tractor idea, he reignited investigations into the idea of using the Holt tractor. The Royal Navy and the Landships Committee at last agreed to sponsor experiments and tests on armoured tractors as a type of 'land ship'. Churchill ordered the building of eighteen experimental land ships.

Construction failed to move forward. Instead of opting for the Holt tractor, the British government chose to involve a British agricultural machinery firm, Foster and Sons, whose managing director and designer was Sir William Tritton. All these projects had failed by June 1915 and any further ideas of grandiose land ships were abandoned.

After these experiments, the committee decided to build a smaller experimental land ship, equivalent to one half of the articulated version and using lengthened US-made Bullock Creeping Grip caterpillar tracks. This new experimental machine was called the No 1 Lincoln Machine. On 11 August 1915, construction began with the first trials starting on 10 September 1915. However, these trials failed again because of unsatisfactory tracks.

Development then continued with new re-engineered tracks and the machine, now renamed 'Little Willie', was completed and tested on 3 December 1915. Trench-crossing ability was deemed insufficient and Walter Gordon Wilson developed a rhomboidal design, which became known as the first of the 'Big Willie' type of a true tank.

After completion on 29 January 1916, very successful trials were undertaken and on 12 February 1916 an order was placed by the War Office for 100 units to be used on the Western Front in France. A second order for fifty additional units was placed in April 1916. The British were the first to put tanks on the battlefield at the Battle of the Somme in September 1916.

The engine was located in the same compartment of the tank as the crew, where the heat, noise and exhaust fumes were almost unbearable. Four members of the crew had to wind a large crank handle to start the engine. The engine was water-cooled with the large radiator situated at the back of the tank, served by a heavy-duty fan that drew air from inside and may have slightly alleviated the dreadful internal conditions.

Fuel was fed to the carburettor by 'gravity feed'. This meant the two internal 25-gallon (113.5-litre) containers had to be situated high up on either side of the front cab. If a tank became stuck in a nose-down attitude it would stall, making it necessary to feed petrol to the engine manually. A far greater danger was fire. If the fuel was ignited by shellfire, the crew had little or no chance of escape. Additionally, the average range of a tank on its internal fuel supply was only 20 to 25 miles, depending on terrain, so crews carried as many extra petrol cans as possible on the roof of the tank where they were extremely vulnerable to damage. Petrol leaking into the tank from the roof could force the crew to evacuate.

Caterpillar tracks were the key to the success of British tanks in the Great War. Commercially-available tracks were simply not up to the job. Albert Tritton of Foster & Co. of Lincoln came up with a new design. This enabled the adoption of the characteristic all-round track layout to give British tanks an unrivalled cross-country performance. Simplicity and strength were the main factors, but there were drawbacks. Small-diameter rollers located along the lower frames were not sprung, so tanks bumped across hard, rough ground, adding further to the discomfort of the crew. A broken or 'thrown' track could disable a tank immediately and replacing it was hard work. To prevent this, adjustable idler wheels at the front were used to keep the tracks taut and track links were flanged so that they would not fall away from the rollers when the tank crossed a trench.

The Mark I had a crew of eight men, four of whom were required just to drive it. The process was complicated. The driver had control of a clutch, footbrake, hand throttle and primary gearbox, which gave two speeds forward and one in reverse. The commander, sitting to the driver's left, operated the brakes. German troops soon learned to fire at the tank's vision devices at the back of the tank, which the crews tried to camouflage with paint. Other apertures, covered by teardrop-shaped flaps, were designed not for vision but to allow members of the crew to use their revolvers.

Conditions inside the Mark I were appalling. Deafening noise, roasting heat, suffocating fumes from the engine and the choking smell of cordite when in action were all part of being a tank crew, but the men learned to live with it and still function as a team. Given that they were often in extreme danger and working in almost total darkness, their commitment was remarkable. Although the tanks were originally regarded as expendable, their crews took great pride in them, christening each one with an individual name and repairing and recovering them after an action whenever possible.

The Mark I crew comprised the following men. The commander (front left) would have been a young officer in 1916. Besides determining the route, watching out for targets and the care of the crew, he was responsible for working a pair of steering brakes in conjunction with the driver. If the ground was bad or the route uncertain, the commander would often get out of the tank and walk ahead, testing the ground with a stick. If it was dark and at the risk of enemy fire and being run down by his own tank, he would hold a lighted cigarette behind his

The British tanks arrive.

back. The driver (seated front right) was regarded as the most skilled and valuable member of the crew. He was responsible for navigating the tank, gear-changing, operating the throttle, applying the foot brake and operating the steering tail device by means of a steering wheel. He also supervised the maintenance of the engine, clutch, gears and tracks. At the rear of the tank, the gearsmen were stationed on each side of the tank. They operated the secondary gearboxes relating to the individual tracks. They also passed forward ammunition, greased the tracks and operated the light machine guns. In a 'male' tank, a gunner and a loader served each six-pounder gun. The gun was moved by the sheer physical exertion of the gunner, using a shaft under his right armpit to elevate and swing the weapon. He aimed using a telescopic sight and operated the firing mechanism manually. As a result, in the killing fields of Flanders in 1915, Holt tractors were the inspiration for British tank development and the first tank crews came from virtually every regiment in the British army. The tanks entered Flers followed by large numbers of British troops. They successfully cooperated with the infantry and, coming as a surprise to the enemy's rank and file, provided invaluable help in breaking down their resistance. The advance met with immediate British success along the line on most of the attacking front. Fighting continued in Flers for some time, but by 10:00 hours British troops had reached the north side of the village. By midday they had occupied great stretches of the enemy's trenches. After many hours of very severe fighting, High Wood was carried at last.

The result of the fighting on 15 September and the following days was a gain more considerable than any in the course of a single operation since the commencement of the offensive. In the course of one day's fighting, two of the enemy's main defensive systems were broken and an advance on a front of over 6 miles to an average depth of a mile had been achieved. All of this had been accomplished with a small number of casualties in comparison to the number of troops employed. Despite that fact, it was afterwards discovered that the attack had not come to the enemy as a complete surprise.

Around 100 years later, the tank has altered beyond all recognition but the basic principles of firepower, protection and mobility remain unchanged.

A change in command of 33rd Division

In September 1916 Major General Landon was relieved of his command of the 33rd Division. It was arranged that he would exchange with Major General Sir Reginald John Pinney, KCB (*c*.1863–1943) from the 35th Division, and the transfer was made on 23 September 1916.

The reason for rotating commanders appears to have been to give Landon a less active command in the 35th, as it was occupying a quieter sector. It was felt that Major General Pinney was a more effective commander for such an active division.

When the major general met the officers of one of his new battalions in early October 1916, it was recorded that he seemed 'pleasant and human' and 'not too old'. However, some of his habits were most unpopular with his men, as he

The rum jar.

stopped the regular issue of rum shortly after taking command, replacing it with tea.

The supply sergeants were in charge of the rum jar and were often accused of stealing its contents. Much affection was lavished on the rum jar and humorous ditties were made up about what it meant to the lads. The infantry were greatly displeased and one NCO described Pinney as 'a bun-pinching crank, more suited to the command of a Church Mission than troops'.

There was some justification for this remark because as well as being teetotal, the major general did not smoke and was devoutly religious. He was the son of the Reverend John Pinney, vicar of Coleshill, Warwickshire, while his maternal grandfather, John Wingfield-Digby, was also a previous vicar of Coleshill.

Following Pinney's arrival, the division was withdrawn for two months to re-organize, thus missing the Battle of Flers-Courcelette. Among the officers Pinney first encountered in the 33rd was Bernard (later Field Marshal) Montgomery, recently posted as brigade major of the 104th Brigade, who would later serve under him as GSO2 (General Staff Officer (Grade 2)) in the 33rd Division.

In memoriam: the neck of a rum jar.

For his service at the Battle of Hazebrouck, Pinney, along with the commanders of the 12th, 55th and 61st divisions, was appointed a Knight Commander of the Order of the Bath.

The advance is renewed: Combles

Situated some 30 miles (48km) north-east of Amiens, Combles is a commune in the Somme department in Picardy in northern France. It was the operations centre for the Battle of Bapaume during the Franco-Prussian War of 1870–71, and was now at the centre of much fighting during the Great War. Many of its buildings were badly damaged and many of its residents injured or killed. Also there were many, many casualties among the forces in combat there and many of the British soldiers who fell are buried in the local cemetery.

Preparations for a further British advance were again hindered by bad weather. A bombardment commenced early in the morning of 24 September, but at 12:35 on 25 September a general attack by the allies was launched on the whole front between the Somme and Martinpuich. The objectives on the British front included the villages of Morval, Les Boeufs, Gueudecourt and a belt of country about 1,000 yards deep, curved round the north of Flers, to a point midway between that village and Martinpuich. By nightfall all of these objectives were in British hands, with the exception of the village of Gueudecourt.

Combles was almost totally surrounded by the allied forces and, in the early morning of 26 September, the British to the north and the French to the south of the railway occupied the village simultaneously. The capture of Combles in this inexpensive fashion was considered to be a considerable tactical success. Underground, the enemy had constructed exceptionally large cellars and galleries at a great depth. These were sufficient to give effective shelter to enemy troops and matériel under the heaviest bombardment. Great quantities of stores and ammunition of all sorts were found in the cellars when the village was taken after the protecting trench to the west had been captured in a somewhat interesting fashion.

On that same day, the 21st Division carried Gueudecourt. In the early morning a tank started from the north-west, firing its machine guns and followed by bombers down the portion of the trench held by the enemy. The German soldiers had no escape as the trench was also being held at the southern end. At the same time a British aeroplane flew down the length of the trench, firing its machine gun at the enemy who were holding it. The Germans then waved white handkerchiefs as a token of surrender. There was a report from the aeroplane, so the infantry accepted the surrender of the whole garrison. By 08:30 the whole trench had been cleared, great numbers of the enemy had been killed and 8 officers and 362 other ranks taken prisoner. British casualties amounted to just five.

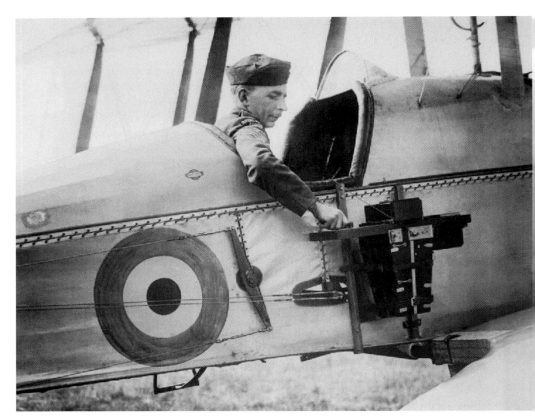

RFC aircraft with aerial reconnaissance camera.

Thiepval

The success of the Fourth Army had now brought British advances to the stage at which Field Marshal Haig considered it advisable that Thiepval should be taken. Possession of this would be of considerable tactical value in future operations. At 12:25 on 26 September, before the enemy had been given time to recover from the blow struck by the Fourth Army, a general attack was launched against Thiepval and the Thiepval Ridge.

The whole of the high ground that extended over a front of some 3,000 yards north and east of Thiepval still remained in enemy hands. In addition, the Zollern Redoubt, the Stuff Redoubt and the Schwaben Redoubt, with their connecting lines of trenches, were also held by the Germans.

As the British crept towards Thiepval from the direction of the Leipzig Redoubt, it seemed as dauntingly impregnable as it had been on 1 July. So long as the Germans still held it, they could overlook almost the whole of the British advance and direct their guns in its direction.

Blasted almost to obliteration, a treeless swampland stretched across the Ancre Valley. More than two months of incessant bombardment had reduced the battlefield to a wasteland and razed the British trenches almost out of existence. It was impossible to clear the land between the lines of the dismembered dead. The old front line was so damaged and choked with bodies that it could only be held as an outpost and garrisoned by very small parties of men.

It was hoped that a short, sharp rush behind the creeping forces would overwhelm the enemy. At the same time, the troops up the hill on the right were to rush the German line and swarm across the Schwaben Redoubt. Their previous attempt at this had failed, but they had done it before so they could do it again and this time they would hold on to it.

The attack was a brilliant success. Tanks again gave valuable assistance to the British troops and by 08:30 on 27 September, the whole of the village of Thiepval was in British hands. Some 2,300 prisoners were taken in the course of the fighting on the Thiepval Ridge, bringing the total number of prisoners taken in the battle area in the operations between 14 September and 30 September to nearly 10,000. In the same period 27 guns, more than 200 machine guns and 40 trench mortars were also captured.

Also on 27 September, the south and west sides of the Stuff Redoubt were carried by British troops, together with the length of trench connecting that strongpoint with the Schwaben Redoubt. To the west, they also carried the greater part of the enemy's defensive line eastwards along the northern slopes of the ridge.

On the Fourth Army front a further portion of the enemy's fourth system of defence north-west of Gueudecourt was carried. The enemy fell back from their fortifications that ran in front of Eaucourt l'Abbaye and Le Sars. On the afternoon and evening of 27 September, British troops were able to make a very considerable advance in this area without encountering serious opposition until within a few hundred yards of the line.

The British artillery barrage was extremely accurate and contributed greatly to the success of the attacks. At the end of September Field Marshal Haig handed over Morval to the French in order to facilitate their attacks on Sailly-Saillisel.

The situation
With the exception of Germany's positions in the neighbourhood of Sailly-Saillisel and their scanty foothold on the northern crest of the high ground above Thiepval, the enemy was driven from the whole of the ridge lying between the Tortille and the Ancre. The enemy had made desperate efforts to cling to their last remaining trenches. In the course of the three weeks following the British advancement, they had made repeated counter-attacks at heavy cost in the vain hope of recovering the lost ground. Bomb-fighting continued among the buildings during the next two days, but by the evening of 3 October the whole of Eaucourt l'Abbaye was in British hands.

Pending developments elsewhere, all that was necessary was to carry on local operations to improve the British positions and to keep the enemy fully employed. It was important to gain ground on the eastern flank, as the Germans still possessed a strong system of trenches covering the villages of Le Transloy, Beaulencourt and the town of Bapaume.

Although the Germans were digging with feverish haste, they had not yet been able to create any very formidable defences behind this line. The resistance of their troops had seriously weakened in the course of recent British operations. In view of the enemy's efforts to construct a new system of defence behind the Le Transloy line, it was desirable that the British should lose no time in dealing with the situation.

By 7 October, after a postponement was rendered necessary by three days of continuous rain, the allies had made considerable advances. Fighting had taken place during the even worsening weather and the most dreadful battlefield conditions. It didn't stop raining during the night and hampered the removal of casualties and any further forward moves.

The Fourth Army also attacked, on the same day, along the whole front from Les Boeufs to Destremont Farm, in support of the operations of Britain's allies. Unfortunately, very bad weather set in again and continued with scarcely a break during the remainder of October and part of November. Poor visibility seriously interfered with the work of the British artillery and constant rain turned the mass of hastily-dug British trenches into channels of deep mud. Country roads, already broken up by countless shell craters that crossed the deep stretches of lately-won ground, rapidly became almost impassable. The supply of food, stores and ammunition became a serious problem. General Rawlinson inspected both roads and rail lines and found the most appalling desolation. Both links had simply been washed away.

These conditions multiplied the difficulties of attacking to such an extent that it was found impossible to exploit the situation. A rapid attack was urgently needed to enable British forces to reap the full benefits of the advantages already gained.

The condition of the battlefields.

In his diary, General Rawlinson wrote that he considered the weather would bring the battle to a close very soon. With the roads being impassable, ammunition could not be got to the guns. He wrote that British casualties since 1 July had now reached 40,000.

The right flank continued to assist the operations of the allies against Saillisel, and attacks were made whenever a slight improvement in the weather made the cooperation of artillery and infantry at all possible. The unavoidable delay in the British advance had given the enemy time to reorganize and rally his troops. Their resistance again became stubborn, with them seizing every favourable opportunity for counter-attacks.

Trenches changed hands with great frequency, rendering it an easier matter to take a battered trench rather than hold it. The conditions of the ground made it difficult to renew exhausted supplies of bombs and ammunition or to consolidate the ground won. The moment for decisive action was rapidly passing away, while the weather showed no signs of improving. The ground had already become so bad that nothing less than a prolonged period of drying weather, which at that season of the year was most unlikely to occur, would suit the Allied purpose. Under these circumstances, while continuing to do everything possible to improve positions on the right flank, preparations for a favourable situation on the left flank were made.

At midday on 21 October during a short spell of fine, cold weather, the line of Regina Trench and Stuff Trench, from the west Courcelette-Pys road westward to Schwaben Redoubt, was attacked with complete success. Assisted by an excellent artillery preparation and barrage, the British infantry carried all of their objectives very quickly and with remarkably little loss. A new line was firmly established in spite of the enemy's shellfire. More than 1,000 prisoners were taken in the course of the day's fighting, but that figure was slightly exceeded by the number of British casualties.

Beaumont Hamel

The village of Beaumont Hamel was one of the fortress villages located just behind the German lines. The hamlet of St Pierre Divion and the villages of Beaucourt-sur-Ancre and Beaumont Hamel, like the rest of the villages forming part of Germany's original front in this district, were evidently intended by them to form a permanent line of fortifications while they developed their offensive elsewhere. This position commanded the valley over which the attacking troops had to cross.

The British realized that Germany's position had become a dangerous one as they had multiplied the number of guns covering this part of their line. At the end of October they introduced another division on the front between Grandcourt and Hebuterne.

The long-continued bad weather finally took a turn for the better and for some days remained dry and cold, with frosty nights and misty mornings. Final preparations were pushed on for the British attack on the Ancre. However, as the ground was still very bad in places, it was necessary to limit the operations to what would be reasonably possible to consolidate and hold under the existing conditions. On 9 November, the British gunners complained that there were too many German aircraft flying over allied territory.

At 05:00 on the morning of 11 November a preliminary special bombardment commenced prior to the attack. It continued for forty-eight hours with bursts of great intensity until 05:45 on the morning of 13 November, when it developed into a very effective barrage covering the assaulting infantry.

At that hour and through dense fog, British troops advanced on the enemy's position. They speedily entered the first line trenches on almost the whole of the German front line, from east of the Schwaben Redoubt to the north of Serre. South of the Ancre the British assault was directed northwards against the enemy's trenches on the northern slopes of the Thiepval Ridge. It met with an altogether remarkable success for rapidity of execution and lightness of cost.

By 07:20 British objectives east of St Pierre Divion had been captured and the enemy in and around that hamlet were hemmed in between British troops and the river. Many of the Germans were driven into their dugouts before they surrendered. At 09:00 the number of prisoners taken was greater than the attacking force. At the expense of fewer than 600 casualties, one single division took nearly 1,400 prisoners. It was considered a great day for Britain's Fifth Army. All German counter-attacks had failed.

The rest of the British forces operating south of the Ancre attained their objectives with equal completeness and success. North of the river the struggle was more severe but very satisfactory results were still achieved. During the morning, the troops attacking close to the right bank of the Ancre reached their second objectives to the west and north-west of Beaucourt. They held on there for the remainder of the day and night. Their tenacity was of the utmost value and contributed very largely to the success of the operations.

As night approached, British troops were established on the western outskirts of Beaucourt. They were in touch with their own forces south of the river, which were holding a line along the station road from the Ancre towards Beaumont Hamel. Further north, the enemy's first line system for a distance of about half a mile beyond Beaumont Hamel was also in British hands. Next morning, at an early hour, the attack was renewed between Beaucourt and the top of the spur just north of Beaumont Hamel. The whole of Beaucourt was carried and, the British line extended to the north-west along the Beaucourt road and across the southern end of the Beaumont Hamel spur.

The number of prisoners taken steadily rose and, during this and the succeeding days, the British front was carried forward eastwards and northwards up the slopes of the Beaumont Hamel spur. The results of this attack were extremely satisfactory, especially as before its completion bad weather had set in once again.

Command of the Ancre Valley had been secured on both banks of the river at the point where it entered the enemy's lines. Losses had been inflicted on the

Mud, mud and more mud.

enemy, which the Germans themselves admitted to be considerable. The final total of prisoners taken in those operations and their development during the subsequent days exceeded 7,200, including 149 officers.

On 18 November 1916, the British advance north and south of the Ancre had reached the outskirts of Grandcourt. Operations ended during that day and the Battle of the Somme was over.

Main objectives achieved

In all respects, precedence to the needs of the Somme battle was required. British troops were responsible for the security of the line held by them and for keeping the enemy on their front constantly on the alert. Their role was a very trying one, entailing heavy work and constant vigilance on the part of both commanders and staffs. They deserved the highest commendations for their unfailing spirit of unselfish and broad-minded devotion to the general good.

Information obtained both during the progress of the Battle of the Somme and since, has fully established the effect of the British offensive in keeping the enemy's main forces tied to the Western Front. Some 360 raids were carried out, during the course of which the enemy suffered many casualties. The total number of prisoners taken by the British in the Somme battle between 1 July and 18 November 1916 was just over 38,000, including more than 800 officers. During the same period, 29 heavy guns were captured, 96 field guns and field howitzers, 136 trench mortars and 54 machine guns.

The 33rd Division remained on the Somme Front until March 1917, when it was transferred to Amiens to participate in the Arras Offensive.

Britain's army

Preparations for the Battle of the Somme, with the exception of those at Gommecourt, were carried out under Sir Henry Rawlinson's orders. It was not until after the assault of 1 July that Sir Hubert Gough was placed in charge of a portion of the front of attack in order to enable Rawlinson to devote his whole attention to the main area.

The army commanders noted the excellent work done by their staff officers and technical advisers, as well as by the various commanders and staffs serving under them. All through the operations, the whole of the British army worked with a remarkable absence of friction.

The vast majority of British troops had been raised and trained after the Great War began. Many of them could count their service in months, with the Battle of the Somme being their first experience of the most incredible fight they had to face. Those troops accomplished so much, under horrendous conditions, against an army whose chief concern for so many years had been preparation for war.

The men of the many Church Lads' Brigades were among those who were engaged in that tremendous battle. Those who did not have a personal experience of the Battle of the Somme could not possibly imagine the difficulties and hardships that had to be overcome or the utter determination, cheerful endurance and invincible courage shown in meeting the seemingly impossible tasks set before them.

Troops from every part of the British Isles and from every Dominion and quarter of the Empire, whether Regulars, Territorials or lads of the New Armies, bore a share if they took part in the Battle of the Somme. Among the entire long roll of victories borne on the colours of their regiments, there has never been a higher test of the strength and resolution of the British infantry. They showed themselves to be worthy of the highest British traditions and the proud records of former wars. The work of the British artillery was outstanding and the strain on the personnel enormous. The excellence of the results attained was even more remarkable in view of the brief training of most of the men, junior officers and NCOs. Despite this, they rose to a very high level of technical and tactical skill and the cooperation between artillery and infantry, on which every victory depended, was an outstanding feature of every battle. A number of the close-knit units still remaining in the 33rd Division saw some action at the very end of the fighting on the Somme when a plan, thought up by Divisional Command, failed to capture a German trench system at night.

Postscript

Beginning at the height of summer, allied offensive operations on the Somme were brought to an end in just over four and half months by adverse weather conditions. The autumn rains and early winter sleet and snow turned the battle-field into an impossible and disorderly situation. To exist in such conditions became an intolerable physical ordeal. The fighting had led to no significant breakthrough for the allied forces. More than four months of relentless assaults on German defence lines had yielded very few gains.

An area approximately 20 miles wide by 6 miles deep had been wrested from Germany's possession and this at an enormous cost in both lives and casualties. British and Commonwealth forces were estimated to have lost 419,654 (dead, wounded and missing); French losses amounted to 204,253. German casualties were calculated at between 437,000 and 680,000.

On 7 December 1916, David Lloyd George became Great Britain's prime minister. He was 54 years old and at the height of his powers. His energy, eloquence and ability had already made him the leading statesman of the day and his accession to the premiership was highly popular with the country in general. Previously, a body of twenty-three people had conducted the affairs of the war. Lloyd George immediately substituted a small War Cabinet of five, which was to be in constant session. The result was a general speeding-up of decision-making.

The *Wipers Times*

In early 1916, the 12th Battalion was stationed in the front line at Ypres, Belgium. They came across a printing press abandoned by a Belgian who had, in the words of the editor, 'not stood on the order of his going, but gone.'

A British army sergeant who had been a printer in peacetime salvaged it and printed a sample page of what was to become the *Wipers Times*, 'Wipers' being

Tommy slang for Ypres itself. The editor was Captain (later Lieutenant Colonel) F.J. Roberts, and the sub-editor was Lieutenant F.H. Pearson. A notable contributor to the paper was Gilbert Frankau, a novelist and one of the Great War poets.

The paper maintained a humorously ironic style that can be recognized in some of today's satirical magazines. It consisted of poems, reflections, wry in-

The *Wipers Times*.

Lieutenant Colonel F.J. Roberts, editor of *The Wipers Times*.

jokes and lampoons of the military situation faced by the division. The everyday concerns of trench soldiers all made an appearance in the articles, sometimes explicit and sometimes as in-jokes that wouldn't be understood by outsiders. Shelling was referred to throughout the magazine, with various poems complaining about or apologizing for incidents in which British guns had shelled their own lines.

The collections of pornography, known to the division as 'The Munque Art Gallery' and 'Kristine's', were frequently mentioned and occasionally advertised, as were the local brothels. The supply of rum and whisky was a prime concern for all at the Front. In one serial story about Narpoo Rum, a certain 'Herlock Shomes' spent five issues tracking rum thieves round Hooge. Brief references also appeared regarding the panic-buying of supplies by unnamed individuals in the division after rumours of a whisky drought.

The reality of life in the trenches rarely broke through what the editor termed the paper's 'hysterical hilarity' but when it did, the gallows humour was quite clear. The paper was produced at irregular intervals between early February 1916 and February 1918. The title changed each time the division was moved to another part of the line with the old titles carefully incorporated into it. By the last wartime issue its full title was:

THE B.E.F. TIMES
with which are incorporated
The Wipers Times, The 'New Church' Times,
The Kemmel Times & The Somme Times.

Publication was held up after February 1918 by the German offensive on the Western Front in that year, but at the end of the war two issues of the *Better Times* were published. The second of these was entitled the *Xmas, Peace and Final Number*.

Chapter Seven

1917: The Battles at Arras

The British attacks at Arras were part of a larger Anglo-French offensive planned for spring 1917. Arras is the capital of the Pas-de-Calais department, part of the Nord-Pas-de-Calais region. It is France's fourth most populous region and is located in northern France on the Scarpe River, well-known for its architecture, culture and history. It was once part of the Spanish Netherlands, a portion of the Low Countries controlled by Spain from 1556 to 1714.

It was a great relief to all ranks when the long, dark, damp nights began to grow shorter and the trenches and countryside began to show signs that spring had arrived and summer was on its way.

The French had suffered the effects of the brutal war that was still taking place on their land and the whole nation had become increasingly disenchanted with its progress or rather the lack of it. This was particularly so regarding Joffre's handling of the Somme, which led to him being replaced by General Robert Nivelle.

France was cheered when Nivelle recaptured much of the ground previously taken by the Germans at Verdun. Nivelle's plan was to attack, not where Joffre had intended to develop the war, but further to the south. As commander-in-chief of the French armies on the Western Front, Nivelle came up with several new ideas and proposed three separate attacks. Two of these were to be across the Rivers Aisne and Oise and would be led by the French. He believed that the Germans had been exhausted by the battles at Verdun and the Somme and he could not resist organizing a breakthrough offensive, which he thought could be completed in a couple of days.

The main attack on the Aisne would be preceded by a large diversionary attack by the British Third and First armies at Arras. The French War Minister Hubert Lyautey and Chief of Staff General Henri Philippe Pétain both opposed the plan, believing it to be premature. However, the British commander-in-chief, Sir Douglas Haig, supported the concept of a decisive battle, insisting that if the first two phases of Nivelle's scheme were unsuccessful, the British effort would be moved north to Flanders.

Nivelle threatened to resign if the offensive did not go ahead, because he had not yet lost one of his battles. He had the enthusiastic support of the British Prime Minister, David Lloyd George. The French Prime Minister, Aristide Briand, also supported him, but War Minister Lyautey resigned during a dispute with the Chamber of Deputies, causing the Briand government to collapse. A new government, under Alexandre Ribot, took office on 20 March 1917 and Nivelle was allowed to continue with his forthcoming planned offensive.

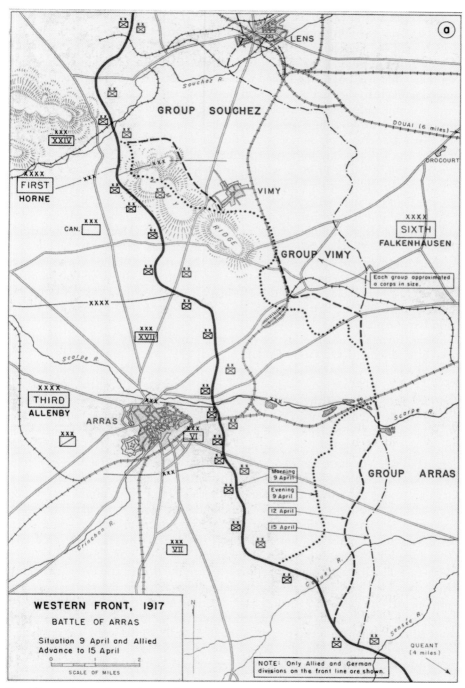

Front lines at Arras prior to the assault.

The attack was to fall on the German positions topping the Chemin des Dames ridge, an area of high ground north-west of Rheims. Closer cooperation of the British with the French was ruled out, as the devastation of the Somme battles in July to November 1916 had destroyed the infrastructure behind the lines. Another offensive, physically linked to the right flank of the French armies, was judged unlikely to succeed. An attack in the Arras region was not the choice of the British commander-in-chief who wanted the main effort of his armies to be directed north around the Ypres Salient. Haig hoped to clear the Belgian coast-line that was increasingly important to the Germans' submarine offensive and to capture the strategically-important railhead of Roulers. If Germany lost this sector of the Western Front it would seriously hamper its war effort.

Britain's Prime Minister Lloyd George overruled Haig's plan. He also tried to put the field marshal under the direct control of France's General Nivelle.

Although much talk had gone on with the French, the Battle of Arras was mainly a British offensive that ran from 9 April to 16 May 1917. British, Canadian, New Zealand, Newfoundland and Australian troops were all engaged to attack the German defences near the city. The offensive had been divided into ten distinct actions comprising battles, flanking, subsidiary and subsequent attacks. The first two actions of the first phase were to be the Battle of Vimy and the simultaneous First Battle of the Scarpe. These were planned to start on Easter Monday, 9 April 1917.

So far, for much of the war, the opposing armies on the Western Front had been at a stalemate. On Good Friday, 6 April 1917, the United States declared war on Germany, having already severed diplomatic relations with them in February. On 10 May, John Joseph 'Black Jack' Pershing, a US army general, was appointed to command the American Expeditionary Forces in the Great War.

The Arras Offensive was to be a combined operation with the French and was conceived as part of Nivelle's plan to bring the war to an end within forty-eight hours, but the Battle of Arras was mainly a British offensive. The French high command was simultaneously embarking on a massive attack (the Nivelle Offensive) about 80km to the south. At Arras, the British allied objectives were to draw German troops away from the ground chosen for the French attack and to take the German-held high ground that dominated the plain of Douai. This was a commune in the Nord department, located on the river Scarpe some 40km (25 miles) from Lille and 25km (16 miles) from Arras. The effort was on a relatively broad front assault between Vimy in the north-west and Bullecourt in the south-east. Finally, after much planning between the British and French, the time of the attack arrived, but the weather had taken a turn for the worse.

In the early morning of 9 April, a fearful whirlwind of artillery fire blasted forth as a prelude to the attack. The number of guns was so great that they could have touched each other from end to end of the line. At 05:30 the word was given and, in the first dim grey light of a rainy, sleet-filled, windy morning, the infantry dashed forward. Grimy, mud-covered, determined lads, soaked to the skin with their feet ankle-deep in mud and with hearts as hard as steel, set about their task in a calm, businesslike fashion.

Some Germans were found scattered in their shattered trenches or cowering in their dugouts. On the left of the 21st Division were the Lancashire Pals of the 30th Division.

The First Battle of Bullecourt
The village of Bullecourt is situated on the flat landscapes of Picardy in north-eastern France. It was the epicentre of the Somme and is located about 25km south-east of Arras and 30km west of Cambrai. A combined force of British and Australian soldiers of the allies' Fifth Army was mostly made up of new conscripts. These young lads were about to face the full force of the professional German troops entrenched within their newly-built line.

Following heavy losses in the fighting on the Somme, the Germans had taken the decision to shorten their lines. For the preceding nine months, Russian prisoners and support troops of the German army had been engaged in building a fearsome new defensive position, called the Hindenburg Line by the British (*Siegfriedstellung* in German). By 18 March 1917, the German army had already completed their withdrawal behind this line. This created serious complications for the British by dislocating their battle plans on the eve of the offensive

For the French the problem was even more acute, as their forthcoming attack was intended as a break-out from a salient that no longer existed. Nevertheless, Nivelle decided to go ahead with the attack. Now committed to the battle, the much larger unopposed French force intended to punch through the German lines to the south and roll up the German army from the rear. This was meant to be the knock-out blow on the Western Front and Nivelle boasted that this offensive would end the war. Of course, this proved not to be the case.

The British were to begin their operations a few days before those of the French, the intention being the hope that the German reserves would be transferred north to counter their attack around Arras. Geographically, much of the battlefield of Arras was relatively flat. To the north of the city was the rise of Vimy Ridge that dominated the countryside and was being held by the Germans. Capture of this ridge was one of the major British objectives because, as long as the Germans held the ridge, British lines of communication were under constant observation.

In the main, the first day's battle by the attacking British and Canadian forces was a success. On the second day of the battle, despite the unseasonable sleet, snow and severe cold, the Canadian Corps captured the vast majority of Vimy Ridge. The reputation of the Canadians as brilliant soldiers had already been solidly established by a long series of military feats beginning with the ever-memorable Second Battle of Ypres. This continued on to the capture of Courcelette and their fine fighting at the Somme.

The whole might of Canada was drawn together in the four excellent divisions that lay facing the historic Vimy Ridge. It was a long gradual slope reaching a height of more than 450 feet at the summit. At its northern tip the ridge rises to a small knoll known to Canadian soldiers in the Great War as 'the Pimple'. From there a high saddle leading to the highest point on the ridge was Hill 145. The

Mortar bursting the barbed wire.

whole terrain was a honeycomb of caverns, trenches and tunnels and it bristled with nests of deadly machine guns.

Moving onwards and fighting with every bit of strength they had left, they overran three lines of German trenches, including the famous La Folie Farm. They captured the village of Farbus and also captured an amazing total of 70 officers and 3,500 men as prisoners. This was the same number taken by their British comrades to the immediate south.

They not only crowned the redoubtable ridge, but as they made their way down the eastern slope, they established their line beyond it. Many of the German infantry were captured in the great chalk excavations in which they had taken refuge. Two large tunnels in particular — the Volker and the Prinz Arnault — were crammed with enemy soldiers. Incredible incidents happened in those subterranean burrows. Small parties of Canadian moppers-up were suddenly faced with large numbers of armed Germans in hiding.

British advances to the south were also impressive with these two battles being considered a great success for the British and Imperial troops. The Canadian and British forces of General Horne's First Army attacking Vimy Ridge and being able to eject the German defenders there saw that worthwhile attacks had been made by General Allenby's Third Army, south of the ridge. A considerable artillery barrage comprising both high explosives and gas preceded an advance of over 3.5 miles by the 9th (Scottish) Division and the 'leapfrogging' 4th Division captured the village of Fampoux. This advance was the longest made in a single attack since the advent of trench warfare in 1914.

All the troops were in high spirits for, although the full extent of the victory had not yet been realized, it was already known that at least 10,000 prisoners and

Celebrating victory at Vimy Ridge.

100 guns had fallen into allied hands. These figures meant that the battle had been the most serious military disaster that had so far befallen the enemy. This sudden triumph seemed to offer the possibility of a break-out and the cavalry were rushed forward in the hope of pouring them through the gap and attacking the enemy's lines of communication. Such hopes, however, proved to be bloodily deceptive.

Despite the rigours of constant treacherous warfare, the troops sang their way through the battles. In 1916, British officer Frederick E. Weatherly had penned the song *Roses of Picardy*. It had become popular and was sung by our lads remembering their wives and sweethearts back home:

> Roses are shining in Picardy
> In the hush of the silver dew
> Roses are flowering in Picardy
> But there's never a rose like you
> And the roses will die with the summer time
> And our roads may be far apart
> But there's one rose that dies not in Picardy
> 'Tis the rose that I keep in my heart.

The view from Vimy Ridge after its capture.

Disaster for the Seaforths

The 2nd Seaforth Highlanders and the 1st Royal Irish Fusiliers were to attack from the sunken lane between Fampoux and Gavrelle. The enemy spotted them on the railway embankment while they were forming up in Roeux. They had advanced over a kilometre of open ground from the railway embankment and the chemical works when they were subjected to immense shellfire and hit by heavy machine-gun fire. The Seaforths had attacked with 12 officers and 420 men, but suffered casualties of all 12 officers and 363 men. Only fifty-seven men survived this attack without being wounded.

Subsequent attacks were equally costly and Roeux was rapidly earning the reputation of being a fortress village. The British attacks were badly planned and not supported by sufficient artillery fire, while the German defences had grown in strength. This action and the casualties from other battalions of Seaforths are commemorated on the Seaforths Cross at Fampoux.

Wednesday, 11 April 1917 was a pivotal day of fighting. General Sir Hubert Gough's Fifth Army attacked in the south at Bullecourt. The hastily-constructed plan had been to use tanks of the Heavy Branch Machine Gun Corps to crush the thick belts of barbed wire protecting the Hindenburg Line. The British effort was a relatively broad front assault between Vimy in the north-west and Bullecourt in the south-east. Following the initial successes, British forces engaged in a series of small-scale operations to consolidate the newly-won positions. In the south the British and Australian forces became very frustrated by the delayed advances, as in the south they had made only minimal gains. Although these battles were generally accepted as being successful in achieving limited aims, they were obtained at the cost of a relatively large number of casualties.

When the tanks failed to arrive on time, the Australian troops broke through the wire, fighting their way into the Hindenburg Line. However, by midday they were faced with the Germans closing in on them from three sides and were forced to retreat across no man's land to their own line. More than 2,000 men were taken prisoner, the largest number of Australians captured during the war.

South of the river, the attacking British divisions fared quite well as Observation Ridge and Battery Valley were captured. However, the planned capture of the villages of Monchy-le-Preux on its hilltop plateau and Guemappe were not realized. Moving south of the Arras-Cambrai road, the successful capture of the Harp and Telegraph Hill can also be viewed as particular triumphs.

South of the Roman Road the British were now attacking the newly-constructed Hindenburg Line. The intelligent siting and design of the line, coupled with the inability of the British artillery to sufficiently destroy the barbed wire, made the attacks in the south a costlier and more difficult task. Neuville Vitasse was captured, but the two divisions to the south of the village suffered grievously in their attacks.

The night of 9 April 1917 had seen Germany's fate hanging in the balance. If the British success could have been exploited, then it is very possible that a potentially disastrous breach in the German lines could have led to their full-scale

The Hindenburg Line at Bullecourt, as seen from the air.

retreat. Sadly for the British, the success of that first day was the highest point of their action in Arras.

Disorganization, breakdown of communications, dreadful weather and the constant problem of moving the artillery forward over heavily-bombarded ground resulted in little concentrated action taking place. This delay was exactly what the Germans needed. It gave them time to reorganize and strengthen their defences.

With the Canadian troops that had captured the strategically significant Vimy Ridge advancing in the north and the British divisions fighting in the centre, after considerable bombardment the battles raged on and significant gains were made astride the River Scarpe. Four days later, the flanking attacks further south by the Australian and British troops of General Gough's Fifth Army at Bullecourt and those of the German forces of General von Falkenhausen's Sixth Army at Lagnicourt remained at stalemate.

Many advances had been accomplished by 11 April, but the uncut wire and a very heavy belt of artillery fire halted the main fighting on the right. The commanding officer and a great majority of the other officers were killed or wounded and the advance was brought to a standstill. An alternative line from Drocourt to Quéant existed some miles to the east. The fall of the front section at a period when much of its wire was still intact proved to the Germans how impossible it was to hold off British troops with mere passive obstacles.

The capture of Monchy-le-Preux

With the help of six tanks, the capture of Monchy-le-Preux by the infantry of the 15th and 37th divisions was an unbelievable feat of British strength. Many of the lads had lain out in the cold and snow for two days and it is a credit to their training and the fighting determination of the British army that their attacks were carried out with such resilience. Friday, 13 April was a day for fresh troops to take the field and carry on the attack. Exhausted and frozen men trudged back to Arras to be replaced by units at full strength. By now it was almost definitely too late for the breakthrough that had appeared so possible on the evening of 9 April 1917.

Despite the undoubted success of the infantry, it is the fate of the cavalry for which Monchy has become so well-known. With the village captured, the cavalry were to advance east to the Green Line, but they were forced back by German machine-gun fire. Subjected to such a barrage from the enemy's artillery, they were unable to escape through the narrow streets that were clogged with horses and cavalrymen. The riders dismounted, hoping to seek refuge in the cellars, but the horses could do nothing and were killed in great numbers as shells rained down on them.

It is recorded that: 'The streets of Monchy, full of horse carcasses and the foul residue of high explosive shells and animals, are said to have run with blood.'

Infantry Hill
An attack was planned from the precarious Monchy salient. Just two battalions of men were to attack Hill 100 (named Infantry Hill by the British). Conditions were appalling as the debris from the horse carcasses blocked the narrow roads through the village. So the attack was postponed until 05:30 on the morning of 14 April.

The plan was to capture Infantry Hill and then send out patrols into the Bois du Sart and Bois du Vert to look for any remaining enemy that were in hiding. The Monchy salient was still surrounded on three sides by enemy forces. The 1st Essex Regiment and Newfoundland Regiment, who went in as prescribed, carried out the attack and by 07:00 the report was that Infantry Hill had been captured.

However, in their first proper use of the new defensive employment called 'elastic defence', meaning that the British were constantly being driven back to where they had started, a German counter-attack was launched. It happened with such speed and precision that over 1,000 Essex and Newfoundlanders were killed, wounded or taken prisoner.

Monchy had been left undefended and was now at the mercy of the advancing German troops. The situation was only saved by the commander of the Newfoundland Regiment, Colonel James Forbes-Robertson, who with eight other men opened rifle fire from the edge of the village. For five hours their fire held back the enemy until fresh troops reached them. These men, known as 'the Men who saved Monchy', were all decorated for this action.

Fighting continued on the Wancourt Ridge with the British capture of the remains of Wancourt Tower. Bitter fighting also continued on the Hindenburg Line with limited piecemeal actions achieving little. Field Marshal Douglas Haig now took control, halting those costly and morale-damaging attacks until a combined offensive could be made. This decision marked the end of the first stage of the Arras fighting and the end of the First Battle of the Scarpe.

'The Men who saved Monchy.'

The Second Battle of the Scarpe, 23–24 April 1917

The results of the First Battle of the Scarpe had been to push the British line 4 miles further east. During that action the 33rd Division was in reserve. On 12 April the 98th Brigade moved into the Cojeul Valley in close support, relieving the 19th Brigade in the Hindenburg Line.

Wide stretches of territory, as well as all the dominating features forming the immediate object of the attack, had been gained. A large number of German divisions had been drawn to the battle area and thousands of German prisoners and guns were taken. Otherwise they would have been diverted further south against the French on the Aisne.

On 16 April, the French offensive was due to take place and the original plan was that it would follow the British offensive within two or three days. However, it had to be postponed due to the weather conditions. In order to assist her allies, British pressure had to be maintained. The First Battle of the Scarpe had scarcely ended when preparations were made for the next operations, but bad weather, the strength already developed by the enemy and the time necessary to complete artillery dispositions interfered with an immediate resumption of the offensive.

18-pounder gun crew in action during the advance near Athies.

It was 23 April before the next great attack took place. At 04:45 hours on a front of about 9 miles from Croisilles to Gavrelle, the German trenches were again stormed after they had been subjected to a perfect tornado of shellfire. Meanwhile, the Canadian Corps (to which the 24th Division was still attached) was engaged in pushing on towards Lens.

Four sectors of the line were of special interest. The Middlesex men were south-west of Cherisy; the 1st Battalion together with other troops of the 33rd Division attacked the enemy east of Monchy; the 29th Division attacked west of Infantry Hill and north of the Scarpe; and the infantry of the 37th Division fought their way towards Greenland Hill.

The men were issued with bombs, rifle grenades, Very lights, ground flares and sandbags. Very lights were so-named after their inventor, the American Edward W. Very. Sometimes these were coloured flares used for signalling emergencies, but more often were in the form of brilliant white flares to provide illumination in trench warfare at night. They were not used to help one's own side but rather to see if the enemy was in no man's land, either working, wiring and digging, or patrolling on a raid. When the Germans or British had their own patrols or working parties out, they did not use Very lights anywhere near them. The lights did not burn for long, unlike the German parachute flares. The best defence was to stand stock still until the flare went out, hoping it didn't fall on your feet. Movement while the flare burned was easily spotted and immediately attracted enemy rifle or machine-gun fire.

The trenches were some 1,500 yards south-east of Heninel, not quite halfway between that village and Fontaine-lés-Croisilles. A Company was on the right and C Company on the left with B and D companies (right and left respectively) occupying the trenches in the rear of the front line. At 16:30, the battalion again marched off to the front line to relieve the Cameronians.

At 23:30 the two latter companies moved into their assembly trenches just behind the front line. By 01:30, all companies had taken up their allotted positions; A and C companies were the first wave and B and D companies the second wave. Zero hour was 04:45. Under cover of the barrage and described in 'The Diaries' as 'excellent', the 98th Brigade attacked the enemy. The 4th Suffolks were on the right, the Argyll and Sutherland Highlanders in the centre and the 1st Middlesex (aka the 'Die-hards') on the left. There were two separate final objectives. The Suffolks had to bomb down the Hindenburg Line to the Sensée River, while the Highlanders and the Middlesex made a frontal attack across open land, the centre of their first objective being a small oblong copse.

The attack of the Suffolks proceeded well down both trenches of the Hindenburg Line, but the Highlanders in the centre and A and B companies of the Middlesex were hung up in front of the copse. The two left companies of the latter battalion (C and D) reached their first objective without much opposition, where thirty prisoners were taken and then sent back. The Suffolks then pressed on to their final objective, which they reached successfully and dug themselves in. A Company of the Highlanders, who had fought their way past the copse, joined them.

But now a serious position presented itself to these three companies. It appeared that they were not only in the air about what was happening, but the enemy was still between them and their original jumping-off line. Captain Beesham had to make his way back along the Hindenburg Line in order to report the situation to Brigade Headquarters.

While he was away, the enemy counter-attacked and succeeded in cutting off a portion of the Hindenburg Line, thus completely cutting all communication with C and D companies in their exposed forward position. To make matters worse, troops on the left of these two companies fell back, taking with them a small party of Middlesex 'moppers-up' that had taken possession of that portion of the first objective captured by C and D companies.

The enemy was again in full possession of his original front line. A and B companies of the battalion were held up in front of the copse and the enemy had regained a portion of the Hindenburg Line. C and D companies had broken through and had reached their final objective, but were entirely cut off as the enemy was both in front of and behind them.

At 12 noon, all units of the 98th Brigade, with the exception of A Company of the 2nd Argyll and Sutherland Highlanders and C and D companies of the 1st Middlesex, were back in their original lines. These very gallant lads, though surrounded and subjected to violent efforts to dislodge them and capture them, resisted every attempt and bloodily repulsed the enemy again and again. The old die-hard spirit once more shone clearly, and the indomitable pluck of the Middlesex and their Highland comrades added yet another splendid incident to their already glorious regimental history.

Another attack by the 98th Brigade was ordered for 18:24 hours to be preceded by and under cover of a heavy barrage. Only a very slight advance was made and by this time orderlies, signallers and officers' servants had all been pressed into the thin line. At 20:00 hours, news was received at 1st Middlesex Battalion Head-quarters that the enemy had formed a barricade in the Hindenburg Line and was advancing towards Brigade Headquarters.

Firstly, the enemy was held up and then driven back to his original position by the Suffolks. Under cover of darkness, the lads who had been lying out all day in shell-holes crawled back and the front line of the brigade now consisted of about 300 men from 1st Middlesex, 2nd Royal Welsh Fusiliers and the 1st Cameronians. However, no word was received of the gallant lads who were surrounded. The barrage for the attack at 18:24 had passed over them, but apart from considerably knocking their trenches about, fortunately there were very few casualties. The night of 23/24 April 1917 passed quietly, but the enemy was obvi-ously nervous because he continued to fire Very lights.

As dawn broke there was almost no movement on the part of the enemy. This gave rise to the suspicion that he had vacated his position. Patrols were sent out and returned with the information that the Germans had fallen back. The 1st Middlesex advanced at once and took possession of the hostile front-line trenches, pushing out other patrols to discover the extent of the enemy's retire-ment. A message now came in from the two forward companies (C and D) that they were still holding on to their position. They had even taken a few prisoners, but both officers had been wounded.

During the morning the 20th Royal Fusiliers relieved the 1st Middlesex, but owing to the enemy's activity it was deemed unwise to withdraw C and D com-panies until nightfall. As soon as possible after darkness had fallen the intrepid Die-hards and Highlanders were also relieved. After forty hours of hard fighting and being completely surrounded, they had reached the sunken roads at 23:00. It is interesting to note that of the sixteen Lewis guns that the two companies had with them, all were brought back, only one having been damaged.

The battalion was now once more united and, on 25 April, marched back from the sunken roads through Henin-sur-Cojeul to Grosville. Before the Die-hards left the line, the GOC visited the battalion and personally congratulated the two companies on their tenacity and success. These congratulations were followed on 1 May 1917 by a letter from the Third Army Commander General Sir E.H.H. Allenby, who had been furnished with a report of that gallant fight: 'I have read this account with great pride and admiration. I congratulate all ranks in the

2nd Battalion Argyll and Sutherland Highlanders and the 1st Battalion Middlesex Regiment on the staunchness and bravery of their two splendid companies.' (Actually there were three altogether.)

After regrouping and with a marked improvement in the weather, the British attacked again on 23 April at the Second Battle of the Scarpe. It was now time for Major General Sir Reginald Pinney commanding the 33rd Division to take over the front from the 21st Division.

General Allenby's Third Army was to undertake phase three of the Second Battle of the Scarpe. There was a renewed advance all along the British line. Its objectives were, counting from the south, Bois du Vert, Bois du Sart, Pelves, Roeux, Gavrelle, Oppy and Acheville. Twelve divisions, with a further five in reserve, were to attack on a 14-mile front between Vimy in the north and Croisilles in the south. The attack was intended to act as a diversion to prevent the Germans feeding reinforcements further south where the French army (commanded by General Nivelle) planned a major offensive on the Aisne. However, the latter was delayed by the German withdrawal to the Hindenburg Line and it was decided that the British attack should go ahead as planned.

Roeux is 4.5 miles east of Arras (in the Scarpe Valley) and was one of the fortified villages that formed part of the German defences behind the German front line. The ground before Roeux posed many difficulties for the British. Two of them were the Arras-Douai railway line which ran north-east to south-west in the cutting, and the embankment of the River Scarpe with its surrounding marshland. Lieutenant General Sir Thomas D'Oyly Snow's 7th Corps in the south had the 33rd Division on its right, the 30th in the centre and the 50th on the left. It was a day of hard fighting with very limited gains. General Snow experienced all the disadvantages that an attack has against the defence as there was no overwhelming artillery to blast a road ahead for the infantry.

All three divisions made some progress in the early hours of dawn when, at about 11:00 and after a good initial advance, a heavy German counter-attack preceded by a terrific shower of shells came rolling down the Cojeul Valley. The whole of the two northern divisions and the centre of the 33rd Division were soon held up and finally driven back to their starting-point by very heavy machine-gun fire. The obstacle in front of the troops was nothing less than the Hindenburg front line.

The 30th Division fell back in touch with the 50th Division, but the 33rd managed to hold on to its gain of ground on the flank, which had brought it into the German front line south of the Sensée River. The position in this part of the line had become serious and was ever more so as the evening passed into night because the forward position of the 33rd Division had exposed its whole left flank. Its advanced units were cut off and the Germans, pushing back the Lancashire men of the 30th Division, had worked forward to such an extent that the British guns were threatened.

If the advance continued, the 33rd Division must either fall back under the most difficult conditions or be overwhelmed by the enemy's onslaught. General

Pinney held his ground and was confirmed right to do so because of the sounds of brisk rifle-fire upon his front that went on throughout the night. However, it was impossible to ascertain which or whose troops were in such isolated positions.

With the first light of morning two battalions, the 19th Brigade, 20th Royal Fusiliers and 2nd Welsh Fusiliers went forward to clear up the situation. After advancing only 1,200 yards they came upon the remains of two grim, battle-stained British companies. One was the 1st Middlesex and the other the 2nd Argyll and Sutherland Highlanders. They had spent some fifteen hours in the heart of the enemy's advance, watching their attacks sweeping past them, but had kept as quiet and steady as two rocks lodged in the ground. Apart from the other hardships of their position, they had endured the whole of the British barrage put down to stop the Germans.

The advance was met by the enemy's extremely heavy machine-gun fire and by a desperately destructive barrage of heavy artillery. In spite of this, the British infantry made good progress at several points. This stout defence not only protected the face of the 33rd Division, but also to some extent covered the flank of the 30th. It was a striking example of what may be accomplished by a small body of determined men who refuse to despair in such a desperate situation.

A score or so of German prisoners were found hiding in their shell-holes that the British had held in their clutches. The 33rd Division gained great distinction

A British machine-gun post near Feuchy.

and, as a visible sign of its expertise, 750 prisoners from the German 61st Division. Further north, General Horne's First Army had been committed to a subsidiary attack on La Coulotte.

A second day of hard fighting was destined to follow that of 23 April, though the advance began later in the day. The day after that (25 April) saw the long struggle still continuing. Another strong German night attack on 27 April broke before the rifle and machine-gun fire of the infantry and at the point of contact between the divisions. The German losses were heavy and they left a few prisoners behind them.

Working in conjunction with the Third Army, both the British and French took part in the Battle of Arleux on 28/29 April, the much larger fourth phase of the offensive. These attacks and the last three major actions of the battle were successful, as they now relieved pressure on the French whose own offensive had run into serious trouble.

British formations were still floundering as the Battle of Arras raged on. One position that had proved troublesome to the British was the Arleux Loop at the village of Arleux-en-Gohelle, which lay at the end of a low spur reaching into the Hindenburg Line at Quéant (12 miles south-east of Arras). Although the Canadian Corps had already taken Vimy Ridge, difficulties in securing the south-eastern flank had left the position vulnerable. To rectify this, British and Canadian troops launched an attack towards Arleux-en-Gohelle on 28 April.

Arleux was captured by Canadian troops with relative ease, but the British troops advancing on Gavrelle met with stiffer resistance from the Germans. The village was secured by early evening, but when a German counter-attack forced a brief retreat, elements of the 61st Division were brought up as reinforcements and the village was held. Subsequent attacks on 29 April were repulsed. Casualties were high and the ultimate result was disappointing.

While advances had been made, it was not the final blow that had been promised by Nivelle. Casualties were excessive and the stark contrast between the promises of the French generals and the realities of the fighting caused a collapse in French morale. On 3 May, the men of the French 2nd Division refused to attack. Many of the units were described as going 'on strike', or to put it more simply, mutinying. The French army was in real danger of disintegration and the offensive was abandoned on 9 May 1917. As the French armies still held over two-thirds of the Western Front, Field Marshal Haig needed to keep up the pressure on the German forces and so prevent any attack on the badly-shaken French.

Concern for the Russian front was also growing as news of the revolution began to arrive in the West. The Russian Revolution of February 1917 had resulted in the overthrow of the autocracy and the establishment of a provisional government. The fate of Nicholas II and his wife Alexandra was bound up in the struggle for power among competing political factions in Russia. Nicholas was convinced that the Russian people would rescue him from his captors. His belief proved to be delusional and the efforts on the part of the liberals, the socialists and some of the Bolsheviks to arrange a trial failed to save the czar and his family.

The relief of the allied armies came at a cost to Haig's own troops. The Third Army was compelled to fight phase five of the offensive because the attack had already been arranged to help the forthcoming French advance that had been due on 5 May. However, 3 May was to be a day of general battle on the British front. The Third Battle of the Scarpe, as the fighting on 3/4 May was named, was an unmitigated disaster for the British army, which suffered nearly 6,000 men killed for little material gain.

In the *Official History: Military Operations France and Belgium 1917* by Cyril Falls, he gives the following reasons for the failure on 3 May 1917 on the 7th Corps frontage:

> The confusion caused by the darkness; the speed with which the German artillery opened fire; the manner in which it concentrated upon the British infantry, almost neglecting the artillery; the intensity of its fire, the heaviest that many an experienced soldier had ever witnessed, seemingly unchecked by British counter-battery fire and lasting almost without slackening for fifteen hours; the readiness with which the German infantry yielded to the first assault and the energy of its counter-attack; and, it must be added, the bewilderment of the British infantry on finding itself in the open and its inability to withstand any resolute counter-attack.

Bullecourt

During any war of consequence there are usually areas of dispute and contention. Even the best of allies have been known to fall out over some failing in the way a particular action was conducted. The matter is liable to become even more contentious when officers from one nation command the army of another nation.

Such an event occurred on the Western Front in April/May 1917. The location was the village of Bullecourt and its environs, south-east of Arras on the Somme battlefield in northern France. The adversaries were the 1st, 2nd, 4th and 5th Australian divisions of the Australian Imperial Forces (AIF). The No.1 Anzac Corps was part of the British Fifth Army commanded by General Hubert de la Poer Gough.

Since the 1916 Anglo-French Somme Offensive had failed to provide recognition of the breakthrough of the German defences on the Western Front, the minds of the allied commanders turned to other possible ventures, including a British-led attack in the Artois Sector (Arras in northern France).

General Gough was convinced that the newly-arrived British tank was the weapon that would open up a whole new means of warfare. As Gough had transferred much of Fifth Army's artillery to Third Army for the Arras operation, he planned to use the tanks instead of artillery. He considered that this would support the troops by tearing down the extensive Hindenburg Line's barbed-wire defences and neutralizing the many machine-gun nests.

The Fifth Army was allotted a company of tanks from the 1st Battalion of Heavy Machine Gun Corps Company. They were given twenty-four Mark I and Mark II tanks, comprising twelve male tanks, with two small mounted cannons, and twelve female tanks with machine guns. Unfortunately, only some of the tanks had armour-plate and all were mechanically unreliable. At the last minute, tank experts convinced Gough that the tanks would make any preliminary artillery bombardment unnecessary. All that was required was supporting barrages by Australia's own artillery and that would be enough to support the advancing infantry. Despite protestations by the Australian commanders about Gough's unorthodox tactics of overriding reliance on the tanks and no preparatory bombardment, he decided to proceed with the attack on 10 April 1917 at 04:30 hours.

The main assault was to be led by the 4th Division of I Anzac supported by the British 62nd Division, with twelve tanks to clear a passage through the heavy barbed-wire defences and to deal with the machine-gun nests. In the midst of a blinding snowstorm, the tanks were delayed and were not in the line by zero hour. So the Australian commanders decided to postpone the attack until the tanks were ready.

Unfortunately, the Australians did not inform their supporting British troops and elements of the 62nd Division advanced as scheduled towards Hendecourt. They walked straight into a hail of machine-gun and artillery fire. It was quite some time before they realized that the Australians had not moved forward. The 62nd subsequently withdrew, having suffered many casualties. The first disaster at Bullecourt was down to the Australians. Gough decided the operation would take place the next day, despite the protestations of the Australian generals.

At 04:30 hours on 11 April 1917, eleven of the tanks were roughly in position. The Australian 4th Division's 12th Brigade decided to wait until all its tanks were properly positioned, but the Australian 4th Brigade decided to press on without the tanks along its planned line of advance to the right of Bullecourt village. This was a risky move since their left flank, where 12th Brigade was supposed to be, was vulnerable to enfilading machine-gun fire. Once again, as planned, there was no preliminary bombardment in order to ensure a surprise element for the tanks. Nevertheless, despite heavy machine-gun and artillery fire, the 4th Brigade reached the first line of the German trenches and occupied them. They then moved off in the direction of the neighbouring village of Riencourt, at which point a well-sited German machine-gun nest brought the brigade to a halt.

Meanwhile, the 12th Brigade finally got the tanks organized by 05:15 hours, and the eleven tanks set off with the men of the 12th Brigade following them. However, the speed of some of the tanks was so slow that the advancing infantry overtook them. The pattern of advance closely mirrored that of the 4th Brigade. After capturing the first line German trench and part of the second, stiff opposition halted the 12th Brigade. Further advance depended on artillery support. None was forthcoming from the Australian artillery.

At 10:00 hours the Germans counter-attacked with their usual fervour and efficacy. In two hours, all of the first line trenches had been retaken and many of the Australian troops in the German second line trench were cut off. All but one of the tanks had either broken down, had ditched or been destroyed by artillery fire. The advancing troops were left without a covering barrage at the most critical points of the advance.

When it came to totalling up the casualties and reviewing the day's events, four facts stood out. Firstly, the British 62nd Division felt badly let down by the Australian commanders and their artillery. Secondly, the Australians' faith in the professional abilities of the British senior commanders, Generals Haig and Gough, was seriously compromised. Thirdly, the Australian casualties were astronomical, representing two-thirds of the strength of the whole of the 4th Division, of whom over 1,000 were taken prisoner. As a result, the division was taken out of the line and remained so for four months until it was entirely rebuilt and retrained.

The Australians were completely disenchanted with the new British tank and for more than a year refused to have anything to do with it. Subsequently, over the next year many Australian lives were lost that probably could have been saved.

The Second Battle of Bullecourt

Despite the disappointments of the First Battle of Bullecourt, the imperative for the attack on the Hindenburg Line remained on the agenda of the British Fifth Army. More careful planning went into a second attempt, although important tactical weaknesses were left unresolved.

This time it was led by the 2nd Australian Division and, once again, was supported by the British 62nd Division. In preparation for the new attack, much of the area in and around Bullecourt village had been heavily shelled and was in ruins. It was accepted that the tanks would support the British 62nd Division, but the Australians insisted that they wanted nothing to do with them.

At 03:45 hours the 5th and 6th brigades of the Australian 2nd Division 'went over the top' towards the eastern edge of what was left of Bullecourt village, when they were hit by heavy machine-gun fire from the front and side and brought to an abrupt halt. Some of the troops started to drift back towards their own lines. Others tried to advance up the German trenches with a bit more success, but they were rigorously counter-attacked as the day went on. The Australian 6th Brigade had more luck on the left of the 5th. The lie of the land gave them more cover and they were able to surprise the Germans in their trenches. Some progress was made. By late morning, lacking support on their left or right, the 6th Brigade was ultimately forced to pull back by vigorous German counter-attacks.

The British 62nd Division was approaching the ruins of Bullecourt village from the left flank and reached the far side of the village. However, despite reinforcements, this position could not be held and the 62nd Division was pushed back through the village, having been reduced to only 100 men. By the end of the day the Australians and British were both grimly hanging on to their limited gains, awaiting their replacement. This came in the form of the Australian 1st Division and the British 7th Division.

Among the ruins of Bullecourt village, a determined German resistance met attempts at further advances by the new divisions with heavy machine-gun fire from their own strong defensive positions. A sort of stalemate situation developed as both sides sought a way out of the costly impasse. At 03:45 hours on 7 May 1917 the British 7th Division made another attempt to take Bullecourt village but, as usual, the German response was vigorous and the village changed hands several times over the next few days with heavy casualties on both sides.

On 12 May the Australian 5th Division gave the British 7th Division strong support. Several troublesome machine-gun positions had been captured or destroyed and the two divisions joined up in Bullecourt village, most of which was now in British hands. Only a small corner in the south-west of the village remained in German hands. On 15 May 1917, efforts by the Germans to oust the British from Bullecourt failed. At 02:00 hours the British dislodged the Germans from their final stronghold.

On the night of 15/16 May, after a heavy German bombardment, a fierce attack was launched along both sides of the railway line to the north of the village, on the village itself and along the northern bank of the River Scarpe. In the dim light of the very early morning of 16 May, after a heavy shell-fall, two separate German divisions burst forward in an attack just north of the Scarpe. In their first ardent advance the attack flowed over the shot-shattered advance posts, but after a long day's fighting they were practically destroyed. The two-month campaign for Bullecourt was over, with the Germans showing no evidence of any further interest in an offensive on the front line at this point. As to the strategic value of the success of the First and Second Battles of Bullecourt, there is little evidence of any great significance. During a long tussle the enemy were shot out of their new positions by the rifles and Lewis guns. However, when evening came they were back where they started and then they finally held.

The capture of Roeux had taken place on 13/14 May. Efforts were made to consolidate the ground and that night the Germans evacuated the eastern half of Roeux and the chemical works. This allowed the line to move forward to the eastern half of the village. However, hopes that the enemy might retire further to the east were dashed. In this brisk action, thousands of the enemy were killed or wounded with nothing to show for it save the substantial losses that had been inflicted. This very severe attack showed once more that British formations, even if penetrated, were very far from being defeated. Initially, these attacks met with some success but the flanks held and the enemy was eventually repulsed from all but the most easterly positions, most of which were regained by the evening.

The Battle of Arras officially ended on 17 May, although a limited attack at Roeux on 5 June regained the remaining ground lost on 15/16 May. It was here that the line stabilized for the remainder of 1917.

The casualty figures were difficult to assess in relation to Roeux alone, but the 4th and 51st Divisions, both of which were involved in much of the fighting at Roeux, recorded some 6,300 and 6,500 casualties respectively in April and May 1917. The 9th Division suffered rather more, at just under 7,000.

Up to this point the new British offensive that had started on 9 April had now practically come to an end and had yielded the splendid results of taking 400 officers and 19,100 men prisoner, together with 98 heavy guns and 159 field pieces captured, plus 227 trench mortars, 464 machine guns and other matériel. The battle of 3 May, which had ended with some gain of ground and by the capture of nearly 1,000 prisoners (as against some 300 British lost that day), was

British troops returning for a rest following the Battle of Arras.

the last general action along the new line. Although it was followed by numerous local engagements, the strain upon the divisions during this continuous fighting had been so great that it was found necessary to give them all rest and relief.

British Empire troops had made significant advances, but had been unable to achieve the hoped-for breakthrough. The 33rd Division fought at the Second Battle of the Scarpe in late April 1917 and suffered heavy losses, but did manage to take 700 prisoners.

New tactics were embodied in the SS135 book, *Instructions for the Training of Platoons for Offensive Action 1917*. The equipment to exploit them, particularly in the first phase, demonstrated that set-piece assaults against heavily-fortified positions could be successful. The platoon would become the principal tactical unit, in four sections – Lewis gun, rifle grenade, bomber and rifle – with the creeping barrage. The graze fuse and counter-battery fire that had already been used reverted to the stalemate situation that typified most of the war on the Western Front.

This offensive was followed by a series of attacks on the Hindenburg Line in late May. Major General Pinney masterminded the first attack, due to take place on the night of 20 May. One observer noted that 'his tail is right up over his back … he was out for a gamble with his troops and he had it.'

Sunday, 20 May 1917 had marked a successful advance by the 33rd Division on the right of the 7th Corps against the Hindenburg Line in the Sensée Valley and southwards towards Bullecourt. On this occasion there was no preliminary bombardment and no creeping barrage. A mist helped the 98th Brigade to deploy unobserved under the bulge of the chalk hills that rise to the south of the Sensée Valley. When the mist rose, the Germans had a fine, if transitory, view of British tactics. The 100th Brigade worked down the Hindenburg Line north of the river, crossing it and joining hands with its comrades to the south. This came as a complete surprise to the enemy and a counter-attack by them was checked by the volume of British gunfire that tore up the whole rear of the German defences. The result was the capture of more than a mile of the front line on either side of the Sensée River, plus half a mile of the support line and the capture of 170 prisoners and many machine guns. This well-managed affair suffered fewer losses than expected. Despite the battle's great success, Pinney still refused to authorize an issue of rum.

A second attack on 27 May 1917 was a complete failure. Pinney later explained the attack as a planned distraction in support of the coming Battle of Messines, an interpretation that was greeted with some cynicism by observers.

Following the fighting around Arras, the 33rd was moved to Nieuwpoort, Belgium, as part of the build-up for another planned British attack. During this period the most enduring description of Major General Pinney was written by the famous war poet Siegfried Sassoon, who was then an officer in a battalion of the 33rd. Sassoon used Pinney as the subject of his satirical poem, *The General*:

> 'Good-morning; good-morning!' the General said
> When we met him last week on our way to the line
> Now the soldiers he smiled at are most of 'em dead
> And we're cursing his staff for incompetent swine.
>
> 'He's a cheery old card,' grunted Harry to Jack
> As they slogged up to Arras with rifle and pack.
> But he did for them both by his plan of attack.

For ten days after this the Southern Front was quiet, and the only change consisted of the withdrawal of the 56th Division with the substitution of the 37th.

Operation HUSH

This was a British plan to make amphibious landings on the Belgian coast supported by an attack from Nieuwpoort and the Yser bridgehead, which had been created by the Battle of the Yser (1914). Several plans had been considered in 1915 and 1916 but were shelved due to operations being carried out elsewhere. Operation HUSH was intended to begin when the main offensive at Ypres had advanced to Roulers and Torhout that were linked in between advances by the French and Belgian armies.

Operation STRANDFEST was a German spoiling attack launched in anticipation of the allied coastal operation due on 10 July 1917. The use of mustard gas for the first time, supported by a mass of heavy artillery, captured part of the bridgehead over the Yser and annihilated two British battalions. The work of the Royal Army Medical Corps was made more difficult by the circumstances of the battle. The gas hung so thickly in the trees and bushes that all ranks were compelled to wear their respirators continuously if they were to escape its effects.

It was necessary to dig trenches to obtain any cover from the persistent shellfire and men could not dig for long without removing their masks. There was a steady stream of gassed and wounded men coming to the regimental aid posts. Their clothes were full of gas and, as the medical officers could not dress wounds without removing their respirators, they also suffered badly. This resulted in several medical officers being hospitalized as a result of being gassed.

Motor ambulances returning for more cases could not reach the dressing stations due to the congested roads, so some of the wounded were sent by horse ambulance to avoid further congestion. The walking wounded cases usually greatly exceeded the stretcher cases and were dealt with fairly rapidly, but in this instance the gas had blinded a great many of them. One of the most pitiful sights of the war was the long queues of temporarily blinded men, their eyes bandaged, linked up together and slowly wending their way through the battlefield guided by RAMC orderlies. The collection and evacuation of these soldiers made as much of a demand on medical personnel and vehicles as if all of them had been stretcher cases. Every form of vehicle was used, even any empty water carts lying by the wayside.

The walking wounded boarding a ship at Le Havre.

After several postponements, Operation HUSH did not meet the objectives required to begin the attack. After the operation was cancelled, the 33rd Division remained at Nieuwpoort, where Pinney was hospitalized and temporarily relinquished command. He remained in hospital for two months, during which time he missed heavy fighting by the 33rd Division at the Battle of Passchendaele.

The Battle of Passchendaele (Third Battle of Ypres)

Field Marshal Haig had mulled over the idea of launching a major offensive in Flanders for a long time. It was his preferred choice for 1916, but the Battle of the Somme had taken precedence that summer.

The Germans had launched the First and Second Battles of Ypres in 1914 and 1915, so the Third Battle of Ypres was intended as Haig's allied forces breakthrough in Flanders in 1917. The French Nivelle Offensive had ended in May and, with such a disastrous failure and mutiny spreading throughout the French army, Haig became determined to press ahead with plans for a major British offensive in the late summer of 1917.

Meticulously planned, the apparent aim of the campaign was to be the destruction of German submarine bases on the Belgian coast. A warning issued by British Admiral Jellicoe followed, saying that the current level of shipping losses would prevent the British from sustaining the war into 1918, so this required the clearance of the bases on the Belgian coast.

Haig recognized the urgency of this requirement and was anxious to finally break the will of the German army, which he believed was near to collapse anyway. This was a view that he had similarly held at the height of the Somme Offensive a year earlier, but without clear results.

British Prime Minister David Lloyd George was opposed to the Passchendaele Offensive and became highly critical of Haig's strategy and tactics, but in the absence of a credible alternative, he felt obliged to sanction the field marshal's plans. He was, however, encouraged by the greatest local success of the war earlier that summer, when the Battle of Messines (7–14 June 1917), conducted by the British Second Army under the command of General Herbert Plumer, resulted in the complete capture of the Messines-Wytschaete Ridge.

The capture of the ridge was a necessary precursor to an offensive aimed at capturing the Passchendaele Ridge. Plumer advocated continuing the attack immediately, arguing that the morale of the German troops was – at least for the present – broken, and that this combined with a shortage of their forces would virtually guarantee the allied capture of the ridge.

Haig disagreed, choosing not to bring forward his plans from the end of July. With the patent instability of Russian forces in the field and the possibility of a Russian withdrawal from the war, action appeared to be mandated in the summer of 1917. If the Russians left the war it would enable Germany to draft its eastern forces into the battle on the Western Front, dramatically increasing Germany's reserve strength.

The Third Battle of Ypres was opened on 31 July 1917 by Sir Hubert Gough's Fifth Army, with one corps of Sir Herbert Plumer's Second Army joining on its

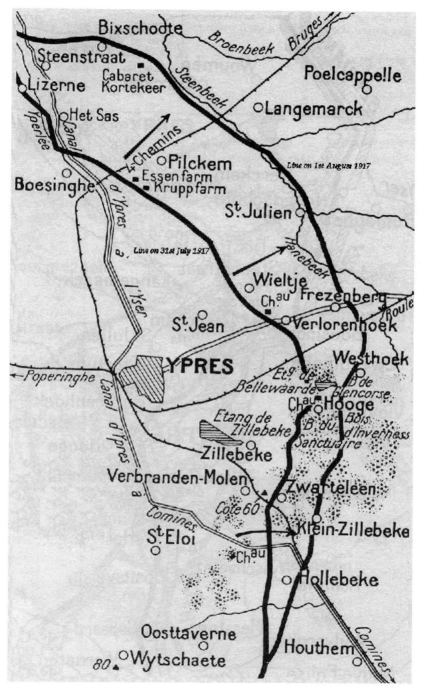

Advance at Ypres, 31 July 1917.

right and a corps of the French First Army on its left. In all, there was a total of twelve divisions. When the attack was launched across an 18km front, the German Fourth Army was in place to hold off the main British advance around the Menin Road. This restricted the allies to fairly small gains around Pilckem Ridge. Similarly, the French were halted further north by the German Fifth Army under General Max von Gallwitz.

British attempts to renew the offensive over the course of the next few days were severely hampered by the onset of heavy rains, the heaviest in thirty years, which churned the Flanders lowland soil into a thick muddy swamp. Tanks were stuck fast in the mud and the infantry also found their mobility severely limited. Ironically the very force of the preliminary bombardment in previous battles had destroyed the drainage systems and exacerbated the problem. The artillery shells launched had peppered the very ground that needed to be crossed by the advancing allied forces.

The disastrous turn in the climate could not have been predicted and the rainfall was by far the heaviest for many years. Fighting had taken place around Ypres since 1914 without experiencing any of the problems encountered during this particular action. As a consequence, no renewed major offensive could be contemplated until 16 August 1917, when the Battle of Langemarck saw four days of fierce fighting that resulted only in small gains but heavy casualties for the British. It was the second allied general attack of the Third Battle of Ypres in Belgian Flanders.

The allied attack had succeeded in the north, from Langemarck to Drie Grachten, but early advances in the south on the Gheluvelt Plateau were forced back by powerful German counter-attacks. Both sides were hampered by rain, which had a greater effect on the British who occupied the lower-lying areas and advanced onto ground that had previously been frequently and severely bombarded. The effect of the battle, the August weather and the successful but costly German defence of the Gheluvelt Plateau during the rest of August, led the British to further revise their methods and main offensive effort.

Dissatisfied with progress, the British commander-in-chief replaced Sir Hubert Gough and moved him and his forces further north with Herbert Plumer. Gough favoured sweeping aggression, but Plumer planned a series of small gains rather than an all-out breakthrough. The attacks began afresh on 20 September with the Battle of the Menin Road Bridge. This was followed by the Battle of Polygon Wood on 26 September and the Battle of Broodseinde on 4 October. These three gains established British possession of the ridge east of Ypres. Encouraged by Plumer's small gains and almost certain that the German army was approaching collapse, Haig decided to continue the offensive towards the Passchendaele Ridge some 10 kilometres from Ypres.

Little progress was made at the Battle of Poelcappelle and the First Battle of Passchendaele on 9 and 12 October respectively. As they poured onto the ridge, the allied attackers were themselves nearing the Eastern Front. The Germans, to further their defence, made full use of mustard gas (as opposed to the chlorine gas used in the Second Battle of Ypres), which resulted in chemical burns. Unwilling to concede to the failure of a breakthrough, Haig pressed on with a further three assaults on the ridge in late October. Passchendaele lay on the last ridge east of Ypres, 5 miles from a railway junction at Roeselare, which was a vital part of the supply system of the German Fourth Army.

The next stage of the allied strategy was an advance to Torhout–Couckelaere to close the German-controlled railway running through Roeselare and Torhout. Further operations and a British supporting attack along the Belgian coast from Nieuwpoort, combined with an amphibious landing, were to have reached Bruges and then the Dutch frontier. The resistance of the German Fourth Army, unusually wet weather, the onset of winter and the diversion of British and

The remains of Chateau Wood, 1917.

French resources to Italy allowed the Germans to avoid the general withdrawal that had seemed inevitable in October.

The campaign ended in November when the Canadian Corps captured Passchendaele. The eventual capture of Passchendaele village by British and Canadian forces finally gave Haig an excuse to call off the offensive by claiming success.

The Third Battle of Ypres was launched on 31 July 1917 and continued right up until the fall of Passchendaele on 10 November 1917. The offensive was by no means the breakthrough that Haig had intended and such gains that were made came at a great cost in human terms. The Battle of Messines had been a prelude to the much larger Third Battle of Ypres campaign, namely the preliminary bombardment that had begun on 11 July 1917. Military analysts and historians disagree on the strategic significance of the battle, although most describe it as a British tactical and operational success.

Today simply referred to as 'Passchendaele', the tactics employed at the Third Battle of Ypres are as controversial as those executed at the Battle of the Somme a little over a year earlier. It was the final great battle of attrition of the war and was, like its predecessors, a costly exercise. The British Expeditionary Force incurred some 310,000 casualties, with a lower number of German casualties at 260,000.

Haig came under intense criticism for persisting with the offensive after it became clear that a breakthrough was unlikely. Critics have argued that the main launch pad for the attack should have been sited at Messines Ridge that was captured by Plumer in June. However, Haig's original plans precluded this with the view that the capture of the ridge was a necessary diversion and he declined to modify his plans. A number of factors were cited to support the decision he took to continue the offensive into the autumn.

Russia had withdrawn from the war. The British were vulnerable to submarine attacks launched from the Belgian coast, and weakened French morale had manifested itself in a widespread mutiny. It became clear that a decisive strike must be attempted before the allied war effort collapsed altogether.

Haig argued that the German forces could less afford the loss of men than the allies, who were being supplemented by the entry into the war of the United States. This view was shared by a number of German contemporaries and the controversy continues to this day. In 1919, German Commander Erich Ludendorff wrote that the British victory cost the German army dear and drained German reserves. Chief of the Greater German General Staff Paul von Hindenburg wrote that the losses at Messines had been 'very heavy' and he regretted that the ground had not been evacuated. In 1920, Field Marshal Douglas Haig's dispatches described the success of the British plan, organization and results, but refrained from exaggerating that the operation was a successful preliminary to the main offensive at Ypres. In 1922, German General Hermann von Kuhl called it one of the worst German tragedies of the war.

Many historians continue to question Haig's decision not to call off the offensive earlier than November, when a number of the core objectives had been attained and it became clear that the French forces would remain in the field.

Until the Spring Offensive of 1918, Roeux was held by the British, but the Germans swept west and re-took much of the old Arras battlefields.

Major General Pinney returned to the division on 30 November 1917 amid rumours that he had gained the return posting through personal influence. The 33rd Division remained in reserve until April 1918.

Shot at dawn

It is at this point in the Great War that I must mention Rifleman Thomas Donovan, service number A/201225, 16th (Service) Battalion The King's Royal Rifle Corps. He had received news from home that yet another of his brothers had been killed in the war. He asked for compassionate leave, but it was refused and he desperately wanted to get back home to be with his mother. He was caught absent without leave and was brutally and mercilessly executed for desertion on 31 October 1917. His mother had now lost three of her sons.

The grave of
Thomas Donovan.

Westhof Farm Cemetery, Belgium.

Thomas was aged 20 and is buried at Westhof Farm Cemetery, Heuvelland, West-Vlaanderen, Belgium, Plot II, D.14. He is also remembered on the British monument at the National Memorial Arboretum near Alrewas in Staffordshire, England.

The Shot at Dawn Memorial is a British monument at the National Memorial Arboretum that memorializes the 306 British and Commonwealth soldiers executed after their courts martial for cowardice or desertion during the Great War. The memorial portrays a young British soldier blindfolded and tied to a stake in readiness for shooting by a firing squad. The memorial was modelled on the likeness of 17-year-old Private Herbert Burden, who lied about his age to enlist in the armed forces and was later shot for desertion. It is surrounded by a semicircle of stakes on which are listed the names of every soldier executed in this fashion.

The families of these lads were only told that they had died in France or Belgium but were never told how or why. Yet even the families of these victims often carried the stigma of the label of 'coward'.

Senior military commanders would not accept a soldier's failure to return to the front line as anything other than desertion. They believed that if such behaviour was not harshly punished, others might be encouraged to do the same thing and cause a breakdown in discipline and the possible collapse of the whole British army.

On 13 January 1915 General Routine Order 585 was issued, reversing the principle of a soldier being innocent until found guilty. Under this order, a soldier was deemed guilty unless sufficient evidence could be provided to prove his innocence. Some men faced a court martial for other offences, but the majority stood trial for desertion from their post. It was given the title of 'fleeing in the face of the enemy'. The court martial itself was usually carried out with some speed and execution followed shortly after with no time allowed for the soldier to establish a defence.

The Shot at Dawn Memorial, Alrewas.

Few, if any, of the soldiers wanted to be part of a firing squad. Lasting emotional pain was caused to those who were ordered into these selected units. Many were just young lads at a base camp recovering from wounds that prevented them from serving at the front, but did not preclude them from firing a Lee Enfield rifle. Some of those in the firing squads were under the age of 16, as were some who were shot for 'cowardice'.

James Crozier from Belfast was shot at dawn for desertion; he was just 16. Before his execution, Crozier was given so much rum that he passed out. He had to be carried, semi-conscious, to the place of execution. Officers present at the execution later claimed that there was a very real fear that the men in the firing squad would disobey the order to shoot.

Private Abe Bevistein, aged 16, was also shot by firing squad at Labourse, near Calais. As in so many other cases, he had been found guilty of deserting his post. Just before his court martial, Bevistein wrote home to his mother: 'We were in the trenches. I was so cold I went out and took shelter in a farm house. They took me to prison so I will have to go in front of the court. I will try my best to get out of it, so don't worry.'

Britain was one of the last countries to still dishonour victims of shellshock. Prime Minister John Major emphasized this in 1993, when he told the Commons that pardoning the 'deserters' would be an insult to those who had died honourably on the battlefield and that everyone was tried fairly.

John Hipkin, a retired Newcastle schoolteacher, organized the 'Shot at Dawn' campaign after reading about a 17-year-old executed for desertion. He campaigned for more than fifteen years before his efforts began to bear fruit. One of the many issues that angered the campaigners is that four times as many men deserted in the United Kingdom than in France or Belgium, but no one was ever actually executed for desertion in Great Britain.

The legal status of a court martial has also been questioned. Those accused lads did not have access to a formal legal representative who could defend them. Some received help from a so-called 'prisoner's friend', but many did not even have this. Legally, every lad who was court-martialled should have had a 'judge advocate' present, but very few did. The night before an execution, a condemned man had the right to petition the king for clemency but none ever did, suggesting that none were aware that they had this right.

The mass pardon of 306 British Empire soldiers executed for certain offences during the Great War was enacted in Section 359 of the Armed Forces Act 2006. This came into effect by Royal Assent on 8 November 2006. Because of the 'crimes' committed by these men, their names were not put on any of the memorials of the Great War.

Anthem for Doomed Youth
What passing-bells for these who die as cattle?
Only the monstrous anger of the guns.
Only the stuttering rifles' rapid rattle
Can patter out their hasty orisons.

No mockeries now for them; no prayers nor bells,
Nor any voice of mourning save the choirs,–
The shrill, demented choirs of wailing shells;
And bugles calling for them from sad shires.
What candles may be held to speed them all?
Not in the hands of boys, but in their eyes
Shall shine the holy glimmers of good-byes.
The pallor of girls' brows shall be their pall;
Their flowers the tenderness of patient minds,
And each slow dusk a drawing-down of blinds.

Wilfred Owen, September 1917.

The Yanks are coming

Returning to 6 April 1917, it was announced that the United States had entered
the war against Germany under the command of Major General John J. Pershing
and had joined her allies, Britain, France and Russia. However, many Americans
were not in favour of the US entering the war and wished to remain neutral.

The Great War was the first time in American history that the United States
had sent soldiers abroad to defend foreign soil. When the US declared war
against Germany, that nation had a standing army of 127,500 officers and
soldiers. Once war was declared, the American army attempted to mobilize its
troops very quickly.

The fatigued British and French troops, who had been fighting since August
1914, sorely needed the relief offered by the American forces. Pershing soon
realized how ill-prepared the United States was to transport large numbers of
soldiers and necessary equipment to the front where matériel, rations, equipment
and trained men were in very short supply.

Transport ships were needed to bring American troops to Europe, but they
were already scarce. Therefore the army pressed cruise ships into service, seized
German ships and borrowed allied shipping to transport American soldiers from
New York, New Jersey and Virginia. The mobilization effort taxed the limits of
the American military and required new organizational strategies and command
structures to transport great numbers of troops and quantities of supplies quickly
and efficiently across the Atlantic.

Although the first American troops arrived in Europe in June 1917, the
American Expeditionary Force did not fully participate at the front until October
1917 when the First Division, one of the best-trained divisions of the AEF,
entered the trenches at Nancy in France. Pershing wanted an American force that
could operate independently of the other allies, but his vision could not be realized until adequately-trained troops with sufficient supplies reached Europe.
Training schools in America sent their best men to the front and Pershing also
established facilities in France to train new arrivals for combat.

By the end of the Great War, 4 million men had served in the United States
army, with an additional 800,000 in other military service branches.

Chapter Eight

The Race to the Sea

The 'Race to the Sea', as it subsequently and somewhat inaccurately became known, was conducted from September to November 1914. It was the name given to the period early in the Great War when Britain and Germany became engaged in mobile warfare on the Western Front. In fact, the 'Race to the Sea' was the actual explanation for Great Britain's entry into the war.

Britain was not under any obligation to support France, let alone Russia, in a war with Germany. However, politically it could not afford to alienate either France or Russia, given its reliance on them for the system of global security that it had constructed. Strategically, Britain's maritime power meant that it could not permit a mighty and hostile European power to dominate the Low Countries and so threaten the English.

Without the navy, Britain could not have stayed in the war. Although it fought only one fleet action at Jutland on 31 May 1916, it prevented the German navy from breaking out of the confines of the North Sea. The degree of the test for the transport services in the Great War was the greatest ever seen in any previous conflict. With the continuing unrest in Europe in 1914, the British government had already foreseen the possibility of having to land an expeditionary force in Belgium.

The exceptional strategic importance of the Channel as a tool for a blockade was recognized by the First Sea Lord, Admiral Fisher, during the years before the war had even started. When the conflict did begin, a Royal Proclamation was issued authorizing the Admiralty to requisition 250 merchant ships as transports.

The chiefs of Cunard, Royal Mail, While Star, Blue Funnel and P&O were called together to formulate practical plans. As a result, the British Expeditionary Force reached Europe three days earlier than expected. Despite a certain amount of confusion, an expeditionary force of 210,000 officers and men, 6,200 horses and 100,000 tons of ammunition was landed across the English Channel within a period of sixteen days.

In the early months of the war, many cross-Channel steamers, not required to maintain essential services, were commandeered either as troopships or hospital ships. Ships previously used on the Thames as London pleasure-steamers now proved to be fine sea-going ships that did magnificent work during the war as cross-Channel troopships.

Many small and efficient steamers, manned by well-trained seamen, were requisitioned early in the war. During the conflict, they carried not only troops but horses, artillery, munitions and stores of every kind across the English Channel. During the four years of the Great War the Transport Department

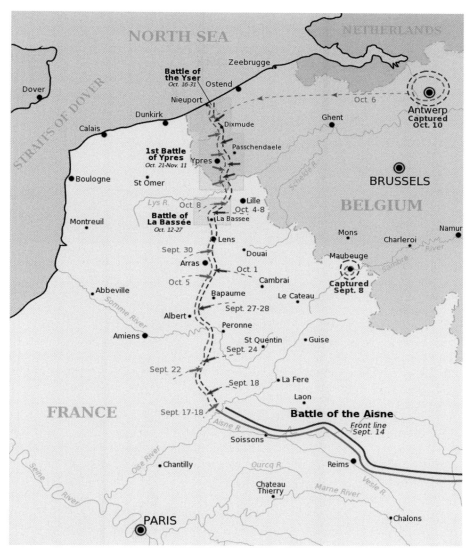

'The Race to the Sea'.

provided 23,700,000 individual passages, in addition to vehicles and guns, not including the work done by British ships for the allies.

The Battle of the Marne, also known as 'the Miracle of the Marne', was a Great War battle fought between 5 and 12 September 1914. It resulted in an allied victory against the German army under Chief of Staff Helmuth von Moltke the Younger. With the German advance stalled at the First Battle of the River Marne, the opponents continually attempted to outflank each other throughout north-eastern France. The battle effectively ended the month-long German offensive

HMS *Warspite* and HMS *Malaya* during the Battle of Jutland.

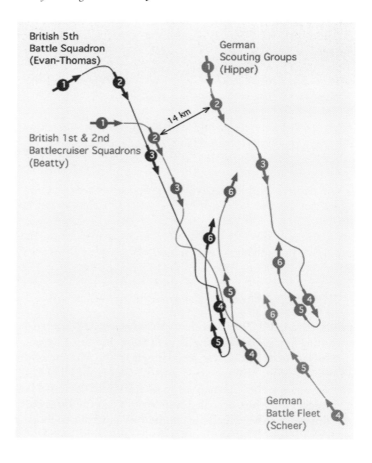

Battle of Jutland
battlecruiser action.

French soldiers waiting for assault behind an embankment, 1914.

that had started the war and had reached the outskirts of Paris. The counter-attack of six French field armies and one British army along the Marne River forced the German Imperial Army to abandon its push on Paris and retreat to the north-east.

The Battle of the Marne was an immense strategic victory for the allies, wrecking Germany's bid for a swift victory over France and forcing it into a protracted two-front war. This brought the forces to positions prepared under British Admiralty guidance, on the North Sea coast in Western Belgium. The nature of operations then changed to extremely large-scale siege warfare. This produced a continuous front line of trench fortifications more than 320km (200 miles) long, which by spring 1915 extended from the coast to the Swiss border.

'The race' had involved a number of battles:

First Battle of the Aisne	13–28 September 1914
First Battle of Picardy	22–26 September 1914
Battle of Albert	25–29 September 1914
First Battle of Artois	27 September–10 October 1914
Battle of La Bassée	10 October–2 November 1914
Battle of Messines	12 October–2 November 1914
Battle of Armentières	13 October–2 November 1914
Battle of the Yser	18 October–30 November 1914

French bayonet charge.

The Imperial German Navy (*Kaiserliche Marine*) could not match the British Grand Fleet, so the Germans developed submarine warfare, which was to become a far greater threat to Britain. The Dover Patrol was set up just before the war began and escorted cross-Channel troopships to prevent submarines from accessing the Channel. This gave the Germans no alternative but to get to the Atlantic by the much longer route around Scotland.

On land, the German army attempted to capture Channel ports, but although the trenches are often said to have stretched 'from the frontier of Switzerland to the English Channel', they actually reached the coast at the North Sea. Much of the British war effort in Flanders was a bloody but successful strategy to prevent the Germans reaching the Channel coast. The route of the race was largely governed by the north-south railways available to each side; the French through Amiens and the Germans through Lille.

At the outset of the war an attempt was made, with naval minefields, to block the path of U-boats through the Dover Strait. By February 1915, this had been augmented by a 25km stretch of light steel netting called the Dover Barrage, which it was hoped would ensnare submerged submarines. After some initial success, the Germans learned how to pass through the barrage, aided by the unreliability of the British mines.

On 31 January 1917, the Germans restarted unrestricted submarine warfare. German Admiralty predictions were that its submarines would defeat Britain by November. This was the most dangerous situation that Britain had had to face to date.

In consequence both sides, most notably the Germans, attempted to gain an advantage by pressing their attacks further north into Flanders. This was the only open flank remaining for any kind of manoeuvre, with each side constantly striving to secure an advantage over the other. All such attempts were thwarted as each side consistently dug in and prepared effective trench defences.

Once the trench lines had reached the coast, the allies switched their focus in the opposite direction. The newly-installed German Chief of Staff Erich Falkenhayn plotted the fierce German attacks. During the battles fought in Picardy, Artois and Flanders, neither side could gain an advantage. With repeated attempts to find the open flank, the line was extended until it reached the coast.

The term 'Race to the Sea' suggests that all the forces began from the Champagne region. In reality, significant German army units arrived from Belgium after the fall of Antwerp and much of the British Expeditionary Force arrived from England by way of the Channel coast of France. The movement towards the North Sea was the result of the continual failed attempts at flanking manoeuvres. Allied attempts to force an extensive German retreat in the wake of the September 1914 battles of the Marne and Aisne had ultimately failed. German defenders had firmly dug in behind previously-prepared trench lines. While the BEF was following previous events to the Marne and returning northwards, there had been coordinated efforts by relatively small forces of the Belgian field and fortress armies.

The French Marines, Royal Marines, the Naval Brigade (reserve sailors half retrained as infantry) and the Royal Naval Air Service (RNAS) mounted in armoured cars and vessels of the Royal Navy. The aim was to screen the Belgian coast and deny the use of its harbours to German forces and their U-boats, with part of the German forces being tied up by the Belgian defence of Antwerp.

Access for supplies from Britain was also needed. The Royal Marines occupied ports such as Ostend, while the RNAS in its armoured cars provided a mobile screen to hinder German movements northwards from the main advance towards Paris.

The flooding of the south-western extremity of Belgium provided an unprepared fortification. The Battle of the River Yser provided an anchor onto which the future Western Front could be locked in by the First Battle of Ypres. The historical importance of the Battle of the Yser is twofold. Firstly, Germany did not manage to defeat the Belgian army and knock Belgium out of the war. Secondly, the German failure to occupy the last corner of Belgium helped to conclude the 'Race to the Sea' and led to the establishment of static trench warfare along the Western Front. The struggle of the Belgian army to hold on to its territory during the remainder of the war – and especially the experiences of ordinary Flemish infantrymen – led to an increase in Flemish national sentiment and the foundation of *Frontbeweging* in 1917. This was the first party of the Flemish Movement.

The importance of the Belgian and French ports such as Calais and Boulogne-sur-Mer in supplying the British Expeditionary Force was to maintain a British army in France. The allies had to have control of the English Channel. To do so, particularly against U-boats, the Strait of Dover had to be controlled. Both Channel coasts had to be occupied by the allies so that a barrage of vessels, mines and nets could be maintained there. Control of the French coast was achieved by coordination between the naval and military forces of Belgium, France and Great Britain with none of the French ports being lost.

To what extent this requirement was understood, before all events, is not clear. It was perhaps so obvious to the Admiralty that it was not stated explicitly. The U-boat threat was well appreciated, but the account of Winston Churchill, who was First Lord of the Admiralty at that time, makes no mention of the need to stop the threat at the Dover Strait. These considerations were crucial to the British Expeditionary Force's return to the north, before the fluid situation there had solidified into a line reaching the coast west of Dunkirk.

The main German forces involved in this aspect of the 'race' came from eastern Belgium, after having been tied up there by operations associated with the resistance of Antwerp. The Belgian army, in conjunction with planning by the British Admiralty and the prepared fortifications of Antwerp and the Yser, played a key role in the progress of the war. During the earlier period, control of the Channel coast was deemed a genuine strategic priority, justifying its tag 'the Race to the Sea'. Ultimately both sides found themselves in possession of certain Channel ports.

'The Race to the Sea' also comprised the last mobile phase of the war up until the German Spring Offensive of March 1918.

The final race to the sea

The German navy had not enjoyed a successful war. Germany's Naval Supreme Commander Admiral Reinhardt Scheer, in conjunction with a few of his close allies including Franz von Hipper and Adolf von Trotha, determined in October 1918 to plan and launch a major attack against the Royal Navy. It was an attempt to restore the lustre of the tarnished German navy.

Scheer was aware that the government of Prince Max von Baden would almost certainly veto plans for a large-scale naval attack at such a late stage of the war. He therefore chose not to inform von Baden of his plans, but word of the impending attack quickly reached the sailors at both key German naval ports, Kiel and Wilmershaven. Determined not to embark upon a mission that they believed would end in disaster and with a belief that the war was approaching its conclusion, many sailors took unauthorized leave or refused to accept orders to put to sea.

Germany began to crumble from within. On 29 October 1918, faced with the prospect of returning to sea, the sailors of the High Seas Fleet stationed at Kiel mutinied. Within a few days, the entire city was under their control and the revolution spread throughout the country. On 30 October, High Seas Fleet Commander Hipper realized that under such circumstances the planned operation could not be executed and it was abandoned. However, this did not bring an end to naval unrest. In spite of the dispatch from Berlin of Kiel's new governor, Gustav Noske, the mutiny began to spiral. Kiel-based commander Prince

The 'end of the line': the Western Front at the end of the Great War reaches the sea near Nieuwpoort, Belgium.

Heinrich of Prussia was obliged to flee under cover of a disguise. Workers' and sailors' councils were formed and actions soon spread to industrial workers at Kiel. Only the U-boat crews remained loyal.

Demands were formulated, calling for both immediate peace and reform. The call spread across Germany and, within the space of a week on 4/5 November, was taken up with revolts in Hamburg, Bremen and Lübeck and, on 7/8 November, in Munich. There was such an air of widespread discontent that on 9 November a group of parliamentary socialists led by Philipp Scheidemann proclaimed the onset of revolutionary action, which finally sealed the fate of both the Kaiser and the end of the Great War.

After the war, British ships carried out the huge task of repatriating British, Dominion and allied troops. At the end of the German advance into France, 'the Race to the Sea' that had begun in September 1914 at Champagne ended at the North Sea in November 1918.

Chapter Nine

1918: The Battle of the Lys

The Battle of the Lys (7–29 April 1918) was also known as the Lys Offensive, the Fourth Battle of Ypres and the Third Battle of Flanders. The Portuguese called it Batalha de La Lys and to the French it was 3ème Bataille des Flandres. The commune is located 16km (10 miles) south-east of Saint-Omer, with several departmental roads by the banks of the Lys and Laquette rivers.

As part of the 1918 German Spring Offensive in Flanders, it was originally planned by General Ludendorff as Operation GEORGE, but became reduced to 'Operation GEORGETTE'. Its objective was to capture Ypres and force the British back to the Channel ports and out of the war.

The German attack zone in Flanders was from about 10km (6.2 miles) east of Ypres to 10km east of Béthune in Belgium. In France, it was about 40km (25 miles) to the south. The front line ran from north-north-east to south-south-west, with the Lys River running from south-west to north-east. It crossed the front near Armentières in the middle of this zone.

The Belgian army held the front in the far north, the British Second Army commanded by General Plumer held it in the north and centre and the British First Army commanded by General Horne held it in the south. The British First Army was a relatively weak force, including several worn-out formations that had been posted to a 'quiet sector'. This included two divisions of the Portuguese Expeditionary Corps, which were undermanned, lacked almost half of their officers, had very low morale and were set to be replaced on the day of the German attack.

In the planning of execution and effects, GEORGETTE was similar to (although smaller than) Operation MICHAEL, fought earlier in the enemy's Spring Offensive. This period incorporated the German attack and subsequent fighting in the valley of the River Lys and in the Flemish hills. During the battle, the Portuguese Expeditionary Corps was effectively wiped out, leaving a 2-mile-wide gap in the British lines.

Field Marshal Haig dispatched the following famous 'Backs to the Wall' message:

> To All Ranks of the British Forces in France
> Three weeks ago today the Enemy began his terrific attacks against us on a 50-mile front. His objects are to separate us from the French, to take the Channel ports and destroy the British Army.
>
> Despite already throwing 106 Divisions into the battle and enduring the most reckless sacrifice of human life, he has as yet made little progress

towards his goals. We owe this to the determined fighting & self sacrifice of our troops. Words fail me to express the admiration, which I feel for the splendid resistance offered by all ranks of our Army under the most trying circumstances.

Many amongst us now are tired. To those I would say that Victory will belong to the side which holds out the longest. The French army is moving rapidly & in great force to our support - - - - - There is no other course open to us but to fight it out! Every position must be held to the last man: there must be no retirement. With our backs to the wall and believing in the justice of our cause, each one of us must fight on to the end. The safety of our Homes and the Freedom of mankind alike depend upon the conduct of each one of us at this critical moment.

D. Haig F.M.

Thursday 11 April 1918.

Despite everything, the British lads remained their usual jovial selves and again found a song they could sing that was suitable for the occasion, *Mademoiselle from Armentières*, also known by its ersatz French line *Hinky Dinky Parlez-vous* and considered to be a risqué song. The tune of the song was believed to be popular with the French army in the 1830s, and the original words told of the liaison of an innkeeper's daughter, named Mademoiselle de Bar le Luc, with two German officers. During the Franco-Prussian war of 1870, the tune was resurrected and

The Portuguese, First World War.

again in 1914 when the Old Contemptibles got to know of it. (It is also the third part of the regimental march of Princess Patricia's Canadian Light Infantry.)

The Australian 1st Division stopped a German attack, whose intention had been to capture Hazebrouck. French reinforcements were sent on their way to the British Kemmel sector, south of Ypres, to help stem the German advance that was threatening Meteren, a commune in the Nord department in northern France. The vital Hazebrouck railhead had to be held, as its loss would have divided the British Expeditionary Force in this area and Field Marshal Haig would not have been able to move his men by rail on a north-south axis, or to the Channel ports.

Early in October 1914, Meteren was occupied by German forces. On 13 October, the British 10th Brigade of the 4th Division captured the enemy's entrenched positions covering the village, which then remained in allied hands until the German offensive of April 1918.

A large gap had to be punched into the line between the join of the 31st and 34th divisions at the site of the 'end of day line'. During the greater part of 12 April 1918, the front line was not continuous. Parts were constantly shifting and divisional staffs did not know at any one time how the front line was situated. The Machine-Gun Companies of the 33rd Division and also the 22nd Corps' Reserve Battalion were rushed into the line and the 33rd Division was ordered into position.

Still fighting with the Vickers gun.

General Pinney personally commanded the divisional Machine-Gun Battalion, which helped turn back the heavy German attack. On 13 April, the 33rd Division held its position against heavy German attacks, but it was lost on 16 April. The sector was then taken over by French troops for a time, but on 19 July the 9th (Scottish) Division (2nd Royal Scots Fusiliers and South African Composite Battalion) recovered the site of the village after a fortnight's bombardment that completely destroyed the houses.

At 17:00 hours on 12/13 April 1918, the 33rd Division had saved Meteren at the Battle of Hazebrouck. The gap was successfully sealed, thus saving the village from being overtaken again. On the afternoon of 12 April 1918, sharp fighting had also taken place in the neighbourhood of Neuve Église. During the night the enemy pressure in this sector had been maintained and extended. By the morning of 13 April the Germans had forced their way into the village, but before noon they were driven out by troops of the 33rd and 49th divisions. It was a most successful counter-attack in which a number of prisoners were taken. During the previous day, the succession of heavy attacks by the 33rd and 34th divisions at Meteren and La Crèche had resulted in the enemy being driven off and with great loss to them. In the evening, further attacks developed on this front and at Neuve Église.

The pressure exercised by the enemy was very great and bodies of German infantry, having forced their way in between La Crèche and Neuve Église, began a strong movement encircling north and east of the former village against the left of the 34th Division. During the early part of the night British troops maintained their positions, but before dawn on 14 April they were under orders to withdraw to a line in front of the high ground known as the Ravelsburg Heights between Bailleul and Neuve Église. During the morning of that day, other troops of the same division were reported to have cleared the village with bombs. However, the enemy persisted in his attacks and by midnight Neuve Église was definitely in German possession.

Other attacks delivered on 14 April between Neuve Église and Bailleul and south-east of Meteren were repulsed. The enemy had again forced his way into the village and heavy and confused fighting took place throughout the night. A party of the 33rd Division, 2nd Battalion, Worcestershire Regiment, maintained themselves in the Mairie until 02:00. Further south, local fighting had taken place on 13 and 14 April at a number of points between Givenchy and the Forêt de Nieppe. In these encounters the enemy met with no success. On the other hand, a local operation carried out by the 4th Division on the evening of 14 April resulted in the recapture of Riez-du-Vinage with 150 prisoners.

Dispatch of Field Marshal Sir Douglas Haig, commander-in-chief of the British armies in France and Flanders:

> The performance of all the troops engaged in this most gallant stand, and especially that of the 4th Guards Brigade, on whose front of some 4,000 yards the heaviest attacks fell, is worthy of the highest praise. No more brilliant exploit has taken place since the opening of the enemy's offensive, though

gallant actions have been without number. The action of these troops, and indeed of all the divisions engaged in the fighting in the Lys Valley, is the more noteworthy because, as already pointed out, practically the whole of them had been brought straight out of the Somme battlefield, were they had suffered severely and had been subjected to a great strain. All these divisions, without adequate rest and filled with young reinforcements which they had had no time to assimilate, were again hurriedly thrown into the fight and, in spite of the great disadvantages under which they laboured, succeeded in holding up the advance of greatly superior forces of fresh troops. Such an accomplishment reflects the greatest credit on the youth of Great Britain, as well as upon those responsible for the training of the young soldiers sent out from home at this time.

On 18 May 1918, the Compulsory Service Act became law in the United States of America. During the spring and summer of that year, lads of the 33rd Division were used to train the American 30th Infantry Division. Throughout 1917 and into 1918, American divisions were usually employed by French and British units to augment in defending their lines and in staging attacks on German positions.

The Battle of Cantigny, fought on 28 May 1918, was the first American offensive of the Great War. The US 1st Division, the most experienced of the seven American divisions then in France and in reserve for the French army near the village of Cantigny, was selected for the attack. The objective of the attack was both to reduce a small salient made by the German army in the front line, but also to instil confidence among the French and British allies in the ability of the inexperienced American Expeditionary Force.

American Expeditionary Force commanders increasingly assumed sole control of American forces in combat. By July 1918, French forces were often assigned to support AEF operations. During the Battle of Saint-Mihiel, beginning 12 September 1918, Pershing commanded the American First Army, comprising seven divisions and more than 500,000 men, in the largest offensive operation ever undertaken by United States armed forces.

The attack at the Saint-Mihiel salient was part of a plan by Pershing in which he hoped that the United States would break through the German lines and capture the fortified city of Metz. It was one of the first American solo offensives in the Great War and the attack caught the Germans in the process of retreating. This meant that their artillery was out of place and the American attack proved more successful than expected. Their strong blow increased their stature in the eyes of the French and British forces, but again demonstrated the critical role of the artillery and the difficulty of supplying the massive armies while they were on the move. The US attack faltered as artillery and food supplies were left behind on the muddy roads.

The attack on Metz was not realized as the Germans refortified their positions and the Americans then turned their efforts to the Meuse-Argonne Offensive. This successful offensive was followed by the Battle of Argonne, lasting from 27 September to 6 October 1918, during which Pershing commanded more than

1 million American and French soldiers. In these two military operations, allied forces recovered more than 200 square miles of French territory from the German army.

The end is in sight

In the last week of September 1918 four separate major allied offensives were launched on the Western Front with the aim of finishing the war before the winter. Officially the four offensives became known as the Battles for the Hindenburg Line and were broken down into the following battles: the Battle of the Canal du Nord, 27 September–1 October (British First and Second Armies); the Battle of the St Quentin Canal, 29 September–2 October (British Fourth and French First Armies); the Battle of Beaurevoir, 3–6 October; and the Battle of Cambrai, 8–9 October.

The Battle of the Canal du Nord

The construction of the Canal du Nord began in 1913 and was intended to link the Oise River to the Dunkirk-Scheldt Canal. However, with the outbreak of the Great War, construction was halted and the work was left in varying stages of completion.

During their retreat, the Germans had made the area along the canal north of Sains-lés-Marquion virtually impassable by taking advantage of the naturally swampy ground and deliberately damming and flooding the entire area. The only passable ground was to the south where a small 4,000-yard (3,700m) section of the canal between Sains-lés-Marquion and Mœuvres remained largely dry on account of its incomplete state. Even in a partially-excavated state, the dry section was still a significant obstacle. The canal itself was approximately 40 yards (37m) wide, with a western bank between 10 and 15 feet (3.0 and 4.6m) high and an eastern bank approximately 5 feet (1.5m) high. The British First Army's General Horne was forced to cease major operations until one could be executed to secure a route enabling him to cross the canal.

As the Hundred Days Offensive of the Great War took place, the battle was fought in the Nord-Pas-de-Calais region of France, along the incomplete portion of the Canal du Nord and on the outskirts of Cambrai. To avoid the risk of having extensive German reserves massed against a single allied attack, the assault along the canal was undertaken as part of a number of closely-sequenced allied attacks at separate points along the Western Front. It began one day after the Meuse-Argonne Offensive, one day before an offensive in the Flanders region of Belgium and two days before the Battle of the St Quentin Canal.

The assault position was along the inter-army boundary between the British First Army and the Third Army. Both were tasked with continuing the advance started with the Battle of the Drocourt-Quéant Line, Battle of Havrincourt and Battle of Epehy. The British First Army was operating in a framework whereby its main task was to lead the crossing of the Canal du Nord and secure the northern flank of the British Third Army as both advanced towards Cambrai. The British Third Army was additionally tasked with securing the Escaut

(Scheldt) Canal so as to be in a position to support the British Fourth Army during the Battle of the St Quentin Canal.

The task of crossing the formidable obstacle of the Canal du Nord required the most careful planning and precisely-organized artillery and engineer support underpinned the success of the attack. At 05:20 on Friday 27 September 1918, following a night of heavy rain, assault troops of the Canadian 4th and 1st divisions left their cramped assembly positions and attacked on a narrow front behind a devastating creeping barrage. The British Third Army's infantry advanced simultaneously, immediately to the right. With dense clouds of smoke blowing towards the enemy lines, the leading Canadian assault troops, assisted by tanks, quickly crossed the canal. Immediately, the Royal Engineers began bridging operations to speed troops, guns and supplies over the captured barrier for the next forward moves. Once over the canal, the plan was to capture the Marquion Line, the villages of Marquion and Bourlon, Bourlon Woods and lastly to secure a general line running from Fontaine-Notre-Dame to Sauchy-Lestrée.

In an attempt to make the Germans second-guess or question the location of the main assault, the 22nd Corps was instructed to engage German positions along the Canal du Nord between Sauchy-Lestrée and Palluel. Likewise, the 7th Corps and the remainder of the 22nd Corps were instructed to carry out minor attacks north of the Scarpe River. This was to prevent the Germans from moving units from that area to the location of the main attack.

If the Canadian Corps was successful in its advance, the intention was to immediately and quickly exploit the territorial gain with the support of the British Third Army's 17th, 6th and 4th corps. After much fierce fighting, later that morning the Marquion Line was passed and the high ground of Bourlon Wood, which was in Canadian hands, was passed by nightfall. The Third Army also made good progress.

Attacks were renewed the next day, although Canadian progress had slowed down somewhat. In the next two days an advance of 6 miles had been made on a 12-mile front. Some 10,000 enemy prisoners and 200 guns were taken. This spectacular success represented a vital preliminary to the Fourth Army's attack on the Hindenburg Line scheduled for 29 September.

The Battle of the St Quentin Canal
This was a pivotal battle of the Great War that involved British, Australian and American forces in the spearhead attack. Under the command of Australian General Sir John Monash, it was a single combined force against the German Hindenburg Line. In spite of heavy German resistance and in concert with other attacks along the length of the line, the assault achieved all its objectives, resulting in the first full breach of the Hindenburg Line. This great offensive convinced the German high command that the writing was on the wall regarding any hope of a German victory.

The 33rd Division had gone over to the offensive in September to see action at the Battle of the St Quentin Canal. The preparatory bombardment had begun on

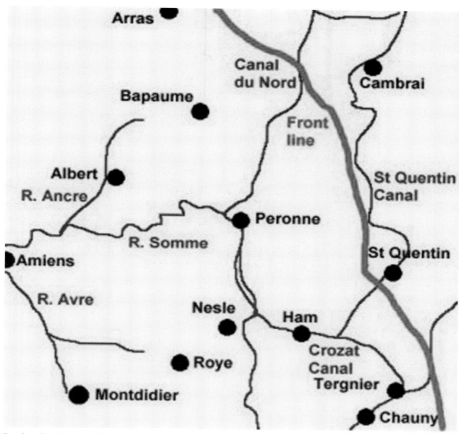

Battle of St Quentin Canal.

the evening of 26 September with gas shells drenching enemy headquarters and gun positions. High explosives wreaked havoc on the German field defences.

American forces were ordered to attack on 27 September to finish clearing German forces from outposts in front of the line. There were only eighteen officers in the twelve attacking companies with the remainder being absent to receive further training. With the corps commander being unsure of where the American troops were and as a result of the confusion it created, the attack had to start on 29 September without the customary and highly-effective artillery support. This had a largely negative effect on the initial operations of the battle. Due to a shortage of American officers, the attack was unsuccessful.

On Sunday 29 September, a series of momentous allied offensives continued with Rawlinson's Fourth Army rejoining the fray. The aim was to break through the main Hindenburg Line between St Quentin and Vendhuile. A strong, well-planned defensive line had been built at relative leisure behind previously-built German front lines.

The defences incorporated the St Quentin Canal and its steep banks. It was at this point that the Hindenburg Line was at its most vulnerable. On the right of the Fourth Army and the French First Army, the attack continued in the St Quentin sector. On the left, both the 4th and 5th corps of the Third Army had attacked at an earlier hour between Vendhuile and Marcoing, with heavy fighting at Villers-Guislain, Gonnelieu and the Welsh Ridge. In the 5th Corps of the Third Army was the 33rd Division, containing the 1st Battalion (98th Brigade) and 18th (Pioneer) Battalion of the Middlesex Regiment. At 05:50, having assembled in rain and darkness, the infantry attacked on a 12-mile front between Holnon and Vendhuile. A portion of the canal went through a 4-mile-long tunnel; an engineering marvel when it was completed in 1810. The core of the defence lay on the canal that was bristling with wire and guns, impervious to tanks and a most formidable barrier for the infantry, except where it ran underground. Through dense fog and smoke and amid the din of machine guns, tank engines and the clamour of the protective artillery barrages, the fight continued.

This time the Australian Corps attacked, with the addition of the 27th and 30th divisions from the American II Corps. They were supported by approximately 150 tanks of the 4th and 5th tank brigades and included the newly-trained American 301st Heavy Tank Battalion. The two US divisions launched the initial attack, with the Australian 3rd and 5th divisions intending to 'leapfrog' through the American forces.

Due to the confusion created during the attack on 29 September, the inexperienced Americans did not clear German positions as effectively as they might have done. This forced the advancing Australians to fight for the ground that the Americans were supposed to have already taken. In the confusion of battle, some American pockets that had been left without effective leadership, willingly went along with the Australians as they advanced. There are documented accounts of soldiers from both nations fighting alongside each other in ad hoc mixed outfits. Their progress was slow and casualties were heavy. Supporting Australian units were drawn into a bitter slogging match for the ridges and by late afternoon had made far less ground than anticipated.

Much greater success was attained by the attack in the south when the 46th Division's 137th Brigade breathtakingly and audaciously overran the German outer defences. They stormed across the canal to Riqueval and captured the surviving bridges in the most dramatic circumstances. Captain A.H. Charlton, 1/6th Battalion the North Staffordshire Regiment, rushed the solid, high-level Riqueval Bridge. He captured a machine-gun post and cut the wires, while an NCO shot the Germans who were trying to explode the mines. Charlton was decorated with the Distinguished Service Order.

By mid-afternoon, when the 32nd Division moved through to continue the advance, the follow-up brigades breached the main Hindenburg system in this sector. Despite some setbacks, the battle turned out to be an outstanding success. The main Hindenburg position had been categorically broken and in an advance of 3.5 miles more than 5,000 prisoners and many guns were captured. Later that same night, Rawlinson issued orders for further forward moves to secure the rest of the Hindenburg Line and the Hindenburg support.

The British high command had fully realized that any success against the formidable defences of the Hindenburg Line could only be achieved with the use of tanks. Defended by fortified machine-gun positions, the British 46th Division crossed the St Quentin Canal and captured 4,200 German prisoners out of a total army of 5,300.

Haig and Joffre at the front.

The Battle of Beaurevoir

In the days immediately following 29 September, General Rawlinson's British Fourth Army sought to exploit its breakthrough of the Hindenburg Line and maintain the allied offensive momentum. Between 30 September and 2 October, Rawlinson's troops gained further ground in difficult piecemeal fighting in which his formations aligned with the leading thrusts of the 9th Corps. The Germans were forced back to their last prepared defensive position at the Beaurevoir Line, roughly 2 miles behind the main Hindenburg system. Eager to push on, Rawlinson initiated a large set-piece assault with the aim of piercing this final barrier. However, despite the desperate state of the enemy, the Fourth Army's attacks met with severe resistance including many counter-attacks.

The fighting for the Beaurevoir Line was ferocious and intense. On 2 October the British 46th and 32nd divisions supported by the Australian 2nd Division planned to capture the Beaurevoir Line (the third line of defences of the Hindenburg Line), the village of Beaurevoir and the heights overlooking the Beaurevoir Line. While the attack succeeded in widening the breach in the line, it was unable to seize the high ground further on. However, the attack had resulted in a 17km breach in the Hindenburg Line. By any measure, and especially by Great War standards, it was a stunning and swift victory.

At 06:05 on Thursday 3 October the assault began with simultaneous attacks by the 9th Australian Corps, well supported by artillery and wire-crushing tanks. On a 10,000-yard attack frontage an advance of 2,000 yards was achieved by nightfall, though neither of the fortified villages of Montbrehain and Beaurevoir was secured. Further attempts to gain these localities failed on the following day as the actions of 4 October, beginning in dense fog, saw very limited gains.

On Saturday 5 October the battle, supported by artillery bombardments and tanks, was renewed with vigour. In the faint dawn light, the Australian 2nd Division moved against Montbrehain and further to the north, the British 25th Division attacked towards Beaurevoir. Toiling through thick barbed-wire entanglements and concentrated German machine-gun fire, the Australian and British infantry pressed forward. Montbrehain was secured by late afternoon and the greater part of Beaurevoir was cleared of the enemy around 19:00 hours. By late evening it was clear that the Beaurevoir Line – the final prepared German defensive position facing Fourth Army – had been broken and open country lay beyond.

Further attacks continued from 6 to 10 October. The British 25th Division managed to clear the fortified villages behind the Beaurevoir Line and capture the heights overlooking it, resulting in a total break in the Hindenburg Line.

Report from *The West Australian* newspaper, Saturday 5 October 1918:

THE BEAUREVOIR LINE. CAPTURE BY AUSTRALIANS.
London, Oct. 4.

Telegraphing from the battle front yesterday, Mr. G. Gilmour says:-
The crumpling of so many other parts of the German front gives the Australians a hope of further successes beyond the Hindenburg line and

assisting in a movement which may develop beyond the present plans and somewhat resemble the Mons retreat reversed. The Australians are already heading towards Le Cateau, and there is the likelihood of the pressure of the Australians and other troops on this sector momentarily effecting a complete break through.

Already the Backbone of the Hindenburg Defence system has been broken along a considerable front. The only line of the Hindenburg system before the Australians east of Bellicourt, Fonsacrane, Beaurevoir, and Mosnieres, is a trench line constituting the last real defence positions and protecting the rear area, which is many miles in extent, and where the enemy will have difficulty in making a stand.

Australian units representing all the States assaulted the Beaurevoir line at dawn on Thursday, advancing from the north-east from positions gained in the neighbourhood of Estrees, some of which were within 1,000 yards of these strongly wired German trenches and then jumping off the line gained in the fighting during the past three days by the Third and Fifth Australian divisions whom General Monash congratulated. The special order says:-
'I wish to convey to the troops my sincere appreciation and thanks for their fine work. Confronted from the outset by a critical situation, and hampered by the inability to make free use of our artillery resources, their divisions have succeeded in completely overwhelming a stubborn defence in a most strongly fortified sector of the west front. This is due to the determination and resource of the leaders, and the grit, endurance and fighting spirit of the troops. Nothing more worthy of praise has been done by the Australians in the war.'

The New South Wales troops after passing through Bellicourt, which the Americans captured showed the Highest Pitch of Fighting Ability, surrounding Nanroy, silencing a score of machine guns and capturing a '77' anti-tank gun which were at the northern corner of the village. This gun was lying in wait for the tanks, whose advance was checked. The New South Wales men immediately summing up the situation arranged with the Americans to guard the flank while they worked forward and round the north side of the village, tackling and bayoneting the machine gunners until they reached the anti-tank gun whose crew with two exceptions, were killed.

Meanwhile other New South Wales troops acted similarly on the southern edge, and finally putting out posts on the farther side where a Victorian unit took over and secured the line. The South Australians and Western Australians, who were cooperating on the right had an equally severe time advanceing against the field guns which were firing at short range. After passing the canal line, where the German dead now lie thickly in the concreted machine-gun posts at the top of the canal the Australians were still under observation from the German gunners on the high ground beyond Mauroy. Yet the Australians, taking advantage of the cover afforded by the newly-won, trench system, pushed on to the east, some reaching Joncourt, which is ours.

The result of the next operation was that the gallant Victorians had probably more hand-to-hand fighting than any other of the Australians. Working out along the old German communication trenches north-east of Bellicourt, they had now gone nearly three miles behind the Hindenburg line. The main fighting occurred round the high ground known as Cabaret Farm. The Victorians resolutely bombed up the trenches, and swarmed into the German positions, killing nearly all the occupants, and gradually pushed out another 1,000 yards. For the next 48 hours little groups of men were feeling their way forward, taking the Sting Out of Numerous Machine-gun Positions, and making sure that no live Germans were overlooked to become a source of trouble. The New South Wales troops, including the unit, which first entered Peronne captured Estrees, where some scattered Germans put up a brief fight. The Western Australians and South Australians delving into the ruins of Joncourt rescued a wounded English lieutenant who had been taken prisoner further south four days previously.

The South Australians, by hard fighting along the strongest German trenches, made steady progress north-east of Bony. The Queenslanders and Western Australians, backing them up, although the going was slow, pressing in the direction of Le Catelet, and then turning more directly to the east. Feeling himself pinched the enemy evacuated a number of positions over the northern end of the underground canal. Already the New South Wales, Victorian, and Tasmanian units had pushed out posts close to the vicinity of the southern outskirts of Le Catelet.

The successful American, Australian, British, and French fighting since Sunday has put our main forces well to the east of the St. Quentin canal. The Australians are making all manner of wagers among themselves regarding the date upon which the Germans will be driven out of France. The signs of German demoralisation continue, notably among the Second Prussian Guards. Batches of this broken division have been taken over a wide front during the past few days.

The Battle of Cambrai
Early October 1918 saw a slow-down in the pace of the combined allied offensives. In the Argonne, on the Aisne and, far to the north in Flanders, logistical difficulties, communications and the onset of autumn rains seriously impeded the transportation of supplies and the forward movement of heavy artillery. Regardless of the problems faced by the Belgian and American forces, Haig remained aggressively confident of what the British armies might achieve within the immediate future. His optimism could only have been enhanced when hearing about the news, made public on 6 October 1918, that the Germans had applied, via US President Woodrow Wilson, for an armistice. Haig seized upon recent British successes, notably the Fourth Army's breaking of the Beaurevoir Line, and sought to further reinvigorate the impetus of allied attacks by initiating a major joint army assault on a 17-mile front, south of Cambrai.

The Hundred Days (18 July–11 November 1918) was the final allied offensive of the Great War on the Western Front. The great German offensives of the spring and summer of 1918 had pushed the allies back for 40 miles and created a series of huge salients in the allied line and the stalemate had been broken. The Battle of Cambrai-St Quentin (27 September–9 October 1918) was the main British contribution to Marshal Foch's all-out attack on the Hindenburg Line. Foch's plan involved a Franco-American attack between Rheims and Verdun (the Meuse-Argonne Offensive), a combined French, British and Belgian attack in Flanders and a mainly British offensive between Cambrai and St Quentin. Here, four allied armies (three British and one French) under the overall command of Douglas Haig would attack the strongest part of the German line.

Haig's four armies, from north to south, comprised the British First Army commanded by General Horne, the Third Army commanded by General Byng, the Fourth Army commanded by General Rawlinson and the French First Army commanded by General Marie-Eugène Debeney. On 25 September the British had twenty-two divisions in the front line, with twenty more in reserve. Among them were two divisions of the American II Corps, the equivalent of four normal divisions. Debeney had a further eight divisions in the line.

The Germans had fifty-seven divisions opposing the British. Germany's General von der Marwitz's Second Army was about to be faced by the British Fourth Army that was gearing up to make the central attack. The German defensive position had been carefully chosen towards the end of 1916. Long sections of it were based on the Canal du Nord and the St Quentin Canal, which ran through steep-sided 60ft-deep cuttings.

The British plan was to launch their main attack between Vendhuile and Bellicourt, where the canal ran through the tunnel. The elite Australian Corps and the fresh US II Corps would carry out the attack. Elsewhere, attacks would be made on the line of the canal. The battle began on 27 September with an attack by the First and Third armies on the Canal du Nord. They advanced 4 miles along a 13-mile front, capturing 10,000 prisoners and clearing the canal.

A preliminary attack on 28 September failed, leaving American troops in an isolated advanced position close to German strongpoints. The artillery bombardment couldn't fire on these strongpoints for fear of hitting the Americans, nor could the first part of the advance be protected by a creeping barrage. The American attack was soon bogged down, forcing the Australians to join in much sooner than expected. The attack on the St Quentin Canal was in serious trouble.

Further south the canal itself was also under attack. The 9th Corps had prepared carefully for the water crossing, providing their men with collapsible boats, life-jackets and even floating piers in the expectation that the Germans would destroy every bridge over the canal. Instead, as the 46th (North Midland) Division advanced towards the canal, they realized that the bridge at Riqueval was still intact. The 137th (Staffordshire) Brigade captured the western bank of the canal, and the 1/6th North Staffords rushed the bridge.

By the end of the day two divisions were across the canal and 9th Corps had captured 4 miles of the main Hindenburg Line. The attack at Riqueval produced one of the most famous pictures of the war. Taken on 2 October 1918 at the conclusion of the fighting, the veterans of 137th Brigade (many still wearing their life-jackets) were photographed on the steep bank of the canal opposite the damaged bridge by British official photographer David McLellan. The following day the Third Army was in the western suburbs of Cambrai and the line of the St Quentin Canal had been captured. General Max von Boehm, commanding the local German army group, was forced to retreat to a new line running south from Cambrai. This line only held for a few days.

At 01:00 on 8 October, in darkness and rain, the first of a series of carefully-phased attacks was led off by the Third Army's 5th Corps in an attempt to seize a northward extension of the Beaurevoir Line which was still in German hands. Though supported by tanks, the infantry's progress was much slowed by uncut enemy barbed wire and intense machine-gun fire. The main Third Army attack was launched at 04:30 behind a protective artillery bombardment. Although the 6th Corps experienced serious mishaps and despite German counter-attacks, the day saw significant advances, some involving the use of their own captured British tanks.

On the right, Fourth Army's attack from south to north, supported by an immense artillery barrage and tanks, commenced at 05:10. French assistance was rather subdued, but hard fighting gained much ground and many prisoners were taken. By the evening, British advances had rendered Cambrai untenable. The British Third, Fourth and the French First armies had launched a set-piece attack along a 17-mile front, forcing the Germans out of the new line. It incorporated many of the newer tactics of 1918, tanks in particular. The attack aimed seriously to imperil the retreating Germans and threaten a decisive breakthrough of their rapidly-improvised defensive line. Although there were three German lines spanning some 7,000 yards (6,400m), the sector had been quiet for some time, so only the German 20th Landwehr and 54th Reserve divisions, supported by no more than 150 guns, lightly garrisoned it.

The Germans defending the sector were unprepared for the 'hurricane bombardment' by 324 tanks, closely supported by infantry and aircraft. The 2nd Canadian Division entering Cambrai encountered only sporadic light resistance. The attack was an overwhelming success and there were fewer than twenty light casualties within an extremely short time. Canadian Frederick Banting (the later co-discoverer of insulin) was wounded in this battle while performing his duties as a medic.

Cambrai was liberated on 9 October and, in a general withdrawal, the Germans were forced to retreat. However, the 2nd Canadian Division rapidly pressed northward, leaving the 'mopping-up' of Cambrai to the 3rd Canadian Division following close behind. When the 3rd Division entered the town on 10 October, they found it deserted and the British Expeditionary Force was on its way back to the battlefields of 1914.

The fighting died down for a few days while the British, having pushed the Germans out of their main defensive lines, prepared to attack their new positions.

A huge mass of 137 Brigade, 46th Division, on the banks of the St Quentin Canal which formed part of the German defence system, the Hindenburg Line, broken on 29 September 1918. They are being addressed by Brigadier General J.C. Campbell VC CMG DSO on the Riqueval Bridge. It remains a compelling image of the Hundred Days campaign and the men who took part in it.

Haig had been determined not to give the enemy time to create strong new lines, and two weeks were needed to prepare for future attacks.

Although the capture of Cambrai was achieved significantly sooner than expected, German resistance north-east of the town stiffened, slowing the advance and forcing the Canadian Corps to dig in.

Cambrai-St Quentin had been a costly battle, with the British suffering 140,000 casualties. They needed time to reorganize and to bring up their artillery. The battle had been Haig's contribution to Marshal Foch's great Autumn Offensive, designed to force the Germans out of the Hindenburg Line. It had succeeded, but the allied advance had then slowed in the face of increasing German resistance and by 10 October the Germans were taking up their new position on the River Selle, close to Le Cateau. They had been obliged to take up this line having been forced out of the Hindenburg Line. In the next five days of fighting and pursuit, the division advanced 11 miles and, at the cost of 536 casualties, inflicted very heavy losses on the enemy as well as capturing 13 field guns and over 1,400 prisoners.

On 17 October Rawlinson's Fourth Army attacked on a 10-mile front south of Le Cateau. Their aim was to reach a line between Valenciennes and the Sambre and Oise Canal. From there the key German railway centre at Aulnoye would be in artillery range. The Fourth Army attack made slow progress, but after two days the right wing had made the biggest advance: a move of 5 miles which was then widened. By the evening of 19 October, the First Army commanded by General Horne had fought its way into a position where it could take part in an attack north of Le Cateau. Early on the morning of 20 October, the First and Third armies attacked north of Le Cateau. By the end of the day they had advanced another 2 miles. In earlier battles, that would have been a dangerous distance to have moved and would have placed the British right in the middle of the German fighting zone. However, the fighting had moved out of the German fortified zone into open country and the Germans had only had ten days to build up their defences on the Selle.

Early in the morning of 23 October, Haig launched a night attack with all three of his British armies: the First, Second and Fourth. This time the British advanced 6 miles in two days. They were now 20 miles behind the rear line of the Hindenburg Line, and the Germans were on the back foot. During the Battle of the Selle, 17–25 October 1918, the British chased the Germans out of a new defensive line they had formed along the River Selle, between Valenciennes and the Sambre.

At zero hour on 26 October, the 18th and 33rd divisions captured Englefontaine and by 02:30 they had taken all objectives. Casualties totalled 109 all ranks. The intense gratitude of the people of Englefontaine found expression in the following message issued to the troops on 26 October: 'The Mairie of Englefontaine, which met this afternoon in a cellar of this village, begs to express to you in the name of the 1,200 inhabitants freed by the British Army its deepest feelings of hearty gratitude.'

That night, the two divisions were relieved by the 38th (Welsh) Division. At dawn on 4 November, seventeen British and eleven French divisions headed the attack. With its resources badly stretched, the Tank Corps could only provide thirty-seven tanks for support. The first barrier to the northern attack was the 60 to 70ft-wide Sambre Canal and the flooded ground around it. The BEF had fought over that very same piece of ground four years earlier.

The 9th and 13th corps reached the canal first. German guns quickly ranged the attackers and, under heavy fire, bodies piled up even before the temporary bridges were properly emplaced. The 1st and 32nd divisions of the 9th Corps lost around 1,150 men in the crossing. After that, amid the small villages and the fields, the German forces defended in depth. It was not until midday that a 2-mile-deep (3km) by 15-mile-wide (24km) breach was secured. Lieutenant Colonel D.G. Johnson was awarded the Victoria Cross for leading the 2nd Battalion Sussex Regiment's crossing of the canal. It was during this battle that the celebrated war poet Wilfred Owen was killed.

Further north, the 4th and 5th corps attacked into Forêt de Mormal. At Le Quesnoy, the German defence was haphazard and the 13th Royal Welsh Fusiliers hardly needed to use their guns, while the 9th Battalion of the 17th Division lost all but two officers and 226 of its 583 soldiers. Despite this, the advance continued and the battle objectives were reached on 4 and 5 November.

After a period of rest at Troisvilles, the 33rd Division re-entered the line on 5 November. It advanced through the Forêt de Mormal and by 7 November was on a line to the east of the Avesnes-Maubeuge road. Once again it was relieved by the Welsh Division and moved to the Sambre valley near Leval.

To the south, the French First Army attacked, capturing the communes of Guise and Origny-en-Thiérache. The Thiérache is a region of France and Belgium united by similar geography and architecture. Located in the north-east of the Aisne department, it also spills over into parts of the Nord and Ardennes departments and the Belgian provinces of Hainaut and Namur. Its overall location is the western foothills of the Ardennes massif. Historically its capital was Guise, although its largest settlement is now Fourmies.

The Castle of Guise was built in the tenth century on the site of an old Gaulish fort. The two Great War battles of Guise left the castle in a pitiful state. The first battle was in August 1914 and the second in November 1917. The damage was so severe that it is now a castle only by name. All that remains to show that it had ever been there are the ruins of the keep and the surrounding brick wall.

From this point, the northern allies advanced relentlessly, sometimes more than 5 miles a day. This resulted in a bunghole bridgehead almost 50 miles (80km) long being made, to a depth of 2–3 miles (3–5km). The British advanced as far between 4–11 November as they had between 27 September and 3 November, until they reached the Armistice Line of 11 November from Ghent, through Hourain, Bauffe and Havré to near Consoire and Sivry.

As the Great War was nearing its end, Valenciennes was liberated. It had remained in German hands from the early days of the war, until it was entered and cleared by the Canadian Corps. The German army had occupied Valenciennes in 1914 and it was only retaken after bitter fighting on 1 and 2 November 1918 by British and Canadian troops. Sergeant Hugh Cairns, a Canadian soldier, was honoured in 1936 when the city named an avenue after him.

Another wartime personality of Valenciennes was Louise de Bettignies. She was fluent in four languages, including German. In 1915 she created and directed the main British intelligence network behind enemy lines, nearly 37 miles (60km) from the front around Lille. She was arrested and imprisoned in Germany at the end of September 1915 and died of mistreatment in September 1918, two months before the Armistice. It is estimated that she saved the lives of nearly 1,000 British soldiers by the remarkably precise information she obtained.

Some 5,000 civilians were found in Valenciennes. In November and December 1918, the 2nd, 57th and 4th Canadian divisions and the 32nd Casualty Clearing Station were posted in the town and the last of them did not leave until October 1919.

German resistance was falling away. Thousands of prisoners were being taken and new attacks quickly prepared. The French First Army and the British First, Third and Fourth armies were tasked with advancing from south of the Condé Canal along a 30-mile (48km) front towards Maubeuge-Mons, threatening Namur. American forces were clearing the forest of Argonne. If this was a success, it would disrupt the German efforts to re-form a shortened defensive line along the Meuse. Several United States army soldiers earned the Medal of Honor there, including Sergeant Alvin C. York, who was portrayed in the 1941 Hollywood movie *Sergeant York* by Gary Cooper.

By 9 November the Canadians had reached the outskirts of Mons. On the morning of 11 November they entered the city, just in advance of the Armistice.

Ironically, this had been the scene of one of the first major battles of the Great War. In 1914 at Mons it was the arrival of the first British soldiers there who discovered the Germans on the Soignies Road. That first encounter introduced Mons to the conflict. So the first involvement of British soldiers had taken place in Mons! Four years later, on 11 November 1918, Canadian troops liberated the city and it became 'the First and the Last' of the Great War for the Commonwealth armies having been the site of the first British 'withdrawal' back in the autumn of 1914.

Liberty!
The liberation meant everything to those Belgian civilians who had suffered so much for so long. One only has to view film footage of the people greeting their Canadian liberators to realize what this action meant to the people of Mons after being in the hands of the Germans for more than four whole years.

In November 1918, the 33rd Division finished the war in the Sambre valley. Ypres had been embroiled in war for more than four years, from 1914 to November 1918, and almost every building had been razed to the ground.

Chapter Ten

Armistice

The massive German attacks in the spring of 1918 came close to breaking through the allied lines and winning the war. Instead, their repulse created a much longer line held by far fewer war-weary troops.

A British counter-attack on 8 August 1918 turned the tide and from then on the allies were advancing. By late September the British were approaching the Hindenburg Line and it was here that the British Fourth Army assigned the attached US 2nd Corps to attack. The 2nd Corps was made up of the 27th and 30th divisions, both National Guard Units, and this line only held for a few days.

The final allied push towards the German border began on 17 October 1918. Towards the first week of November 1918, during the 'war to end all wars', it was deemed by each side to be a draw and they both settled down to a protracted bout of further trench warfare. This was punctuated at various points by concerted allied attempts to decisively puncture the enemy line, as they had done at the Somme, the Aisne and at Passchendaele.

As the British, French and American armies advanced, the alliance between the Central Powers began to collapse. Turkey signed an armistice at the end of October and Austria and Hungary followed suit on 3 November 1918. On 9 November the Kaiser abdicated and slipped across the border into The Netherlands and future exile. A German republic was declared and peace feelers were extended out towards the allies.

Ferdinand Foch, together with Joseph Joffre and Philippe Pétain, had become the most prominent French military officers in the war. At a rail siding just outside of Compiegne, three days of intense negotiations were in progress. A German delegation had been brought to the personal carriage of Ferdinand Foch, who was Marshal of France and overall commander of allied forces during the closing months of the Great War. The Germans were ordered by their government in Berlin to sign any terms put on the table by the allies. Serious social upheaval had forced the Berlin government to give out this instruction, people having taken to the streets as a result of chronic food shortages caused by the British naval blockade.

The German delegation, led by Matthias Erzberger, signed the terms of the Armistice. This was done at 05:10 on 11 November 1918 in a railroad car parked in a French forest near the front lines, and the date would become known as 'Armistice Day'.

However, the cease-fire itself did not take effect until 11:00 hours to allow the information to travel to the many parts of the Western Front. Despite that, on many parts of the front, fighting continued as normal. Even as the people of Paris,

'How much longer?'

American troops in north-eastern France cheer after hearing that the Armistice has been signed.

The allied representatives at the signing of the Armistice. Ferdinand Foch (second from right), is seen outside his railway carriage in the forest of Compiègne.

London and New York were celebrating the end of the fighting, casualties and tragic and unfortunate deaths were still occurring.

Technology had allowed the news to reach the world's capital cities and by 05:40 celebrations had begun, even before very many soldiers knew about the Armistice. Rumours of an armistice had begun to circulate within the ranks without any of the details yet being known. Most British forces, as well as the Germans, had believed that the land occupied at 11:00 on 11 November would remain occupied. On the Western Front, many tens of thousands of soldiers assumed that 11 November 1918 was just another day in the war and officers continued to order their men into combat.

Quite a number of the final casualties were at Mons in Belgium, one of the first major sites of battle in 1914. In a cemetery just outside Mons in the village of Nouvelle, there are nine graves of British soldiers. Five are from August 1914, while four are dated 11 November 1918, the day it was supposed to be 'all over'.

Counting the cost
The Commonwealth War Graves Commission (CWGC) records show that 863 Commonwealth soldiers died on 11 November 1918, although this figure also includes those who died on that day from wounds previously received.

The last British soldier killed in the Great War was Private George Edwin Ellison of the 5th Royal Irish Lancers. He was killed at Mons at 09:30, just ninety minutes before the cease-fire. He had also fought at Mons in 1914.

The last French soldier to die was Augustin Trebuchon from the 415th Infantry Regiment. He was a runner and was in the process of taking a message to his colleagues at the front informing them of the cease-fire. He was hit by a single shot and killed at 10:50. In total, seventy-five French soldiers were killed on 11 November, but their graves are dated 10 November 1918. Two theories have been forwarded for this discrepancy. The first is that by stating they died on 10 November, before the war had ended, there could be no question about their family's entitlement to a war pension. The other theory is that the French government wanted to avoid any form of embarrassment or political scandal should it ever become known that so many had died on the last day of the war.

The last Canadian to die was Private George Lawrence Price of the Canadian Infantry (2nd Canadian Division) who was killed at Mons at 10:58. Officially, Price was the last Commonwealth soldier to be killed in the Great War.

In particular, the Americans took heavy casualties on the last day of the war. This was because their commander, General John Pershing, believed that the Germans had to be severely defeated at a military level to effectively 'teach them a lesson'. By the time Germany had signed the Armistice, the American Expeditionary Force had evolved into a modern, combat-tested army recognized as one of the best in the world. Pershing regarded the terms of the Armistice as being too soft on the Germans. Therefore he supported those commanders who wanted to be proactive in attacking German positions, even though he knew that an Armistice had been signed.

The Americans suffered heavy casualties attempting to cross the River Meuse on the night of 10/11 November, with the US Marines alone suffering 1,100 casualties. They could have crossed the river unhindered – and with no casualties – if Pershing had waited until 11:00. The 89th US Division was also ordered to attack and take the town of Stenay on the morning of 11 November. Stenay was the last town captured on the Western Front but at a cost of 300 casualties.

The last American soldier killed was Private Henry Gunter who was killed at 10:59. Officially, Gunter was the last man to die in the Great War. His unit had been ordered to advance and take a German machine-gun post. It is said that even the Germans, who knew that they were literally minutes away from a cease-fire, tried to stop the Americans attacking. However, when it became obvious that this had failed, they fired on their attackers and Gunter was killed. His divisional record stated: 'Almost as he fell, the gunfire died away and an appalling silence prevailed.'

Information about German casualties is more difficult to ascertain. However, it may well be the case that the last casualty of the Great War was a junior German officer called Tomas, who approached some Americans to tell them that the war was over and that they could have the house he and his men were just vacating. However, no one had told the Americans that the war had ended and, because of a communications breakdown, Tomas was shot as he approached them just after 11:00.

Officially, more than 10,000 men were killed, wounded or went missing on 11 November 1918. The Americans alone suffered more than 3,000 casualties. When these losses became public knowledge, such was the anger at home that Congress held a hearing regarding the matter. In November 1919, Pershing faced a House of Representatives Committee on Military Affairs that examined whether senior army commanders had acted appropriately in the last few days of the war. No one was ever charged with negligence and Pershing remained un-apologetic, still convinced that the Germans had got off lightly under the terms of the Armistice.

He also stated that, although he knew about the timing of the Armistice, he simply did not trust the Germans to carry out their obligations. He therefore, as commander-in-chief, ordered the army to carry on as it would normally do and as any 'judicious commander' would have done. Pershing also pointed out that he was merely carrying out the orders of the Allied Supreme Commander, Marshal Ferdinand Foch, who had ordered that the allies were to 'pursue the field of greys (Germans) until the last minute'.

The terms of the Armistice agreement called for the cessation of fighting along the entire Western Front to begin at precisely 11:00 hours on the morning of 11 November 1918. After more than four years of bloody conflict, the Great War was at an end. In London, Big Ben was rung for the first time since the start of the war in August 1914. In Paris, gas lamps were lit for the first time in four years.

By 4 December 1918 the 33rd Division had moved to Montigny (which is the name, or part of the name, of several communes in northern France) and was inspected by King George V. On 17 December the division was at a rest camp in the village of Hornoy, which is west of Amiens and about 17 miles south of Abbeville.

The Great War was the most devastating conflict in British military history. Almost 4,000,000 men were deployed in the British army alone. Nearly 800,000 men were killed and over 2,000,000 wounded. In the early stages of the war the British Expeditionary Force was virtually destroyed, but volunteer forces and then conscripted men reinforced and rebuilt it.

The devastation was nowhere more apparent than on the main Western Front, where the German army had placed its main body and where that army alone could be decisively engaged. Out of more than 8.5 million men of the British Empire who put on a uniform during the Great War, almost 5.5 million served, at some time or other, on the Western Front. The remains of some of the trenches are still very much in evidence 100 years after being dug by our reluctant lads who had donned khaki in order to show their allegiance to their country.

Dulce Et Decorum Est
Bent double, like old beggars under sacks,
Knock-kneed, coughing like hags, we cursed through sludge,
Till on the haunting flares we turned our backs
And towards our distant rest began to trudge.
Men marched asleep. Many had lost their boots
But limped on, blood-shod. All went lame; all blind;
Drunk with fatigue; deaf even to the hoots
Of tired, outstripped Five-Nines that dropped behind.
Gas! Gas! Quick, boys! – An ecstasy of fumbling,
Fitting the clumsy helmets just in time;
But someone still was yelling out and stumbling,
And flound'ring like a man in fire or lime …
Dim, through the misty panes and thick green light,
As under a green sea, I saw him drowning.
In all my dreams, before my helpless sight,
He plunges at me, guttering, choking, drowning.
If in some smothering dreams you too could pace
Behind the wagon that we flung him in,
And watch the white eyes writhing in his face,
His hanging face, like a devil's sick of sin;
If you could hear, at every jolt, the blood
Come gargling from the froth-corrupted lungs,
Obscene as cancer, bitter as the cud
Of vile, incurable sores on innocent tongues, –
My friend, you would not tell with such high zest
To children ardent for some desperate glory,
The old Lie: Dulce et decorum est
Pro patria mori.
Wilfred Owen (1893–1918).

This poem was written between 8 October 1917 and March 1918. Wilfred was killed in battle aged 25 on 4 November 1918 at the Sambre–Oise Canal, France. He was one of Great Britain's greatest war poets. After recovering from previous wounds, he was sent back to the trenches in September 1918. In October, he won the Military Cross for seizing a German machine gun and using it to kill a number of Germans. On 4 November 1918, he was shot and killed near the village of Ors. The news of his death reached his parents' home as the church bells were ringing to celebrating the Armistice on 11 November 1918.

Chapter Eleven

Those Who Came Home

There were fears that Germany would not accept the terms of any peace treaty and, therefore, the British government decided it would be wise to be able to quickly recall trained men in the eventuality of the resumption of hostilities. Soldiers who were being demobilized, particularly those who had agreed to serve 'for the duration', were at first posted to Class Z Reserve that was authorized by an Army Order of 3 December 1918. They returned to civilian life but with an obligation to return if called upon. Authorization was given in early December 1918 for all classes of the P and W Reserves (with the exception of conscientious objectors in the latter case) to be discharged forthwith, irrespective of their original terms of engagement.

On 28 February 1919, Divisional Headquarters moved to Le Havre. Demobilization continued throughout the first months of 1919 and on 30 June 1919, the 33rd Division ceased to exist. All those brave lads of the Church Lads' Brigade who had managed to survive the Great War came home. The Z Reserve was abolished on 31 March 1920.

Every lad from the CLB who served in the Great War was awarded the 1914–15 Star, the British War Medal 1914–1918 and the Allied Victory Medal. Report in the *News of the World*, 26 October 1919:

> Around one of the oldest Field Marshals in the British Army last night, sat 200 young and hefty fellows to celebrate the first re-union dinner of the survivors of the 16th Battalion of The King's Royal Rifles Corps (Church Lads' Brigade Battalion) formed in the opening days of the war.
>
> In proposing the toast to 'The Battalion', Lord Grenfell pointed out that he had nothing but praise for their splendid gallantry in France, notably at High Wood, Bullecourt, and Neuve Eglise.
>
> A famous general had told him that, at the latter place, it was to a large extent due to the gallant fighting of the battalion that the ill attempt of the German Army to force its way through to Calais was defeated.

Seven good men and true
Of those eight brave lads who travelled to France in November 1915, not knowing what their fate was to be, all but one came home. The seven had left their homes as young lads, ready to experience a new life and discover new surroundings. They found a country torn up by a vicious war. They ate and slept in rat-infested mud-holes for days on end. They came home, battered and bruised in mind, body and spirit, but they had become MEN.

Service medals.

Rifleman Harry Barber C428 was badly wounded at the Battle of the Somme and lost one of his arms. No doubt he had to undergo months of treatment and was eventually fitted with a prosthetic limb, which he wore for the rest of his life. Because of this he struggled to find work, but was eventually given a job at Cressbrook Mill. He married Maria Longstone in 1917 and they had one son (Harry Stanley) who was born in 1924. Harry senior lived for many years in Wesley Cottage, next door to Tideswell Methodist Church in Fountain Square. In his later life he was the caretaker there. Harry died in 1973 aged 82 and is buried with his wife in Tideswell Cemetery.

Rifleman Joseph Isaac Boller C730 returned home from the war suffering from the effects of being gassed. He returned to his job as a nickel-plater in the jewellery quarter of Birmingham. However, this was to be short-lived as he developed tuberculosis. Joe was engaged to be married and while waiting for Joe to come home from the war, his girlfriend already had her wedding dress hanging on the back of her bedroom door. As his condition worsened, he refused to marry her, knowing that he would never recover. Joe died at home on 18 March 1920 aged 25. He is buried in the family grave at Witton Cemetery in Birmingham.

Captain Jesse Robert Brightmore C480 was also gassed in the war and came back to England lying on his back on a stretcher and spent time in Wharncliffe War Hospital, Sheffield. He married his cousin, Emily Walton, who was headmistress at Litton Mill School in 1918 and they had one son, Vernon Jesse Robert. Eventually, Jesse returned to work for the Westminster Bank in Manchester, where he became chief cashier. He retired in 1954 aged 60. In later life he was chairman of Derbyshire County Council. Jesse died from a severe stroke in March 1965 aged 71. He is buried in Tideswell Cemetery.

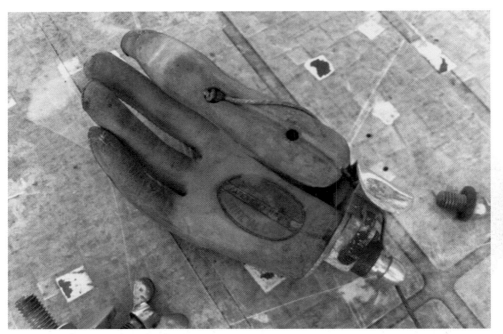

A photo of Harry Barber's hand.

Joseph I. Boller's grave.

Tideswell ex-servicemen's club, with possibly Jesse Brightmore standing.

Rifleman Matthew Ferguson C1647 married Margaret Dunham in 1923 and they had a son, John T., born in 1923 and a daughter, Ann, born in 1925.

When Rifleman Sydney Goodwin C432 returned from the war it is believed he opened a grocer's shop. He was a keen gardener and became a judge at local horticultural and agricultural shows. He was a co-founder of the Tideswell Well Dressing Society in 1946 and was also an active local councillor. He married Edith Bramwell in 1920. Later he moved to Winchester, where he got a job as a gardener at the Royal Hotel. Sydney died in Winchester in 1978 at the age of 85.

When Rifleman Henry Thomas Gwinnell C1316 joined the army, he was only 17 years old. He was stationed at Uxbridge, where he met Mildred Annie Sims. When he went off to war in 1915 Mildred was pregnant and gave birth to Alice Lucy. Henry returned from the war and married Mildred in 1920. They had another daughter, also named Mildred, in 1921. The family lived at 2 Haig Cottages, Uxbridge for the rest of Henry's life. He died on 24 June 1937, aged 40.

Lance Corporal John Henry Norman C657 returned to his home town of Worksop in Nottinghamshire. He married Doris Brown in 1925 at Basford in that county. They had a daughter, Annie M. Norman, in 1926. He died on 31 August 1957, aged 64.

Sydney Goodwin outside his greenhouse.

Other notable survivors ...
Field Marshal Francis Wallace Grenfell GCMG (1841–1925). During the remainder of his life, he devoted himself to work on behalf of the Church Lads' Brigade, the Royal Horticultural Society, of which he was president, and various other voluntary services. He was a colonel commandant of the 60th Rifles from 1899 until his death on 27 January 1925 at Windlesham, Surrey.

Major General Herman James Shelley Landon, CB, CMG (23 August 1859–16 October 1948). From August 1917 to May 1918 Herman Landon commanded the 64th Division in the Home Forces. His health had forced him to retire from active service and he finally retired from the army on 19 August 1919. After the war, he was appointed a Companion of the Order of St Michael and St George (CMG). He also received the Croix de Guerre and was appointed a Commander of the Belgian Order of Leopold. Following his death in October 1948, his obituary was published in *The Times* on 20 October 1948.

Major General Sir Reginald John Pinney, KCB (2 August 1863–18 February 1943). The 33rd Division finished the war in the Sambre valley. In February 1919, with the division mostly demobilized, the major general retired from the army, aged 56, after thirty-five years of service. Following the end of his army career, he took up residence at Racedown Manor in the village of Broadwindsor, Dorset, where he lived the life of a retired country gentleman. He became a Justice of the Peace and Deputy Lieutenant for the county, and served as its High Sheriff in 1923. He did not return to an active army post, although he held the ceremonial colonelcy of the Royal Fusiliers from 1924 to 1933, as well as the honorary colonelcy of the Dorset Coastal Brigade, Royal Artillery, and the 4th (Territorial) Battalion of the Dorsetshire Regiment.

Reginald Pinney died on 18 February 1943, survived by his wife and five of his children. All three of his sons served in the Second World War; his eldest son, Bernard, was killed in action in November 1941, commanding J Battery Royal Horse Artillery at Sidi Rezegh in North Africa. His daughter Rachel, who hit the headlines in the interwar years, was part of the notorious Ferguson's Gang, an anonymous and enigmatic group who raised funds to support the National Trust's acquisition of properties.

A scholarship fund to provide access to higher education for the children of Dorset's ex-servicemen was established in Pinney's name in June 1943, and still remains in existence.

Siegfried Sassoon (1886–1967). In March 1919, Sassoon resigned his commission and left the army. He spent a brief period as literary editor of the *Daily Herald* before going to the United States and travelling the length and breadth of the country on a speaking tour. Sassoon had a number of homosexual affairs, but in 1933 surprised many of his friends by marrying Hester Gatty. They had a son, George, but the marriage broke down after the Second World War. He continued to write both prose and poetry. In 1957, he was received into the Catholic Church. On 1 September 1967, Siegfried Sassoon died one week before his 81st birthday of stomach cancer and is buried at St Andrew's Church, Mells, Somerset, close to Ronald Knox. Ronald Arbuthnott Knox (17 February 1888–24 August 1957) was an English priest and theologian. He was also a writer and a regular broadcaster for BBC Radio.

Field Marshal Douglas Haig, 1st Earl Haig (1861–1928). Haig served as commander-in-chief of British Home Forces from 1918 until his retirement in

Flanders poppy.

1921. He also helped establish the Royal British Legion and worked hard to raise funds for its charity. The Earl Haig Fund is a charity set up in 1921 to assist ex-servicemen. Today the Haig Fund continues to support veterans from all conflicts and other military actions involving British armed forces. Its members sell reproduction Flanders poppies in the weeks before Remembrance/Armistice Day. The 'Haig Fund' is no longer inscribed on the black button in the centre of each poppy; instead it reads 'Poppy Appeal'. Haig was created an Earl in 1919 and died on 29 January 1928.

*   *   *

In October 1916 the British government set up a committee regarding the idea for a commemorative memorial plaque that could be given to the relatives of men and women whose deaths were attributable to the Great War of 1914–18. In October 1917 it was announced that the committee had also decided to issue a commemorative scroll to the next of kin in addition to the bronze plaque. One of those approached for suggestions of the wording on the scroll was Rudyard Kipling, whose only son John was missing in action, believed killed, at the Battle of Loos in late September 1915.

Commemorative memorial plaque.

The accepted final wording agreed by the committee was:

He whom this scroll commemorates was numbered among those who, at the call of King and Country, left all that was dear to them, endured hardness, faced danger, and finally passed out of the sight of men by the path of duty and self-sacrifice, giving up their own lives that others might live in freedom. Let those who come after see to it that his name be not forgotten.

The National Memorial Arboretum

Hundreds of cemeteries in France and Belgium are home to the graves of thousands of brave lads who travelled across the sea to a strange country that had previously meant very little to them. Their quest was to protect Britain and put up an incredible fight to free other nations from the tyrannical rule of Germany.

On a 150-acre site in Staffordshire, close to the heart of England, is a living and growing tribute to the servicemen who sacrificed so much to retain the freedom

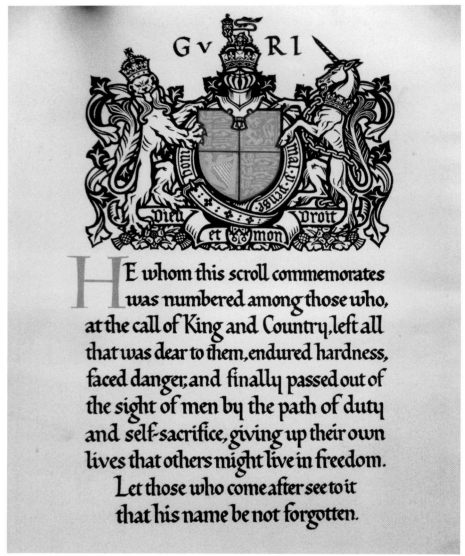

E whom this scroll commemorates was numbered among those who, at the call of King and Country, left all that was dear to them, endured hardness, faced danger, and finally passed out of the sight of men by the path of duty and self-sacrifice, giving up their own lives that others might live in freedom. Let those who come after see to it that his name be not forgotten.

Commemorative scroll.

of Great Britain and her people. The landscape is ever-changing, land and rivers meet, and wildlife, birds, trees and wild flowers thrive. Behind every monument and memorial are stories of heroism, selfless devotion and sadness.

The Orange Zone (Plot 206), is the Memorial Garden of the Church Lads' & Church Girls' Brigade. The Church Lads' & Church Girls' Brigade Memorial Garden was a project undertaken by members of the Brigade Association. It is located next to the south wall of the Millennium Chapel of Peace and Forgiveness that holds two minutes of silent remembrance every day. The garden is one of the first memorials to be created after the National Memorial Arboretum was opened to the general public.

The garden was dedicated on 22 June 2002 by the Right Reverend Paul Barber, Honorary Assistant Bishop in the Diocese of Bath and Wells (Bishop Barber is a Vice President of the Brigade Association). Also dedicated during the ceremony was the Lectern Bible, donated by the Brigade Association for use in the Millennium Chapel in Advent 2001.

Having been offered a very rough rectangular plot of land, there was much work to be done but with the help of contractors the garden was levelled off and block-paved pathways now take the form of a Christian cross. Its design was the idea of Avril Scott of Emmanuel Parish Church, Gorton, who is also a member of the Emmanuel Gorton Church Lads' and Church Girls' Brigade Company.

Twenty-two berberis shrubs were selected to represent the brigade's military past but, more specifically, to represent its twenty-two Victoria Cross recipients. The shrubs are purple and similar in colour to the medal ribbons awarded to Victoria Cross recipients, i.e. 'The Colour for Valour'. The berberis plants are of a variety that will not grow higher than 18 inches. This is to ensure that people sitting on the benches have an unrestricted view over the plants to the rest of the Arboretum.

The Christian cross form of the pathways represents the brigade's present path through life. In a sense we all have to 'walk the Cross'. The two rowan trees

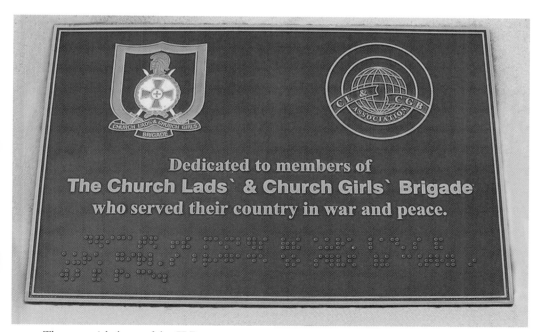

The memorial plaque of the CLB.

The garden was dedicated on 22 June 2002 by the Right Reverend Paul Barber, Honorary Assistant Bishop in the Diocese of Bath and Wells.

represent the brigade's future because, as they grow, they will always be greater than the past.

Originally the garden had two rustic benches donated by the London Branch of the Brigade Association, but after six years of valuable service these were replaced in 2008 by more modern benches with cast-iron end frames complete with the brigade logo on the end of each. The end frames are also painted green to commemorate the uniform worn by the King's Royal Rifle Corps.

Although the brigade is a Church of England organization, its Memorial Garden is intended to be a place where people of other Christian denominations and other faiths can feel comfortable and welcome. The brigade feels honoured to have been allocated such a wonderful location, which they see as an extension to the chapel. Effectively it is the chapel's churchyard, where people can sit to relax and contemplate in the normally peaceful surroundings.

The Brigade Memorial Garden would never have been created without the help of its many sponsors. In recent years, the brigade has held its own annual Service of Remembrance in the Millennium Chapel and in the Brigade Memorial Garden where wreaths are laid to honour the fallen. Those members of the brigade family who have passed away in the preceding twelve months are also remembered by the reading of names being added to the Roll of Remembrance. This service takes place on the nearest Saturday to 11 November, which is the anniversary of the opening of the first Brigade Company at St Andrew's, Fulham in 1891.

The Church Lads' Brigade is one of the founding members of the National Council for Voluntary Youth Services (NCVYS). The Church Lads' and Church Girls' Brigade remains a member by virtue of its work towards the personal and social development of young people. The Church Lads' Brigade showed its strength during the first part of the twentieth century when it was at its peak as a major youth organization. To commemorate the Great War link to the King's Royal Rifle Corps, Church Lads' Brigade members wear a rifle green tie as part of their uniform to this day.

The brigade's patron saint is St Martin of Tours. A banner depicting St Martin, which was presented by the brigade in 1921 to honour those members who lost their lives in the Great War, is kept at Westminster Abbey.

Memorial services are held on the nearest Saturday to 11 November, the anniversary of the opening of the first Brigade Company at St Andrew's, Fulham in 1891.

The Church Lads' Brigade at a drum parade competition at Belle Vue speedway track in 1968.

St Martin's banner.

The banner of St Martin is of white silk brocade embroidered in rich silks with designs of roses, thistles, shamrocks and leeks, with a figure of St Martin on horseback in the centre in the act of dividing his cloak with the beggar. Designed by the Reverend E.E. Dorling, the banner was presented in November 1921 by the Church Lads' Brigade as a memorial to those who died in the Great War. The Latin inscription on the reverse can be translated as 'In eternal memory of members who recently so splendidly died in war for God, King and Country the CLB gave this banner 1921.'

Line of Descent

1755	The 62nd (Royal American) Foot
1757	renumbered The 60th (Royal American) Foot
1824	The 60th, Duke of York's Own Rifle Corps
1830	The 60th, The King's Royal Rifle Corps
1881	The King's Royal Rifle Corps
1958	redesignated 2nd Green Jackets (The King's Royal Rifle Corps)
1966	succeeded by 2nd Battalion, The Royal Green Jackets (The King's Royal Rifle Corps)
1968	renamed 2nd Battalion, The Royal Green Jackets 1992: renamed 1st Battalion, The Royal Green Jackets 2007: succeeded by 2nd Battalion, The Rifles

Order of Battle of the 33rd Division

98th Brigade

18th Bn, the Royal Fusiliers	(1st Public Schools) to 19th Bde, 27 Nov 1915
19th Bn, the Royal Fusiliers	(2nd Public Schools) left 28 Feb 1916
20th Bn, the Royal Fusiliers	(3rd Public Schools) to 19th Bde, 27 Nov 1915
21st Bn, the Royal Fusiliers	(4th Public Schools) left 28 Feb 1916
1st Bn, the Middlesex Regiment	from 19th Bde, 27 Nov 1915
2nd Bn, the Argyll & Sutherland Highlanders	from 19th Bde, 27 Nov 1915
4th Bn, the King's (Liverpool Regiment)	joined 27 Feb 1916
1/4th Bn, the Suffolk Regiment	joined 28 Feb 1916, left Feb 1918
98th Machine Gun Company	joined 28 Apr 1916, moved to 33rd Bn, MGC, 19 Feb 1918
98th Trench Mortar Battery	formed by 30 Jun 1916

99th Brigade

Brigade left to join 2nd Division on 25 Nov 1915

17th Bn, the Royal Fusiliers	(Empire)
22nd Bn, the Royal Fusiliers	(Kensington)
23rd Bn, the Royal Fusiliers	(1st Sportsmen's)
24th Bn, the Royal Fusiliers	(2nd Sportsmen's)

100th Brigade

13th Bn, the Essex Regiment	left 22 Dec 1915 (West Ham)
16th Bn, the Middlesex Regiment	left 25 Feb 1916 (Public Schools)
17th Bn, the Middlesex Regiment	left 8 Dec 1915 (1st Football)
16th Bn, the King's Royal Rifle Corps	(Church Lads' Brigade)
1st Bn, the Queen's	joined 15 Dec 1915, to 19th Bde, 14 Feb 1918
2nd Bn, the Worcestershire Regiment	
1/6th Bn, the Cameronians	joined and left Feb 1916
100th Machine Gun Company	joined 28 Apr 1916, moved to 33rd Bn, MGC, 19 Feb 1918
1/9th Bn, the Highland Light Infantry	joined 29 May 1916
100th Trench Mortar Battery	formed by 13 Jun 1916

19th Brigade

Brigade joined from 2nd Division on 25 Nov 1915

1st Bn, the Middlesex Regiment	to 98th Bde, 27 Nov 1915
2nd Bn, the Argyll & Sutherland Highlanders	to 98th Bde, 27 Nov 1915
2nd Bn, the Royal Welsh Fusiliers	left 4 Feb 1918
1st Bn, the Cameronians	
1/5th Bn, the Cameronians	became 5/6th Bn, May 1916
18th Bn, the Royal Fusiliers	from 98th Bde, 27 Nov 1915, left 26 Feb 1916
20th Bn, the Royal Fusiliers	from 98th Bde, 27 Nov 1915, disbanded Feb 1918

19th Machine Gun Company	formed 24 Feb 1916, moved to 33rd Bn, MGC, 19 Feb 1918
19th Trench Mortar Battery	formed by 24 Jun 1916
1st Bn, the Queen's	joined from 100th Bde, 14 Feb 1918

Divisional Troops

18th Bn, the Middlesex Regiment	joined as Divisional Pioneer Battalion, Jul 1915 (1st Public Works Pioneers)
19th Motor Machine Gun Battery	joined Nov 1915 but left and moved independently to France, 6 Feb 1916
248th Machine Gun Company	joined 21 Jul 1917, moved to 33rd Bn, MGC, 19 Feb 1918
33rd Battalion MGC	formed 19 Feb 1918

Divisional Mounted Troops

F Sqn, the North Irish Horse	joined Jan 1915, redesignated at B Sqn on 25 May 1916, left 19 Apr 1916 for 1st Cavalry Division
33rd Divisional Cyclist Company, Army Cyclist Corps	left 19 Apr 1916

Divisional Artillery

The original divisional artillery was designated 'Camberwell' as it was raised there by the mayor and a committee between January and June 1915. Initial assembly and training took place in Dulwich. It joined the division at Bulford between 5 and 8 August 1915. However, the artillery did not proceed to France with the division. Instead, it took the artillery of the 54th (East Anglian) Division. The 33rd divisional artillery (as shown below) crossed to France and rejoined its division in December 1915.

CLVI Brigade, RFA	
CLXII Brigade, RFA	
CLXVI Brigade, RFA	broken up 12 Sep 1916
CLXVII (Howitzer) Brigade, RFA	broken up 12 Sep 1916
126 (Camberwell) Heavy Battery RGA	left for XXII Heavy Artillery Group on 2 May 1916
33rd Divisional Ammunition Column RFA	
V.33 Heavy Trench Mortar Battery, RFA	formed by 29 May 1916; broken up Feb 1918
X.33, Y.33 and Z.33 Medium Mortar Batteries, RFA	formed by 4 May 1916; in Feb 1918, Z broken up and batteries reorganized to have 6 × 6-inch weapons each

Royal Engineers

212th (Tottenham) Field Company	
222nd (Tottenham) Field Company	
226th (Tottenham) Field Company	left for 2nd Division, 2 Dec 1915
33rd (Tottenham) Divisional Signals Company	
11th Field Company	

Royal Army

99th Field Ambulance	
100th Field Ambulance	left for 2nd Division late Nov 1915
101st Field Ambulance	
73rd Sanitary Section	left 31 Mar 1917
19th Field Ambulance	joined from 2nd Division late Nov 1915

Other Divisional Troops

33rd Divisional Train ASC

originally 225, 226, 227 and 228 companies. Embarked for France 12 Nov 1915 but transferred in Mar 1916 to 29th Division. 170, 171, 172 and 173 companies, formerly the 28th Divisional Train, joined on 13 Nov 1915. 172 Company switched with 8 Company from 2nd Divisional Train in late Nov 1915

43rd Mobile Veterinary Section AVC
230th Divisional Employment Company
33rd Divisional Motor Ambulance Workshop

joined 1 Jun 1917
absorbed into Divisional Supply Column on 31 Mar 1916

The King's Royal Rifle Corps: Great War Battle Honours 1914–18

1914   The Battle of the Marne (6–10 September)
       The Retreat from Mons (23 August–5 September)
       The First Battle of Ypres (19 October–22 November)
       The Battle of Langemarck (21–24 October)

1915   The Second Battle of Ypres (22 April–25 May)
       The Battle of Aubers Ridge (9 May)
       The Battle of Festubert (15–27 May)
       The Battle of Hooge (30 July)
       The Battle of Loos (25 September–18 October)

1916   The Battle of the Somme (1 July–18 November)
       The Battle of Albert (1–13 July)
       The Battle of Bazentin Ridge (14–17 July)
       The Battle of Delville Wood (15 July–3 September)
       The Battle of Pozières (16–28 July)
       The Battle of Guillemont (3–6 September)
       The Battle of Flers-Courcelette (15–22 September)
       The Battle of Morval (25–28 September)
       The Battle of Transloy Ridges (1–20 October)
       The Battle of Ancre Heights (1 October–11 November)
       The Battle of Ancre (13–18 November)

1917   The First Battle of the Scarpe (9–14 April)
       The Battle of Arleux (28–29 April)
       The Battle of Arras (9 April–16 May)
       The Battle of Messines (7–14 June)
       The Battle of Pilckem Ridge (31 July–2 August)
       The Battle of Langemarck (16–18 August)
       The Battle of Menin Road Ridge (20–25 September)
       The Battle of Polygon Wood (26 September–3 October)
       The Battle of Broodseinde (4 October)
       The Battle of Poelcappelle (9 October)
       The Battle of Passchendaele (31 July–6 November)
       The Battle of Cambrai (20 November–6 December)

1918   The Second Battle of the Somme, also called the Battle of Saint-Quentin (21 March–5 April)
       The First Battle of Bapaume (24–25 March 1918)
       The Battle of Rosières (26–27 March)
       The First Battle of Arras (28 March). Arras 1918 was a battle honour awarded to units of the British and Imperial armies that took part in one or more of the following engagements: The Battle of Avre (4 April); The Battle of Ancre (5 April); The Battle of Messines (10–11 April); and The Battle of the Lys (9–29 April).

The complexity and intensity of the fighting was acknowledged by the post-war Battles Nomenclature Committee who identified eight separate battles in the period 9–29 April. Therefore in the official Battle Nomenclature the following local names are allotted to the Battle of the Lys: Estaires (9–11 April); Hazebrouck (12–15 April); Scherpenberg (29 April); and two subsequent actions: La Becque (28 June) and Meteren (19 July). The Hindenburg Line: Havrincourt; St Quentin Canal; Beaurevoir; Courtrai; the Battle of Bailleul (13–15 April); Béthune (18 April); First Kemmel Ridge (17–19 April); Second Kemmel Ridge (25–26 April).

The Battle of Albert (21–23 August)

The Second Battle of Bapaume (21 August–3 September)

The Second Battle of Arras (26 August–3 September)

The Battle of Drocourt-Quéant Canal (2–3 September)

The Battle of Havrincourt (12 September)

The Battle of Epehy (18 September)

The Battle of St Quentin Canal (29 September)

The Battle of the Canal du Nord (27 September–1 October)

The Battle of the Beaurevoir Line (3–5 October)

The Battle of Courtrai (14–19 October)

The Battle of the Selle (17–25 October)

The Second Battle of the Sambre (4 November)

Comparison of Casualties from major Western Front Battles

Battle	Year	Allies	German
1st Marne	1914	263,000	220,000
First Battle of Ypres	1914	126,921–161,921	134,315
Verdun	1916	400,000–542,000	355,000–434,000
Somme	1916	623,907	465,000–595,294[97]
2nd Aisne	1917	118,000	40,000
3rd Ypres	1917	200,000–448,000	260,000–400,000
Spring Offensive	1918	851,374	688,341
Hundred Days Offensive	1918	1,069,636	1,172,075
Total Casualties	1914–18	3,652,838–4,077,838	3,334,731–3,684,025

Bibliography

Anderson, Janice, *World War 1 Witness Accounts* (Abbeydale Press, 2009).

Balcon, Jill, *The Pity of War* (Shepheard-Walwyn Publishers Ltd).

Duncan, the Reverend James, *With the CLB Battalion in France* (Skeffington & Son, 1917).

Edmonds, Brigadier General Sir James E., *Military Operations, France and Belgium, 1918*, Vol. II (Macmillan, 1937).

Hallows, Ian S., *Regiments and Corps of the British Army* (New Orchard Editions, 1994).

Ivelaw-Chapman, John, *The Riddles of Wipers* (Pen & Sword Books, 2010).

MacDonald, Lyn, *Somme* (Michael Joseph, 1983).

McNab, Chris, *Tommy, First World War Soldier* (Pitkin Guide, 2012).

Moore-Bick, Christopher, *Playing the Game* (Helion & Co., 2011).

Norman, Terry, *The Hell They Called High Wood* (William Kimber, 1984).

Roynon, Gavin, *Ypres Diary 1914–1915* (The History Press, 2010).

The War on Hospital Ships with Narratives of Eye-witnesses and British and German Diplomatic Correspondence, Second & revised edition (Harper & Brothers Publishers, New York & London, 1918). (A summary of the war on hospital ships since May 1917, with brief narratives from survivors, will be found in an additional chapter, 'The Second Year'. That story has been compiled from accurate and authenticated narratives of eye-witnesses. This brings the blacklist up to 10 March 1918 and shows a record of ruthlessness that has revolted the world.)

Index

Abbeville, 228
Abbeville Communal Cemetery, 24
Acadians, 7, 9
Accrington Observer & Times, 40
Acheville, 176
Aegean Sea, 55
Afghanistan, 18
Africa, 41
Aisne, 97, 172, 199, 201, 216, 223
Albert, 98, 107–109, 113–19, 124–9, 199
Allenby, Gen E., 167, 175–6
Alrewas *see* National Memorial Arboretum
American Expeditionary Force (AEF), 138, 164,
    190, 195, 208–16, 222–7
American Revolution, 17
American War of 1812, 18
Amherst, Gen J., 14
Amiens, 97–8, 151–8, 200, 228
Ancre, 144, 153–7
Andover, 50, 60
Anglican Church *see* Church of England
Antwerp, 201–202
Appalachian Mountains, 17
Argonne, 208–209, 216–17, 222
Arleux, 178
Armentieres, 199, 204
Arras, 108, 158, 162–5, 169–71, 176, 178–84,
    191
Arras Memorial, 59
Artois, 179, 199, 201
Asquith, Herbert, 22, 69
Asturias see Hospital Ships
Athies, 172–3
Aulnoye, 220
Australia, 41, 108, 138, 164–5, 169–70,
    179–81, 206, 210, 212, 214–16
Austria, 1, 18, 32, 223
Austrian Succession War, 1
Awoingt British Cemetery, 50

Baden, Prince Max von, 202
Baden-Powell, R.S.S., 28
Bailleul, 108, 207
Baker, Ezekiel, 17

Baker Rifle, 17–18
Banting, F., 218
Bapaume, 119, 127, 151, 154
Barber, H., 47, 74, 230, 232
Barber, Rev'd P., 239–40
Baring-Gould, S., 86
Battalions,
    1/6th Cameronians, 96, 174–5
    1/9th Glasgow Highland Light Infantry, 96,
        130
    1st Heavy Machine Gun Corps, 206–207
    1st King's Royal Rifle Corps, 19–20
    1st Leicestershire, 19
    1st Middlesex, 173–7
    1st The Queen's, 96, 132
    1st Royal Irish Fusiliers, 19–20, 169
    2nd Argyll and Sutherland Highlanders,
        176–7
    2nd Royal Dublin Fusiliers, 19–20
    2nd Royal Scottish Fusiliers, 207
    2nd Royal Welsh Fusiliers, 132, 175, 177
    2nd Seaforths, 169
    2nd Worcestershire, 96, 207
    4th Suffolks, 174–5
    14th (Service) Welsh (Swansea), 122
    16th (Service) King's Royal Rifle Corps, 96,
        113, 128, 132, 191
    17th (Service) Middlesex, 96
    20th Royal Fusiliers, 175, 177
Bay of Fundy, 7–9
Bazentin Ridge, 98, 107, 113, 124–5, 127–30,
    132–3, 140, 145
Beaubassin *see* Bay of Fundy
Beaucourt, 156–7
Beaulencourt, 154
Beaumont Hamel, 156–7
Beauquesne, 117
Beaurains Cemetary, 23
Beaurevoir, 108, 209, 214–16, 218
Bedson, A.C., 59
Beitzen, Curt, 69
Belgium, 32–3, 56, 60, 82, 92, 96, 99, 159, 164,
    184, 186, 188–90, 192, 194, 196, 199,
    201–204, 209, 216–17, 222, 226, 237

Bellamy, Rev'd R.L., 28
Bellicourt, 215–16
Berlin, 223
Bernafay Wood, 122–3
Bethune, 94, 204
Bethune Town Cemetery, 61
Bettignies, Louise de, 222
Bevistein, A., 194
Biggarsberg Mountains, 18
Blood River Poort, 21
Boehm, Gen Max von, 218
Boer War, 18–21, 28, 58, 64, 97
Boller, J.I., 48–9, 59, 231–2
Bois du Sart, 171, 176
Bois du Vert, 171, 176
Bois Français, 135
Bonnie Prince Charlie, 1
Boone, Daniel, 10
Boritska trench system, 98, 108, 113
Boston, Mass, 4, 7
Boulogne, 96, 201
Bouquet, Lt-Col Henri, 12, 14–17
Bourlon, 210
Bowman, H.F., 59
Boyd, G.F., 109
Braddock, Maj-Gen E., 1, 3, 9–10, 12
Braemar Castle see Hospital Ships
Braithwaite, Cmdr W., 109
Briand, A., 162
Brigades,
  2nd, 175
  3rd, 96
  4th, 160, 307
  5th, 96–7
  6th, 95–6
  10th, 206
  11th, 109
  12th, 180
  19th, 95–6, 108, 172, 177
  23rd, 96,
  24th, 108
  25th, 96
  86th, 96
  98th, 95, 108, 172, 174–5, 184
  100th, 77, 95–7, 108, 113, 128
  154th, 96
  Highland Light Infantry, 96, 108
  Scottish Rifles, 96, 108
Brightmore, Capt J.R., 48, 231, 233
Brinn, F.J., 59
Britannic see Hospital Ships
British Columbia, 17
British, the, 7, 9–10, 14–17
British North America, 6

Brodie helmets, 106
Broodseinde, 187
Bruges, 189
Bullecourt, 164–5, 169–71, 180–2, 184, 230
Burden, H., 192
Burma, 18
Bushy Run, 15–16
Butler, Lt-Col R., 97
Byng, Gen, 217

Cairns, Sgt H., 222
Calais, 25, 201, 230
Cambrai, 108, 165, 169, 209, 216–18, 220
Cambrai East Military Cemetery, 23
Cambrin Churchyard Extension, 61
Campbell, Brig-Gen J.C., 219
Campbell, Maj-Gen John, 12, 14
Canada, 17–18, 29, 41, 108, 138, 164–6, 170,
    178, 190, 210, 218, 220, 222
Canal du Nord, 209–10, 217
Cantigny, 208
Cape Maringouin *see* Bay of Fundy
Cape Breton Island, 12
Carlton, Capt A.H., 212
Chambon, M. de Vergor du, 7
Champagne, 203
Chappell, W., 36, 59–61
Charleston, South Carolina, 12
Chateau Wood, 189
Chelmsford, Lord F.T., 28, 30, 41
Chemin des Dames Ridge, 164
Cherisy, 173
China, 18
Chitral, 21
Church Lads' Brigade, 27–30, 32–4, 36–7, 39,
    41–6, 48, 59, 69–70, 73, 76, 93, 98, 113,
    128, 158, 172, 230, 234, 238–9, 241–3
Church of England, 27, 72, 77, 240, 242
Churchill, W.L. Spencer, 33, 146, 202
Citadel Cemetery, 136
Cléry, 142–4
Clipstone Camp, 60, 77–8, 95–6
Colenso, Battle of, 21
Cojeul Valley, 172, 178
Combles, 140–2, 145, 151
Commonwealth War Graves Commission
    (CWGC), 226
Compiegne, 223, 225
Condé Canal, 222
Connaught, Duke of, 28, 31
Cooper, James Fenimore, 1
Courcelette, 141–2, 144, 150, 155, 165
Crimean War, 58
Croisilles, 173–4, 176

Crown Point, 4–6
Crozier, Brig-Gen F.P., 105
Crozier, J., 194
Crum, Maj. F, 22
Cumberland, Duke of, 1, 3, 6, 12
Curlu, 119
Curzon, Lord G.N., 68

Daily Chronicle, 45
Daily Express, 45
Daily Herald, 45
Daily Mail, 45, 134
Daily Mirror, 45
Daily News, 33
Daily Telegraph, 45
Debeney, Gen, 217
Delaware tribe, 16
Delville Wood, 129–33, 140–3
Denham camp, 37, 48, 59–60, 69, 72–3, 76–7, 96
Derby, Earl E.G.V.S., 39, 41, 122
Dewdrop Trench System, 98, 108, 113, 122
Dieskau, Baron, 6
Divisions,
    1st, 96, 109
    2nd, 95–7, 119
    4th, 167, 182, 206
    5th, 131, 144
    6th, 109
    7th, 127, 130, 181–2
    8th, 96, 108
    9th, 130, 167, 182, 207
    14th, 142
    15th, 170
    18th, 109, 127
    21st, 130, 152, 165, 176
    24th (Canadian), 173
    25th, 96
    29th, 96, 173
    30–35th, 95, 165, 176–7, 206–208
    33rd, 77, 95–8, 108–109, 111, 128, 131–2, 142, 145, 149–50, 158–9, 172–3, 176–7, 183–4, 186, 191, 206–208, 210, 222, 227, 230
    35th, 142
    37th, 170, 173, 184
    38th (Welsh), 109, 111, 122
    40th, 95
    46th, 109
    49th, 207
    50th, 176
    51st (Highland), 96, 182
    54th, 95
    56th, 184
    58th, 96
    62nd, 180–1
    63rd, 178
    Lowland, 96
Donegal see Hospital Ships
Donovan, T., 191–2
Dorling, Rev'd E.E., 243
Dover, 200, 202
Dover Castle see Hospital Ships
Drie Grachten, 188
Drocourt, 170, 209
Dundee, 18–20
Dunean, Rev'd J., 113
Dunkerque, 95, 202, 209
Dutch Republic, 1

Ecole, 22
Egypt, 66, 68
Ellison, G.E., 226
Englefontaine, 109, 220
Englefontaine British Cemetery, 110–11
Epehy, 108, 209
Erasmus, Gen 'Maroela', 18, 20
Erzberger, M., 223
Escaut, 209
Estrees, 215–16
Eton, Buckinghamshire, 50

Falfemont Farm, 140–4
Falkenhayn, Gen Erich, 201
Falls, Cyril, 179
Fampoux, 167, 169
Farbus, 166
Ferdinand, Archduke Franz, 30
Ferguson, M., 50, 233
Feuchy, 177
Field Service Regulations, 63
First Nations governments. 17
Fisher, Adml, 196
Flamborough Head, 55–6
Flers, 149–51
Foch, Gen, 143, 217, 220, 223, 225, 227
Fonsacrane, 215
Fontaine-Notre-Dame, 210
Forbes, Gen J., 14
Forbes-Robertson, Col J., 171
Forêt de Mormal, 109
Forêt de Nieppe, 207
Ford, E.A., 28
Fort Beauséjour, 7, 9
Fort Bedford, 14, 16
Fort Cumberland, 9
Fort Detroit, 16
Fort Duquesne, 9–10, 14

Fort Edward, 5
Fort Lawrence, 7, 9
Fort Ligonier, 16
Fort Michilimackinac, 16
Fort Oswego, 10
Fort Pitt, 14, 16
Fort Presque Isle, 16
Fort Sandusky, 16
Fort William Henry, 6
Foureaux Wood, 133, 137
France, 1, 7, 10, 14, 18, 32, 50, 56, 60, 65,
    79–80, 82, 92, 95, 97, 124, 127, 147, 162,
    179, 192, 194–7, 199, 201, 203–204, 206,
    216, 223, 227, 230, 237
Frankau, Gilbert, 160
Franklin, Benjamin, 10
French, 1, 3–7, 9–10, 12, 14, 16, 32, 44, 56,
    98–9, 107–108, 113–14, 118, 121–2,
    134–5, 140–1, 143–5, 154, 159, 162,
    164–5, 172, 178–9, 184, 188, 190, 195,
    199–200, 202, 204–209, 216–18, 222–3
French-Indian War, 1, 3, 6, 14, 16–17
French, Sir J.D.P., 68

Gallipoli, 66
Gallwitz, Gen Max von, 188
Gas (masks), 99–100, 123, 130, 133, 185, 188,
    211
Gavrelle, 169, 173, 176, 178
Gee, W. Mallock, 27–30
Geneva Convention, 56–7
Germans, 43–4, 54–7, 88–9, 107–109, 113–14,
    119–25, 127–35, 139, 141, 143, 145,
    152–4, 156, 159, 162, 164–6, 169, 171–3,
    176–8, 180–2, 185–6, 188–91, 195, 197,
    199–202, 206–12, 214–18, 220, 222, 226–8
Germany, 32–3, 45, 54, 57, 64, 99, 137, 159,
    164, 186, 195–6, 199, 201–203, 222–3,
    230
Gheluvelt Plateau, 188
Gibb, Phillip, 134
Ginchy, 140–4
Givenchy, 207
Glenart Castle see Hospital Ships
Glencoe, the battle of, 18
Gloucester Castle see Hospital Ships
Gloucester, Duke of, 5–6
Godewaersvelde British Cemetery, 23
Gonnelieu, 212
Goodwin, S., 50–1, 233–4
Gordon Boys' Brigade, 28
Gough, Gen. H., 114, 158, 169–70, 179–81,
    186, 188
Gough, Brig-Gen J.E., 119

Grandcourt, 156, 158
Graves, Robert, 102, 107–108, 132
Great Britain, 7, 18, 28, 32–3, 44–5, 58, 64,
    68–9, 92, 137, 139, 194–6, 200, 202, 208,
    210, 230, 236
Great Lakes, 1, 4, 16
Great War, 21–2, 25, 30, 32, 37, 43–4, 58, 62,
    67–8, 76, 82, 92, 97, 101, 103, 109, 111,
    113–14, 124, 136, 138, 147, 151, 158, 160,
    164–5, 191–2, 194–7, 203, 208–10, 214,
    217, 222–3, 226–8, 230, 236, 241, 243
Green Jackets Museum, 26
Greenland Hill, 173
Grenfell, Lord F.W., 37–9, 41, 73, 96, 230,
    234
Grosville, 175
Guemappe, 169
Gueudecourt, 151–3
Guillemont, 123, 133, 140–3
Gunter, H., 227
Gurney, Ivor, 131
Gwinnell, H.T., 50, 233

Hague Convention, 56–7
Haig, Gen D, 65, 113, 117, 119–22, 125, 127,
    130, 133, 135–6, 142–3, 153–4, 162, 164,
    171, 178–9, 181, 186, 188–90, 204–207,
    213, 216–17, 220, 235–6
Haldane, R.B., 64
Hamel, 144
Hampshire, HMS, 69
Hampshire, W., 61
Hankey, Sir M., 146
Hardecourt, 119
Harp Hill, 169
Havrincourt, 209
Hazebrouck, 108, 206–207
Hebuterne, 156
Hendecourt, 180
Henderson, Maj-Gen D., 97
Heninel, 174
Henin-sur-Cojeul, 175
High Wood, 98, 107–108, 113, 124, 127–34,
    136–7, 141–5, 149, 230
Hindenburg Line, 108, 165, 169–72, 174–6,
    178–9, 181, 183–4, 209–17, 219–20, 223
Hindenburg, Gen Paul von, 190
Hipkin, J., 194
Hipper, Franz von, 202
Hissey, T., 29
Hodgson, W.N., 112–13
Hohenberg, Duchess of, 30
Holnon, 212
Horne, Gen H., 166, 178, 204, 209, 217, 220

Hornoy, 111, 228
Hornsby, Ruston, 146
Hospital Ships, 54–8
  Asturias, 57–8
  Braemar Castle, 58
  Britannic, 55–6, 58
  Donegal, 58
  Dover Castle, 58
  Glenart Castle, 58
  Gloucester Castle, 57–8
  Lanfranc, 58
  Portugal, 58
  Rewa, 58
  Saita, 57
  Vperiod, 58
Hudson River, 5
Hungary, 223
Hunter-Weston, Lt-Gen Sir, 109
Hush, 108, 184
Hussars, 18th Squad, 20

Illinois, 16
Impati, 18, 20
Imperial War Museum, 25
India, 18, 21, 25, 64, 66, 68, 97
Infantry Hill, 171, 173
Ireland, 25
Iroquois, 4, 9
Isthmus River, 7
Italy, 21, 190

Jacobite Rebellion, 1
Jellicoe, Adml J.R., 186
Joffre, Gen, 125, 135, 142–3, 162, 213, 223
Johnson, Sir William, 4–6
Joncourt, 215–16
Jutland, 196, 198

Kaiser William II, 32, 35, 203, 223
Kemmel Ridge, 108, 206
Keogh, Sir A., 58
Kiel, 202–203
Kindersley-Porcher, Lt-Col C., 69, 79
King Albert, Belgium, 135
King George II, 5, 12
King George III, 17
King George V, 25, 32–3, 84, 111, 135–6, 227
King George's War, 1
King's Royal Rifle Corps (KRRC), 1, 18, 21–6,
    30, 37–9, 42, 45, 50, 59, 61, 71, 75–7, 80,
    82, 92–3, 98, 108, 115, 128–9, 132, 230,
    240–1
King William's War, 1
Kipling, Rudyard, 236

Kitchener, Earl H.H., 22, 39, 41–2, 44, 68–9,
    95, 137
Krupp, German field gun, 19
Kuhl, Gen Hermann von, 190
KwaZulu-Natal, 18

La Bassée, 199
La Belle Alliance Memorial, 22
La Boiselle, 122, 125
La Coulotte, 178
La Crèche, 207
La Ferte sous Jouarre Memorial, 24
La Folie Farm, 166
Ladysmith, 19, 21
Lagnicourt, 170
Lake Champlain, 5
Lake George, 5–6
Lake Lac Saint-Sacrement *see* Lake George
Landon, Maj-Gen H.J.S., 95, 97, 131, 149, 235
Land's End, 55
Lanfranc *see* Hospital Ships
Langemarck, 188
Laquette, 204
Last of the Mohicans, 1
Le Cateau, 215, 220
Le Catelet, 216
Le Forêt, 142, 144
Le Havre, 60, 80–1, 93, 96, 111, 185, 230
Le Touret Memorial, 23
Le Transloy, 154
Le Transloy Cemetery, 108
Leipzig Redoubt, 119, 133, 153
Lens, 173
Les Boeufs, 108, 151, 154
Les Tuileries British Cemetery, 111
Leuze Wood, 143–4
Leval, 111
Lijssenthoek Military Cemetery, 24
Lille, 200, 222
Limburg, 25
Lloyd George, D., 122, 136, 159, 162, 164, 186
Lomas, N., 50
Lomas, R., 50, 52
Lomax, Maj-Gen S., 97
London Gazette, 21, 45
Longueval, 123, 127, 130–1, 140, 145
Loos, 68, 97, 236
Louage Wood, 144
Louisbourg, 7, 9, 12–13
Loyalhanna, 14
Ludendorff, Gen, 204
Luxemburg, 32
Lyautey, H., 162
Lys, 108, 204, 208

Macedonia, 21
Mackay, Lt-Col J.J., 95
Maine, 7
Major, J., 194
Mametz Wood, 107, 119, 122
Manchester Guardian, 45
Marcoing, 212
Marden, T.O., 109
Marne, 97, 197, 199, 201
Marquion, 210
Martinpuich, 142, 145, 151
Marwitz, Gen von der, 217
Massachusetts Bay, 3–4
Maubeuge-Mons, 222
Mauroy, 215
McLellan, D., 218
Menin Road, 188
Menin Gate Memorial, 23–4
Mesopotamia, 66
Messines, 108, 184, 186, 190, 199
Meteren, 206–207
Methuen, Lord P.S., 30, 41
Metz, 208
Meuse, 217, 222, 227
Meyer, Gen. Lukas, 19–20
Mickley, Northumberland, 50
Middlesex Advertiser, 73
Mingo tribe, 16
Mirage Trench, 108
Mississippi River, 9
Moeuvres, 209
Mohawk, 4–6
Moltke, Helmuth von, 197
Monash, Gen Sir J., 210, 215
Monchy-le-Preux, 169–73
Monckton, Col Robert, 6–7
Monongahela River, 10
Monro, Maj-Gen C.C., 119
Mons, 97, 215, 222, 226
Monsell, J.S.M, 27
Montagu, E.S., 122
Montauban, 119–20, 123, 140
Montbrehain, 214
Montcalm, Louis Joseph du, 10
Montgomery, FM Bernard, 150
Montigny, 111, 227
Montreuil, 114
Morval, 138, 142, 151, 154,
Mosnieres, 215

Namur, 222
Nancy, 195
Nanroy, 215
Napoleonic Wars, 17–18

National Archives War Diaries, 23.
National Memorial Arboretum, 192–3, 237–40
National War Museum, 25
Native Americans, 1, 3, 5, 7, 10, 14, 16–17
Netherlands, 223
Neuve Eglise, 108, 207, 230
Neuville Vitasse, 169
Newbolt, H., 45
New England, 7
New England Provincials, 5, 7
Newfoundland, 29, 41, 108, 164
New France, 1
New York, 4, 6, 12
New Zealand, 108, 138, 164
News of the World, 230
Niagara, 4
Nicholas II, 178
Nieuwpoort, 184, 186, 189, 203
Nivelle, Gen R., 162, 164–5, 176, 178, 186
No Man's Land, 99, 127, 169
Norman, J.H., 52
North America, 1, 3, 12, 15–17
Noske, Gustav, 202
Nouvelle, 226
Nova Scotia, 1

Oak, HMS, 69
Ohio Valley/River, 1, 9, 11, 16
Oise Canal, 209, 220, 229
Ovillers, 122
Ontario, 17
Oppy, 176
Ors, 229
Ostend, 201
Ottawa tribe, 16
Owen, Wilfred, 106, 195, 228–9
Oxfordshire & Buckinghamshire Light
    Infantry, 25

Palastine, 25
Palluel, 210
Pals Battalions, 39, 98, 120, 165
Partridge, Eric, 101
Passchendaele, 24, 186, 188–90, 223
Pearson, Lt F.H., 160
Pelves, 176
Peninsula Barracks, 26
Peninsular War, 17–18
Penn Symons, Maj-Gen Sir William, 18–20
Pennsylvania, 14
Pensacola, 17
Pepperrel, Sir William, 10
Perham Down, 60, 79, 96
Peronne, 118

Perceval, Maj-Gen E., 119
Pershing, Gen J.J., 164, 195, 208, 226–7
Pétain, Gen H.P., 162, 223
Philadelphia, 12, 16
Picardy, 108, 151, 165, 168, 199, 201
Pilckem Ridge, 188
Pinney, Maj-Gen Sir R.J., 95, 149–50, 176–7, 183–4, 186, 188, 191, 207, 235
Pittsburgh, 14
Plumer, Gen H., 186, 188, 190, 204
Poelcappelle, 188
Polygon Wood, 188
Pontiac's Rebellion, 14, 16–17
Portugal *see* Hospital Ships
Portuguese, 204–205
Powell, G.H., 114
Pozières Ridge, 132, 135, 143
Prevost, Jacques, 12
Price-Davies, Maj-Gen L.A.E., 21
Price, G.L., 226
Prince William *see* Cumberland, Duke of
Prince William Henry *see* Gloucester, Duke of
Princip, G., 32, 34
Prinz Arnault Tunnel, 166
Prussia, 18

Quéant, 170, 178, 209
Quebec, 7, 14
Quebec, Battle of, 6
Queen Anne's War, 1
Queen Victoria, 28, 32, 39

Ravelsburg Heights, 207
Rawlinson, Gen H., 107–108, 114, 117, 122, 127, 135–6, 142, 145, 154–5, 158, 211, 213–14, 217, 220
Rayleigh, Essex, 60, 73, 74, 76, 96
Regiments,
    Argyll and Sutherland Highlanders, 174
    Devonshires, 112
    1st Essex, 171
    13th Essex (West Ham) Bt, 95
    16th (Service) Middlesex (Public Schools), 95
    Newfoundland, 171
    1st Queens, 108
    1st Royal Irish Fusiliers, 169
    2nd Seaforths, 169
    2nd Royal West Kents, 108
    Welsh, 122
    Worcesters, 108
    7th Dragoon Guards, 128
    20th Deccan Horse Guards, 128–9
    60th of Foot, 17
Regina Trench, 155

Reserves, 63–8, 230
Rewa see Hospital Ships
Rheims, 164, 217
Ribot, A., 162
Richards, Frank, 132
Richthofen, Manfred von, 145
Ridley, E., 50
Riencourt. 180
Riez-du-Vinage, 207
Rifle Battalions,
    1/7th Rifle Battalion, 18
    1st Cameronians (Scottish Rifles), 108
    95th Rifles, 18
    King's German Legion Rifles, 18
Rifles, the, 25, 66, 108
Riqueval Bridge, 212, 217, 219
Roberts, Lt-Col F.J., 160–1
Roeselare, 189
Roeux, 169, 176, 182, 191
Roulers, 164, 184
Royal American Regt, 1, 12, 15, 18
Royal Army Medical Corps, 58, 185
Royal Defence Corps, 67
Royal Green Jackets, 25
Russia, 18, 38, 69, 165, 178, 186, 190, 195–6

Sailly-Saillisel, 154–5
Sains-lés-Marquion, 209
Saint-Mihiel, 208
Saita see Hospital Ships
Salisbury Plain, 60, 95
Sally Port, 22
Sambre Valley, 111, 220, 222, 229
Sandhurst, Royal Military College, 21, 97
Sarajevo, 30
Sassoon, Siegfried, 106, 136, 184, 235
Sauchy-Lestreé, 210
Scapa Flow, 69
Scarpe, 108, 162, 164, 170–3, 176, 179, 182–3, 210
Scheer, Adml R., 202
Scheidemann, P., 203
Schwaben Redoubt, 153, 156
Scott, Avril, 239
Scott, George, 7
Scottish Highlanders, 16
Scrabster, 69
Sellars, A., 61
Selle, 108, 220
Sensée River, 174, 176, 184
Serbia, 32
Serre, 120, 156
Seven Years War *see* French Indian War
Shawnee tribe, 16

Shellshock (CSR), 105
Sherston Roberts, Hon Lt F.H., 21
Shirley, Col William, 3–5, 10
Shot at Dawn Memorial, 193
Sitwell, Maj F., 69
Snow, Lt-Gen O.T., 176
Soignies Road, 222
Somme, 37, 39, 61, 98, 107, 111–14, 116,
    118–19, 121–2, 124, 127–9, 132–3, 140–3,
    145, 151, 158–9, 162, 164–5, 179, 186,
    190, 208, 223
Sonning, Berkshire, 21
St John River, 7
St Lawrence, the Gulf of, 7, 12
St Martin's Banner, 242
St Pierre Divion, 156
St Quentin canal, 108, 209–13, 217–19
South Africa, 18, 130, 207
Stenay, 227
Strandfest, 185
Strickland, E.P., 109
Stuart, House of, 1
Stuff Redoubt, 153, 155
Swinton, Lt-Col E., 146
Switch Line, 128–9, 132, 145
Switzerland, 200

Talana Hill, Battle of, 18–20
Tanks, 146–9, 153, 169, 179–81, 188, 212–14,
    218
Territorial Cadet Force, 28–9, 37, 41, 43
Territorials, 37, 48, 63–7, 69, 95, 159
Terschelling, 55–6
The Times, 45, 107
Theyanoguin, Hendrick, 6
Thiepval, 119, 122, 142–3, 153–4, 156
Thiepval Memorial, 124–5
Thirteen Colonies, 1–2, 12, 14
Thundersley, Essex, 74, 76
Tideswell, Derbyshire, 45, 48, 50, 52, 231, 233
Tin Hats, 105
Tomas, 227
Torhout, 184, 189
Tortille, 154
Trebuchon, A., 226
Trench Fever, 100–102
Trench Foot, 102–105
Trenches, 54, 89, 99–100, 102–103, 113, 118,
    120, 126, 152, 155, 166, 181, 185, 201
Tritton, A., 147
Troisvilles, 109
Trônes Wood, 123–4, 127
Trotha, Adolf von, 202

Tuileries British Cemetery, 110
Turkey, 223
Tuscarawas River, 16
Tyne Cot Memorial, 23–4, 59

Ushant, 55
Uxbridge, 50, 69, 73, 77, 233
Uxbridge Record, 29

VAD Nurses, 55
Valenciennes, 220, 222
Vaudreuil, Gov Pierre de, 14
Vendhuile, 211–12
Verdun, 107, 135, 162, 217
Very, E.W., 173
Vienna, 18
Villers-Guislain, 212
Vimy Ridge, 165, 167–70, 178
Volker Tunnel, 166
V period see Hospital Ships

Wancourt Ridge, 171
Washington, George, 9–10
Watts, Maj-Gen, 127
Weatherly, F.E., 168
Wellington, 1st Duke of, 18
Welsh Ridge, 212
West, Benjamin, 6
West Indies, 18, 41
Western Front, 21, 41, 45, 87, 111, 114, 130,
    132, 136–7, 146–7, 158, 161–2, 164–5,
    179, 183, 186, 196, 201, 203, 209, 217,
    223, 226–8
Westhof Farm Cemetery, 192
Wilmershaven, 202
Wilson, W.G., 147
Wilson, Woodrow, 216
Winchester, 18, 21, 25–6, 41
Winslow, John, 7
Wipers Times, 159–61
Wolfe, Maj-Gen James, 6
Wyandot Tribe, 16
Wyld, Maj. C., 69, 73, 79

York, Sgt A.C., 222
York's Own Rifles, Duke of, 16

Ypres, 21–2, 24, 97, 99, 159–60, 164–5, 184,
    186–90, 201, 204, 206, 222
Yser Bridge, 184–5, 199, 201–202
Yule, Brig-Gen James Herbert, 20

Zollern Redoubt, 153